W9-AOI-546

FOR REFERENCE

———

NOT TO BE TAKEN FROM THE ROOM

Congregation Shaare Shamayim - G.N.J.C.
Verree Road above Welsh Road
Philadelphia, Penna.   19115

JUNIOR JUDAICA
ENCYCLOPAEDIA JUDAICA
FOR YOUTH

JUNIOR JUDAICA
ĒJ ENCYCLOPAEDIA JUDAICA
FOR YOUTH

editor in chief
Rabbi Dr. Raphael Posner

4
Ju-Net

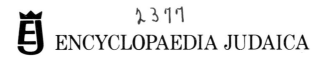
ENCYCLOPAEDIA JUDAICA

Second, updated edition

Exclusive distribution rights reserved by MACCABEE PUBLISHING, INC.

ISBN   0-942500-00-8
ISBN   0-942500-04-0
Library of congress catalog number 82-80118

Printed and bound by Keterpress Enterprises, Jerusalem
Printed in Israel

There are many Hebrew words in *Junior Judaica;* some are printed in Hebrew letters but all are given in transliteration, that is, spelled out in English. The following table shows the system we have used in all cases except in a very few where there is an accepted English spelling.

Consonants:

א	not transliterated
ב	b
ב	v
ג	g
ד	d
ה	h
ו	v; when it is not a vowel
ז	z
ח	h; pronounced like the "ch" in Loch Lomond
ט	t
י	y; when it is not a vowel
כ	k
כ	kh; pronounced like the hard German "ch" as in *Ach!*
ך	kh; this is the final from of כ, i.e., the way it is written at the end of a word.
ל	l
מ	m
ם	m; final form of מ
נ	n
ן	n; final form of נ
ס	s
ע	not transliterated
פ	p
פ	f
ף	f; final form of פ
צ	z; pronounced "ts" as in tsetse fly
ץ	z; final form of צ
ק	k
ר	r
ש	sh
ש	s
ת	t
ת	t

Vowels:

a; as in calm
e; as in bed
i; as in tin
ei; like the "a" in take
o; as in or
u; as in zoo

א and ע as pronounced by most Hebrew speakers have no sound but take the sound of the vowel. Occasionally, when they appear inside a word we use an apostrophe (') to indicate that the two vowels should be pronounced separately.

JUDAH HALEVI and MAIMONIDES.
Detail from the Benno Elkan *Menorah* which stands outside the Knesset building in Jerusalem, depicting two of the giants of medieval Jewish life: Judah Halevi, the poet and singer of Zion (at right, with harp) and Moses Maimonides, the philosopher and halakhist (with a volume of the Greek philosopher Aristotle and a volume from his monumental halakhic code, *Yad Ha-Ḥazakah*).

JUBILEES, BOOK OF. A work dating from the middle Second Temple period, the Book of Jubilees purports to be the secret revelation of the angel of the "Divine Presence" to Moses on his second ascent of Mount Sinai. Although the original version (entitled "Book of the Divisions of the Seasons According to their Jubilees and their Weeks") was in Hebrew, all the surviving versions are translations from Greek. Fragments of the original Hebrew version have been discovered in the Qumran caves.

The book, which is the work of an unknown Jewish sect, is in the form of an angelic monologue on the contents of the Bible, providing exact dates for the events and stories, calculated according to the Jubilee year, the sabbatical year and the year of the sabbatical cycle, sometimes giving even the months and days. According to the author, the commandments were written on the "tables of heaven" before they were given to man; some apparently are also practiced and upheld by the angels (for instance, *circumcision, the *Sabbath and *Shavuot), and some were also kept by the patriarchs. In contrast to the traditional view, Shavuot is said to commemorate the renewal of the covenant between God and man after the *Flood, and the *Day of Atonement is said to date from the sale of Joseph into slavery.

The book opposes close links with gentiles and is extremely strict in its interpretation of Sabbath laws. The author notes four different "new years" — the first day of the first, fourth, seventh and tenth months. Their significance relates, not to the agricultural cycle, but to cosmic events which occurred at the time of the Flood — the beginning of the construction of the ark, the day the land became dry, the day the waters began to recede into the mouths of the abyss, and the day when the tops of the mountains became visible. Jubilees also maintains the literal observance of "an eye for an eye" against the Pharisaic interpretation. At the *end of days the author envisages a *Messiah from the tribe of Judah, and another from the tribe of Levi.

The beliefs expressed in Jubilees (the immortality of the soul, the rule of Belial, Prince of Evil, on earth, and the calendar) are similar to those held by the community of Qumran, and the work was most probably a product of the *Essenes and one of their basic texts. The author probably lived at the end of the reign of John Hyrcanus (135-104 b.c.e.). The book had a particularly profound influence on the *Falashas, whose rites and calendar are based on it.

The *sha'ar* or title page of Judah Halevi's *Kuzari*, printed in Venice in 1547. Written in the form of a dialogue between a Khazar king who converted to Judaism and a rabbi who instructed him in the tenets of Judaism, the *Kuzari* projects in vivid fashion Judah Halevi's national and religious philosophy.

JUDAH HALEVI (before 1075-1141). Born in Spain, Judah Halevi was one of the greatest poets and philosophers that the Jewish people has produced.

About 800 of his poems are known, from his youthful love and friendship poems to the *piyyutim* which are among the greatest religious poetry since the Psalms. But though these poems reached great artistic perfection, Judah Halevi is most famous for his *Shirei Zion*. In these songs of Zion, he concludes that the only place for the Jew is Erez Israel, an idea still uncommon in the 12th century, and sings with pride of the glorious past of Erez Israel, with anguish at its present desolation, and with longing for a return to the Holy Land:

"O city of the world, with sacred splendor blest,
My spirit yearns to thee from out the far-off
   West;
Had I an eagle's wings, straight would I fly to
   thee,
Moisten thy holy dust with wet cheeks streaming
   free.
In the East, in the East, is my heart, and I
   dwell at the end of the West;

How shall I join in your feasting, how shall I
    share in your jest,
How shall my offerings be paid, my vows with
    performance be crowned,
While Zion pineth in Edom's bonds, and I am
    pent in the Arab's bound!
All the beauties and treasures of Spain are
    worthless as dust in mine eyes;
But the dust of the Lord's ruined house, as a
    treasure of beauty I prize."

Halevi's philosophy was expressed most clearly in the *Kuzari,* in which he stressed the unity of God and His chosen people, Israel. His ideas are presented in a lively and interesting manner in the form of a dialogue. The king of the Khazars, after being told by an angel in a dream that while his intentions were acceptable to God, his actions were not, wants to discover how he should lead his life and invites an Aristotelian philosopher, a Christian, a Muslim and a Jew to discuss their respective beliefs. In this way Halevi compares their teachings, and concludes that Judaism is superior.

Believing as he did that Erez Israel has a special holy character, and that the ideal existence for the Jews was attainable only in their own land, Judah Halevi decided that he must journey there to spend his last days. This decision was not an easy one, since Israel at that time was a desolate and dangerous place, and it meant sacrificing his comfortable life, his beloved family, friends, students, and admirers in Spain. After a difficult ocean voyage he finally reached Egypt where, unfortunately, he died before being able to complete his journey.

JUDAH HA-NASI (second to third century c.e.), *Nasi* (president of the Sanhedrin and leader of Judea) and editor of the Mishnah. Referred to also as *"rabbenu ha-kadosh"* ("our holy teacher"), or simply as "Rabbi," Judah was the son of Rabban Gamaliel and a descendant of Hillel. He was regarded in his own generation and later as a savior of Israel, and his wisdom and humility as well as his wealth and close friendship with the Roman Emperor Marcus Aurelius became the subject of numerous legends.

Judah lived most of his life in *Bet She'arim where he had his yeshivah, but moved in his later years to *Sepphoris. As *nasi* he applied himself to strengthening the economic position of the Jews in Erez Israel, to settling them on the land, and to shaping the country's national religious institutions. Recognition of his position by the Roman authorities

enabled Judah to invest his office with quasi-royal status. According to the *aggadah* the Roman Antoninus befriended Judah, gave him the tenancy of estates in the Golan, and was partner in a cattle-breeding enterprise with him. Judah may also have met the Roman emperors Septimus Severus and Antoninus Caracalla on their visits to Erez Israel. Nonetheless, he apparently believed that the "destroyers of the Second Temple [were] destined to fall into the hands of Persia."

Judah did what he could to keep as much as possible of Erez Israel in Jewish hands, especially following the *Bar Kokhba revolt, and tried also to mitigate the heavy tax burden which fell on the Jews. He concentrated all the power of the *bet din* in his own hands and held sway over the south as well, showing especial interest in Jerusalem. To enhance the prestige of the patriarchate, whose seat was in Galilee, the intercalation of the year (adjustment of the lunar to the solar calendar) was transferred there from Judea. Judah opposed those who tried to lower the status of Babylonian Jewry in relation to that of Erez Israel, instead stressing the need for unity. He also encouraged the use of Hebrew over the vernacular Aramaic. He exempted sages from city tax, numbered the rich among his companions at table and gave generous assistance to students from his own wealth. He is reported to have said, "Trouble comes to the world only on account of the unlearned," toward whom he showed no sympathy. Certain of the sages opposed Judah's opulent and regal style of life but he always managed to avoid open conflict with his critics.

Judah's redaction of the *mishnayot* into the classic standard Mishnah laid the foundation for development of the *halakhah* in the Talmud. When Judah died contemporaries said of him "not since the days of Moses were learning and high office combined in one person until Rabbi," and "the angels and the mortals took hold of the holy ark. The angels overpowered the mortals and the holy ark has been captured."

JUDAH MACCABEE, one of the great warriors of history, and the founder of the *Hasmonean kingdom. Among the many explanations of how he came to be called Maccabee, two are most common: that the name represents a transliteration of the Greek work meaning "hammer," signifying Judah's military prowess; or that it comes from the first letter of each word in the biblical verse, "Who is like you, O Lord, among the mighty," indicating Judah's religious devotion.

In the second century b.c.e., Judea was under *Seleucid rule, and the Seleucid leader Antiochus IV Epiphanes, tried to turn Erez Israel into a secular, Hellenistic state (see *Hellenism). He prohibited the practice of Judaism, desecrated the Temple, and forced Jews to worship idols and eat prohibited food. Instead of submitting, however, the Jews of Judea rose in revolt, and Judah Maccabee, the third son of Mattathias the Hasmonean, became the military leader of the rebellion.

Judah was a military genius. Aware of the superior strength of the Seleucid forces, he avoided engaging them in open battle but instead devised a series of daring ambushes and night attacks. At a crucial battle near Beth-Zur, Judah defeated the numerically superior Seleucid force and the road was opened to Jerusalem. On the 25th of Kislev, 164 b.c.e. Judah Maccabee led his army in a triumphant return to Jerusalem, where he purified the Temple and instituted a festival of eight days (see *Hanukkah).

Judah's aim was the independence of Judea, and to this end he went to the aid of Jewish settlements in Gilead, Transjordan and the Galilee. His successes were extraordinary, but hard on the heels of these

An illustration from the *Low German Bible,* printed at Quental and Cologne, 1478-1480, depicting a scene from the first Book of Maccabees: an encounter between the Hasmonean and Seleucid armies.

challenges to Judea's autonomy came an internal struggle between the Jewish nationalists, led by Judah, and those who wished to submit to Hellenistic culture. Because the nationalists had the upper hand, the Hellenists continually appealed to Seleucid leaders for help. Judah was able to withstand attacks from several of the armies sent from Syria, but finally was overcome in 161 b.c.e. and died with his men on the field of battle. After his death his brothers succeeded him and ensured the independence of Judea under the Hasmonean dynasty. The story of Judah Maccabee is told in the Books of the Maccabees in the *Apocrypha.

JUDAIZERS. Persons who, without actually being Jewish, follow Jewish practices or claim to be Jews are termed Judaizers. The model of the Judaizer was Naaman, minister to the king of Syria around 850 b.c.e. who, after being cured of leprosy by the prophet *Elisha, worshiped the God of the Jews while continuing outwardly to pray to the idols of the state religion. In the classical period, both the principles and certain practices of Judaism attracted some segments of even Rome's population, who became "God fearers," rejecting pagan worship and observing the Sabbath. The requirement of circumcision for full conversion to Judaism was a distinct deterrent to adult male sympathizers with Judaism, who therefore frequently contented

1. Judah Maccabee portrayed on an enamel plaque produced in France in the 16th century.

2. Pilgrimage from Japan of contemporary Judaizers, a group called the Original Gospel Tabernacle, praying for the peace of Jerusalem and for Soviet Jewry, at the Western Wall, Jerusalem, 1971.

themselves with a half-way conversion.

During the early Christian period the Church violently suppressed Christian Judaizers who wore Jewish ritual dress, followed some of the dietary laws, kept the Sabbath, celebrated Easter on *Passover, or observed other Jewish rites. Later the Church developed an organized answer to Judaizers in the form of the *Inquisition. During the period of Puritanism in England and North America, the Christian interest in the Bible led to a revival of Judaizing. Extremists demanded that the Christian liturgy be written in Hebrew, that the constitution be modeled on biblical law, that Sabbath be observed on the seventh day, and that there be rigorous abstention from blood in food. Some English, Hungarian and Russian sects of Judaizers formally adopted Judaism.

The first open appearance of Judaizers in Russia occurred in Novgorod in the 15th century, when two clergymen were "corrupted to Judaism" by Skhariya Zhidovin, a local Jew. They later influenced many members of the court of the Grand Prince Ivan Vasilevich of Moscow, but were persecuted by the authorities, some being restricted to monasteries; even Zosima, the Metropolitan of Moscow, was accused of being one of their number, and was deposed. After the leaders of the sect were burned at the stake in 1504, it rapidly disappeared from the scene.

During the second half of the 18th century a revival of Judaizing occurred in Russia, the most prominent sect being the Molokans. In the 19th century Judaizers were again persecuted, and this time either brought back into the Church or conscripted into the army. Those unsuitable for military service were exiled to Siberia and denied passports. Jews were expelled from all areas where Judaizers were discovered. Thus, whole villages were depopulated and destroyed. But flourishing villages of banished Judaizers grew up beyond the Caucasus, where they spread their religion among the local population.

On October 17, 1905 a manifesto declaring freedom of religion to all Russians abolished discriminatory legislation against Judaizers and Sabbath Observers, and the government took pains to point out that anti-Jewish legislation no longer applied to these sects. Some Judaizers married into Jewish families and settled in Erez Israel, becoming completely absorbed into the Jewish population.

The present-day Seventh Day Adventists, while

adopting certain Jewish practices based on the Bible, are yet a separate, and Christian, sect. To what extent certain Mexican Indians or the "Black Jews" of the United States should be considered true Jews is undecided.

In the southern Chilean province of Cautin a group of about 1,000 people form the Iglesia Israelita, some of whom joined the Zionist movement and settled in Israel. In *Japan several Christian sects are deeply interested in Judaism and their members often visit Israel. A small Judaizing sect in Uganda, known as the Bayudaya, was founded in the 1920s and officially recognized by the Uganda government in 1964.

JUDITH, BOOK OF, an historical narrative dating from Second Temple times. Holofernes, commander-in-chief of the army of *Nebuchadnezzar, king of Assyria, was sent by his master on a campaign of conquest, in the course of which he overcame all the countries between Persia and Sidon and Tyre. When he reached the Valley of Esdraelon he found his way

to Judea and Jerusalem barred by the Jewish strongholds of Bethulia and Betomesthaim. Holofernes laid siege to Bethulia. Within the town there lived a young, rich and beautiful Jewess named Judith. She obtained permission to leave and go into Holofernes' camp. Impressed by her beauty, he invited her to a feast. When, overcome by wine, he had fallen asleep, Judith took his dagger, cut off his head and, handing it to her maid, returned to Bethulia. The leaderless Assyrians, now panic-stricken, fled.

No one knows if this story is based on events which really happened. It may be no more than a historical novel written in the time of the *Hasmoneans to inspire courage. However, a Cappadocian prince named Holofernes did fight under Artaxerxes III against the Egyptians in 352 b.c.e. The story may therefore derive from a Persian source.

From the literary standpoint, the Book of Judith is one of the most finished productions of the Second Temple period. A prose work, it embodies two poems: Judith's prayer before setting out for Holofernes' camp, and Israel's rejoicing at her victory. The book exists in four principal Greek versions, all based on an original Hebrew one, now lost. An abridged Aramaic translation also existed in ancient times, from which St. Jerome made a Latin translation.

JULIAN THE APOSTATE (Flavius Claudius Julianus, 331-363 c.e.), Roman emperor from 361 to 363. The nephew of Constantine the Great, Julian received a Christian education, but was greatly influenced by Greek philosophy and ideas. In 355 he was appointed governor of Gaul, where he proved to be a popular and outstanding soldier and administrator. In 361 he became ruler of the entire Roman Empire.

The driving passion in Julian was his intense hatred of Christianity. His uncle Constantine had made Christianity the official religion of the empire and done much to spread it; Julian now sought to undo this work. He established a pagan cult in opposition to Christianity, and forbade certain books and practices as inimical to pagan religious belief. He argued that Christianity had adopted the worst aspects of Judaism and paganism, and that within a generation it had gone from a persecuted religion to become an official belief persecuting others.

Julian's attitude toward Jews was colored by his

An oil painting by the 15th century Italian artist Botticelli, showing Judith returning to Bethulia with the severed head of Holofernes.

Julian the Apostate.

hatred of Christianity. He tacitly accepted Jewish monotheism by rejecting the Christian claim that Jesus is God, arguing that the Bible says there is but one God. At the same time, he argued that all religions and cults have their gods — Judaism has its deity, and other cults and religions have their own. He concluded that paganism was superior to Judaism because pagan countries had produced greater military leaders, philosophers, scientists, lawmakers and other intellectuals. In spite of this, Julian promised to abolish the anti-Jewish laws and to rebuild the Temple in Jerusalem. This, however, was never accomplished.

JULIUS CAESAR (c. 100-44 b.c.e.) was emperor of Rome and a political and military leader of almost legendary proportions. Caesar was favorably disposed toward the Jewish people. During his civil war against Pompey in 49 b.c.e., Caesar freed Aristobulus II, the deposed ruler of Judea, and planned to send him to Syria to aid him in recovering his throne. This was thwarted when Pompey's supporters poisoned Aristobulus before he could leave Rome. Once Caesar had conquered the entire Orient, Hyrcanus, the ruler of Judea, supported him. In return, Caesar attempted to correct some of Pompey's abuses against the Jews. He permitted the reconstruction of the walls of Jerusalem, restored to Judea the port of Jaffa, and confirmed Hyrcanus and his descendants as high priests and ethnarchs of Judea. Thus, Caesar granted to Hyrcanus and his descendants Judea, Jaffa and the Jewish settlements in the Galilee and Transjordan, as well as in the Jezreel Valley. Judea was taxed at 12.5% of the produce of the land and was exempted during *Sabbatical years. Extortion by the military was absolutely prohibited. In addition, Caesar permitted Jewish organization in the *Diaspora. Caesar's enmity toward Pompey, who had conquered Jerusalem and defiled the Holy of Holies, made him popular among the Jews. His restoration of Judea, his deference toward the high priest Hyrcanus II, and his tolerant attitude toward Diaspora Jewry increased the sympathy of the Jewish masses for him, and when he was assassinated, he was deeply mourned by Jews.

JUSTICE is the fair administration of the law. It means that a judge must not show special favor to a litigant or a defendant for any reason at all, and that nobody — not even the king — is above the rule of the law. This concept of even-handedness is, in the Jewish view, absolutely essential for the existence and progress of society. The Bible quite clearly states "Justice, justice shall you pursue, that you may thrive and occupy the land that the Lord your God is giving you" (Deuteronomy 16:20). The prophets castigated Israelite society for its lack of justice and described most of the troubles the Jews suffered as divine punishment for the rampant injustice. See also *Bribery; *Courts.

Judaism, as a religion which embraces all aspects of life, believes that the law by which man must live is that which was given by God and has been correctly interpreted. For more on this, see *Law, Jewish.

The Hebrew word for justice is צֶדֶק, *zedek,* and indicative of Judaism's attitude is the fact that another form of the same root צְדָקָה, *zedakah,* means "charity." For justice must be tempered with mercy and indeed the main attribute of God is His integration of justice and mercy. Yet another Hebrew word derived from the same root is צַדִּיק, *zaddik,* which means "righteous." The righteous man is one who is both just and merciful.

One of the main problems of theology is the apparent injustice of some of God's actions, such as the suffering of the innocent and the success of the wicked. This is a problem that has occupied the attention of religious people throughout the ages and many great personalities in the Bible such as *Abraham, *Moses and *Job accused God of not acting justly. The prophet *Habakkuk, in answer, stated that "the righteous shall live by his faith" (2:4), suggesting that man cannot understand God's actions and must have faith that justice is being done. Jewish philosophers throughout the ages have proposed different answers such as that the suffering of the innocent is a trial and test, as it was in the case of Job, and that they will ultimately be rewarded if they keep their faith. See also *God; *Suffering.

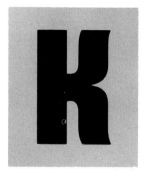

KABBALAH. The word *kabbalah* comes from the root which means "to receive" and should be translated literally as "that which is received." Kabbalah has several usages in the Hebrew language and the intention can only be understood by the context of the sentence. Kabbalah means "tradition" and as such refers to the oral law which was received by tradition. It is also the name of the certificate of competence given to a *shoḥet,* ritual slaughterer, and in modern Hebrew means a "receipt." The best-known use of the word, however, is as the name of a mystical system within Judaism and this entry is about that system. A person who believes in, studies and practices the Kabbalah is known as a kabbalist, which is often used in the English language for someone with a mystical tendency.

In a sense, mysticism is a very natural phenomenon. A human being finds himself born into the world and he knows that sooner or later he will die. It is natural that he should want to know how he was created and where he is going. When he looks around himself, he sees an astonishingly complex world and wants to know how it came into existence. If he believes that God created the universe he wonders how He did it since He is infinite and the world is finite. He also thinks about man's relationship with God and how evil and imperfection can exist in the world when it was created by God who is wholly good. Mysticism tries to provide answers to these questions and to many more like them.

There is evidence that mysticism existed in Judaism from very early times and, indeed, early Jewish mysticism had a great influence outside Judaism, particularly on Christianity. In the Talmud there are discussions about the Chariot of God, the Throne of God and the "size" of God. These are based on various passages in some of the later prophetic Books of the Bible. The term Kabbalah began to be used for Jewish mysticism from about the year 1200 c.e. and as such the inference is that the doctrines of this mystical system have been handed down by tradition from generation to generation. Kabbalistic tradition therefore attributes some of the main kabbalistic books to important figures in the early history of the Jewish people. Modern scholarship, however, dates those books to various periods in the Middle Ages.

Mysticism was an important subject during the geonic period in Babylonia (see *Gaon). It is possible that the Jews became very interested in the subject because of their contact there with Oriental mystical religions, particularly Zoroastrianism which taught that there is a constant struggle in the world between the powers of good and evil. This doctrine of course highlights the problem of how evil came into existence in the first instance and how it can continue to exist. *Saadiah Gaon wrote a commentary to a famous mystical work called *Sefer ha-Yeẓirah* ("The Book of Creation"), the authorship of which was attributed to the patriarch Abraham. This book and Saadiah's commentary on it became one of the most important texts in the subsequent development of Jewish mysticism.

With the decline of the Babylonian center of Jewish life, immigrants took their doctrines with them to Europe and North Africa. The *Ḥasidei Ashkenaz movement in northern France and Germany developed its own brand of mysticism and Provence, in southern France, was the source of one of the main texts of Kabbalah, *Sefer ha-Bahir* ("The Book of Brightness") which was attributed to the mishnaic sage, Neḥunyah ben Hakanah. In Spain too the Kabbalah gained a tremendous impetus, particularly because of the great Bible and Talmud commentator *Naḥmanides, who was a major kabbalist.

It was in medieval Spain that the most important work of the Kabbalah, the *Zohar* ("The Book, of Splendor") originated. The book is written in Aramaic

Drawing of a man holding a tree of the ten *Sefirot,* showing their hierarchical relationship. From the title page of *Portae Lucis,* a Latin translation of *Sha'arei Orah,* by the 13th-century kabbalist Joseph ben Abraham Gikatilla.

"The Kabbalist," detail from Benno Elkan's *Menorah* standing outside the Knesset building in Jerusalem.

and is a mystical commentary on the Torah. It was "discovered" by Moses de Leon and attributed to *Simeon bar Yoḥai, the second-century rabbi. Modern scholarship believes that the main part of the *Zohar* was written between 1270 and 1300 and that Moses de Leon may have been the author and not the "discoverer." The *Zohar* is the chief text of Kabbalah and all subsequent systems rely on it.

The expulsion from Spain in 1492 led to the spread of Kabbalah. The refugees took their beliefs and knowledge with them, and so Safed in Ereẓ Israel became an important center of the mystical doctrine. Indeed, Safed is known to this day as "the city of the kabbalists." An amazingly talented group of people came together in this city led by a young man, Isaac *Luria who, although he wrote no books and was only active for a few years, completely revolutionized Kabbalah. His pupils, Moses Cordovero and Ḥayyim Vital, handed kown their master's teachings in a series of books which are standard for the study of Kabbalah. It was in the Luria school that Kabbalah

ceased to be a purely theoretical discipline and that the idea of practical Kabbalah started. This involved the use of kabbalistic invocations to heal the sick, to perform miracles and particularly to hasten the "end of days" and the coming of the Messiah.

Lurianic Kabbalah had an important influence on subsequent Jewish history. There is no doubt that *Shabbetai Ẓevi was to a great extent motivated by it and the messianic movement he started used kabbalistic doctrines, albeit in a perverted form, in formulating its own philosophy. *Ḥasidism also leaned heavily on the Kabbalah and many kabbalistic notions became basic beliefs for hundreds of thousands of simple folk in Eastern Europe even though they certainly did not understand the whole complicated system of Kabbalah.

Some Basic Concepts of the Kabbalah. One of the chief problems that the Kabbalah seeks to solve is how God who is infinite created the world. The doctrine of ẓimẓum ("contraction") teaches that God the *Ein Sof* ("The Infinite") "contracted" Himself in order to leave room for the world. God then "sent out" of Himself ten creative powers – known as *sefirot,* spheres – and created (and rules) the world through them. These *sefirot* are connected one to the other "like a flame to the wick" but each has a distinct function. Together they are like a chain joining God and the world. Each *sefirah* has a separate name (in different texts the names vary) and a specific place in the hierarchy. The commonly accepted order (descending) of the *sefirot* and the names usually given to them are: 1) *Keter* (Supreme Crown); 2) *Hokhmah* (Wisdom); 3) *Binah* (Intelligence); 4) *Gedullah* (Greatness; 5) *Gevurah* (Power) or *Din* (Judgement); 6) *Tiferet* (Beauty) or *Raḥamim* (Compassion); 7) *Neẓaḥ* (Lasting Endurance); 8) *Hod* (Majesty); 9) *Ẓaddik* (Righteous One) or *Yesod Olam* (Foundation of the World); 10) *Malkhut* (Kingdom) or *Attarah* (Diadem).

The *sefirot* also form groups within themselves, and in kabbalistic literature they are often depicted as forming a human body or a tree. From *sefirah* 5, *gevurah,* the powers of evil emanate, creating the *sitra ahra* ("the other side") which is often the name given to the devil. When men behave well and do God's will, that is communicated upwards through the *sefirot* and then God sends down through them His goodness and benefits. However, when men behave badly the *sefirah gevurah* intensifies its activities which result in even greater evil. Man's role in the universe is to "correct" evil by his good actions and his inner purity. He can repair the "broken vessels" of evil. The body is considered to be the "garment" for the soul which at death returns to its source, God, and is recycled until it performs its mission. It is from this doctrine that the theory of transmigration of souls and exorcism of evil spirits developed and was widely believed. For more on this, see *Dibbuk.

The doctines of Kabbalah are extremely complicated and a great deal of intensive study is required to master them. In the 20th century Kabbalah has become a subject for academic research and many scholarly books have been written describing it and evaluating its influence. The major figure in this area is Gershom Scholem (1897-   ) who was professor of Jewish mysticism and Kabbalah at the Hebrew University in Jerusalem from 1933 until his retirement in 1965.

KAFKA, FRANZ (1883-1924), Czech-born German novelist who had a great influence on Western literature, especially on the development of the "Theater of the Absurd." Born and raised in Prague, he studied law and worked in a law office and an insurance company, writing in his spare time. A tyrannical father had a profoundly disturbing influence on him. Although he never married, two women were influential in his life: the journalist Milena Jesenska, and the Polish Jewess Dora Dymant, who nursed him in his final illness. For years Kafka suffered from migraine and insomnia, and in 1917 was diagnosed as tubercular. He spent most of his remaining life in a sanatorium. Although Kafka had instructed his friend, Max Brod, to burn all his writings at his death, Brod realized their importance and succeeded in getting them published.

Kafka's central theme seems to be the search for personal identity. Obstacles are constantly placed in the paths of his heroes, who never succeed in attaining their goals. Most interpreters see in Kafka's works a symbolic representation of the spiritual plight of modern man, although some lay greater emphasis on the author's personal psychology, and others on his alienated Jewish identity.

Kafka's most famous novels are *Der Prozess* (1925: "The Trial," 1937), *Das Schloss* (1926: "The Castle," 1930), and *Amerika* (1927: "America," 1938).

Kafka studied Hebrew, became interested in Hasidism and toyed with the idea of settling in Palestine. His progress toward a deeper understanding of Judaism paralleled his search for truth and purity. His novels have been adapted in many languages as

Franz Kafka

plays, operas, and movies. The Czech Communist government rehabilitated him from the category of "decadent genius" in 1964.

KAHANEMAN, JOSEPH (1888-1969) was a rabbi and yeshivah leader who founded Torah institutions both in Lithuania and later in Erez Israel. He was known as the Ponevezher Rav, i.e. the rabbi of Ponevezh, a city in Lithuania.

Rabbi Kahaneman received his education at the yeshivah of Telz and then at the *kolel* of the Ḥafeẓ Ḥayyim. In 1916 he was appointed head of the yeshivah of Grodno. Soon after, he founded similar centers of learning throughout Lithuania, including a preparatory yeshivah in Ponevezh. After the rabbi of Ponevezh, Isaac Rabinowitz, died in 1919, Rabbi Kahaneman was appointed the Ponevezh Rav in his place. With his dynamic personality and great organizational ability, Rabbi Kahaneman devoted himself to establishing centers of Torah learning, among them the yeshivah in Ponevezh which became the largest in Lithuania. As an active community leader, he served as head of Agudat Israel and as an elected member of the Lithuanian parliament. In addition, he administered the Ponevezh yeshivah and lectured there twice a week.

When World War II broke out, Rabbi Kahaneman was on a mission abroad, and never returned to Lithuania. In 1940 he settled in Erez Israel, and from there directed his efforts towards rescuing Lithuanian Jews from the Nazis. Afterwards, he spent his life reestablishing a network of Torah institutions in Israel. In 1944 he laid the foundation of the

The "Ponevezher Rav," Rabbi Joseph Kahaneman, 1888-1969.

Ponevezh Yeshivah in Bene Berak, Israel, and traveled throughout the Jewish world to enlist support for his cause. The result was Kiryat Ponevezh where more than 1,000 students study, and where there are hostels for children and adults, an extensive library and a memorial to Lithuanian Jewry. Furthermore, Rabbi Kahaneman formed the *yarḥei kallah*, a refresher course in talmudic studies for adults to attend each year. He used to say that all his work was done "with 21 fingers" — those of his hands and feet and the finger of God.

KAHN, LOUIS I. (1901-1974), U.S. architect and designer of synagogues. Born in Estonia, Kahn was brought to the U.S. at a young age, and after receiving training as an academic architect he became an expert in city planning. He has held positions as resident architect of the American Academy in Rome, design critic at Yale University, and professor of architecture at the University of Pennsylvania. Many of his projects have won design awards, among them the Yale Art Gallery in New Haven and the Richards Medical Research Building at the University of Pennsylvania. His designs which strive to combine service to functional needs with an attempt to create a flamboyantly picturesque effect have placed him in the forefront of modern international architecture. Among the many synagogues which he has designed is the Mikveh Israel Congregation in Philadelphia. It is fortress-like, featuring a series of massive, repetitive, round block stones, and rounded walls broken up by arched openings which let in natural light. He also designed a model of the Ḥurvah synagogue in the Jewish Quarter of the Old City of Jerusalem.

Charcoal drawing of the interior of the Mikveh Israel Synagogue in Philadelphia, Pennsylvania, designed by the architect Louis Kahn, 1961.

KAIROUAN, *Tunisia,was the commercial meeting place of East and West, and Jews settled there as early as the seventh century c.e. The community became the leading Jewish economic and cultural center in North Africa during the Middle Ages, and a center of Jewish learning. An important correspondence was kept up between the Jews of Kairouan and the Babylonian academies. Kairouan scholars were also in contact with Erez Israel, where there were many immigrants of North African origin. Toward the end of the tenth century, Ḥushi'el ben Elḥanan arrived in Kairouan and from then on the city became an important center of Jewish learning. Ḥushi'el established an academy of unusual spiritual and intellectual ability. At his death he was succeeded as head of the academy by his son Ḥananel who was one of the greatest Jewish scholars of the Middle Ages. The academy was well-known throughout the Jewish world and attracted Jews from many places. According to legend, Ḥushi'el was one of the four rabbis who had set sail from Bari in southern Italy on a mission on behalf of the Babylonian academies to raise funds for the dowries of poor brides, was captured by a Muslim sea raider, and ransomed and redeemed by Jewish communities. He was said to have been sold in Tunisia and so to have become leader of the Kairouan rabbis. For more on the legend, see *Four Captives.

From the end of the first half of the 11th century, Rabbi Nissim ben Jacob ibn Shahin held a prominent position in Kairouan as a result of his vast learning and his many connections. He was the teacher of the Spanish poet Solomon ibn *Gabirol. Rabbi Nissim succeeded his friend Ḥananel ben Ḥushi'el as representative of the Babylonian academies in Kairouan. From his writings can be traced the history of the Jews of North Africa. He was also important in the field of *halakhah.* Sadly, he witnessed the destruction of his community when the Arabs invaded from Egypt in 1057.

Jews again settled in Kairouan after the French conquest in 1881, and two synagogues were founded. But the communities were small and did not take root; today there are no Jews in Kairouan.

KALISCHER, ẒEVI HIRSCH (1795-1874) was a Polish rabbi and Zionist thinker. In addition to his books on *halakhah* and Jewish philosophy, Kalischer's great contribution to Jewish thought was his belief that the settlement of Erez Israel was a necessary first step before the coming of the Messiah.

He believed that there had to be an active human element in the redemption of the Jewish people, expressed in a national movement of the Return to Zion. Pointing to the ongoing struggles of European nations for their independence, Kalischer criticized his fellow Jews for being the only people without national aspirations. In his book *Derishat Ziyyon,* he explained his idea of the return to Erez Israel and stated his theory that redemption would come in two stages: the natural one through return to Erez Israel and working on the land, and the supernatural one which would follow. Furthermore, he preached that the first stage should involve a healthy economic foundation for the *yishuv,* a foundation which could only come about through the development of agriculture on a large scale. Accordingly, he recommended the establishment of an agricultural school for the younger generation.

From the time he published *Derishat Ziyyon,* Kalischer devoted his life to traveling through Europe to enlist support for his idea from the Jewish groups and leading Jewish personalities of the time. In addition, he continued to write sermonizing articles for many Hebrew newspapers and journals as well as works in the field of *halakhah.* Shortly before his death, Kalischer saw the beginning of his ideal realized when an agricultural school was opened at Mikveh Israel in 1870. Although Kalischer had planned to settle there to supervise the observance of the *mitzvot* connected with Erez Israel, his plan was not realized. After his death, his son Ze'ev Wolf Kalischer continued his father's activities, and at his initiative a tract of land near Rachel's tomb was purchased from the funds of Kalischer's estate.

KALLIR, ELEAZAR is the author of numerous *piyyutim,* or liturgical poems in the Jewish prayer book. Although very little is known about his personal personal history, he was the most prolific of the early Jewish poets, who left a tremendous wealth of poems. Kallir's *piyyutim* were widely known in the Orient, the Balkans, Italy, France, Germany and Eastern Europe, and more than 200 such *piyyutim* may be found in various prayer rites. They include poems for all the major festivals, for the special Sabbaths, for fast days and for the prayers for rain and dew. Many of these remained classic models of his particular style, which came to be known as *Kalliri.*

Although biographical facts about Kallir are sparce, various scholars have conjectured about when he lived. Some sources place his lifetime around the year 750 c.e., while others believe he lived as early as 635 c.e. Still others believe him to have lived in the tenth century c.e. It is generally believed that he lived in Erez Israel and resided in Tiberias. According to a 12th century source, he was killed by his teacher *Yannai who was jealous of his talents.

There are also debates about the source of the name Kallir. Some authorities believe the name was derived from the poet's father's hometown which might have been Cagliari, Calais, Cologne or Kallirrhoe, all of which bear a resemblance to Kallir. Other scholars believe Kallir was a nickname derived from Latin, meaning "the fast one." The interpretations of the name Kallir are as numerous as the guesses about the time in which he lived.

KALONYMUS, an eminent German-Jewish family which flourished from the ninth until the 13th century, especially in the cities along the Rhine. Its members included rabbis, preachers, poets, teachers, authors, moralists, and theologians, and most of the prominent communal leaders of the time. The family originated in eighth-century Italy, although the name Kalonymus appears in talmudic literature. Some members migrated from south Italy to Germany in

1. Rabbi Zevi Hirsch Kalischer (1795-1879), one of the earliest of the 19th-century thinkers who advocated active Jewish resettlement of Erez Israel.
2. A reconstructed section of the house in the city of Mainz which belonged to the Kalonymus family.

the ninth century (probably on the orders of Holy Roman Emperor Charles the Bald) and led the German Jewish community through the tragic period of the Crusades and the subsequent upheavals of the 12th and 13th centuries.

*Eleazar ben Judah of Worms mentions in a tract that the family received "secrets" orally from the Babylonian scholar Aaron ben Samuel; many of the most prominent halakhists and talmudic scholars of the time were among its members. Samuel ben Kalonymus he-Ḥasid founded the *Ḥasidei Ashkenaz, and the family led and directed it, and formulated its mystical theology and pious code of behavior. The family also dominated the political and cultural life of German Jewry of the period.

Kalonymus ben Meshullam ha-Parnas, the leader of the Mainz community, was martyred with all his people in the massacres of 1096.

KAPLAN, MORDECAI MENAHEM (1881-   ), a
rabbi and controversial figure; the founder of
*Reconstructionism, a branch of *Conservative
Judaism. He was born in Lithuania and was brought
to the United States at the age of nine. His early
religious education was Orthodox, but during his high
school years he was attracted to other conceptions
of religion. He was ordained at the Jewish Theological
Seminary and served as rabbi of Kehillath Jeshurun
in New York, an Orthodox synagogue. In 1909 he
was appointed dean of the new Teachers' Institute of
the Seminary, and began also to teach in the
rabbinical school. Kaplan was one of the founders of
the New York *Kehillah*, an attempt in 1909 to
organize religious community services. Its pronounced
success was its Bureau of Education. Since Kaplan
believed that the synagogue must serve as the focal
point of all Jewish and related activity, he organized
the first Jewish Center and served as its rabbi from
1917 to 1922. In 1935 he founded the Society for
the Advancement of Judaism and its magazine *The
Reconstructionist.* His teachings had wide influence
and also stirred deep controversy in religious and
Zionist circles, even among his colleagues.

Kaplan argued that many Jews had remained loyal
to their faith despite great hardship because it
assures them salvation in the world to come. He
taught that the focus of Jewish life should be on
people rather than texts and that Judaism should
adapt some of its beliefs and practices to help man
attain salvation in this world. He produced new
editions of the daily and festival *prayer books in

which those passages not in accordance with his philosophy of religion were deleted. This resulted in 1945 in a *ḥerem, or ban, proclaimed by the organization of ultra-orthodox rabbis. Two colleagues at the Seminary, Louis *Ginzberg and Alexander Marx, published an "adverse statement" of criticism. Although Kaplan was an ardent supporter of Jewish settlement in Palestine, he antagonized many Zionists by preaching that the creative survival of the Jewish people in the Diaspora was both possible and desirable.

Kaplan was assisted in his work, and on retirement succeeded, by his son-in-law Ira Eisenstein.

KARAITES are members of a Jewish sect established
in the eighth century c.e. which rejects the rabbinic interpretation of the Bible as put forward in the Talmud and Midrashim. The Karaites claimed that the founder of the sect was *Anan ben David and their oldest document is his *Sefer ha-Mitzvot* ("Book of Commandments") which lists the rules of the Bible without taking the Oral Law of the rabbis into consideration. As it developed, Karaism believed that each teacher of the law could interpret the Bible as he saw fit although certain rules of interpretation did develop.

The name Karaite derives from the Hebrew word *mikra*, scriptures, as opposed to Rabbanite, which denotes a follower of Orthodox rabbinic Judaism.

1. Pillar believed to be from the Kalonymus house in Mainz, dating from the 10th century, the period when the family settled in Germany. The royal symbol of the eagle on the capital is a mark of privilege.
2. The founder of Reconstructionism, Mordecai Kaplan.
3. Photo taken in September 1967 showing the ruins of the Karaite synagogue in the Old City of Jerusalem, which was built in 1864.

The Karaites never considered themselves as outside the Jewish people; in fact they felt that they were the original Jews and that the rabbis of the Talmud had perverted pure Judaism.

Karaism reached its peak during the Geonic period in Babylonia (see *Gaon) and was involved with the traditional leadership in what were often very bitter controversies. The Karaites concentrated on Bible studies, particularly Hebrew language, and their interest stimulated the Rabbanites to work in those areas. Very many books were written by the Karaites against the Rabbanites and *vice versa*. *Sa'adiah Gaon was one of the chief opponents of Karaism.

The Karaite calendar is somewhat different from the accepted Rabbanite calendar. The Karaites fixed the beginning of the month by visual sighting of the moon even after traditional Judaism had ceased that practice. The result is that Karaite holidays do not fall on the same days as do holidays for other Jews (see also *Calendar). They keep the same laws as other Jews but in a different manner since they disregard all the rabbinic interpretations and regulations. Their laws as to what constitutes incest are very different, and in many cases Karaite observance is much stricter. The Karaites do not observe the festival of *Ḥanukkah because it is not in the Bible.

The Karaites always had a deep love for and

attachment to Ereẓ Israel and considered it a great *mitzvah* to live there, particularly in Jerusalem, where they maintained a congregation during the entire Middle Ages and into the modern period.

Although there were acrimonious disputes between them, the Karaites and Rabbanites did try to live in peace in various periods and localities. At times they even intermarried and occasionally in the marriage document the Rabbanite bridegroom promised to allow his Karaite bride to observe the festivals according to the Karaite dates on condition that she also observed the Rabbanite dates. During the later Middle Ages, however, the Rabbanites took a harder position on the Karaites and pronounced that, because of their different marriage laws, they could not be considered Jews. The Karaites themselves were also not eager to be absorbed into the general Jewish population and so the gap widened.

Besides Babylonia, there were important centers of Karaism in Egypt (in all periods until and including the 20th century), Turkey (12th to 16th centuries), and in various parts of what is now Russia, particularly the Crimea (17th to 20th centuries). In 1932 there were approximately 12,000 Karaites in the world. The Nazis did not classify them as Jews and so they were spared in the Holocaust. Their own attitude to the fate of the Jews vacillated between indifference and some cases of actual collaboration with the Germans. In the Arab states, however, after the establishment of the State of Israel, they were persecuted as Jews and most emigrated to Israel where they were welcomed and enabled to settle in compact communities that run their own affairs. It is estimated that there are 7,000 Karaites in Israel. For various aspects of Karaite history and life, see *Anan ben David; *Firkovich, Abraham; *Passover; *Sabbath.

KATZIR, AHARON (1914-1972). Israel has produced a number of scientists of international repute. Aharon Katzir was among the most respected of them.

Katzir was born in Lodz, Poland, and was brought to Ereẓ Israel at the age of 11. He studied at the Hebrew University in Jerusalem and for a few years was a member of the university staff. In 1948 he became head of the Polymer Research department of the Weizmann Institute of Science at Rehovot, and in 1952 was appointed professor of physical chemistry at the Hebrew University. Katzir was a pioneer in the study of the electrochemistry of biopolymers. He

1. Lithograph of a Crimean Karaite woman and her children, by Raffet, published in a travel book in the middle of the 19th century.
2. Professor Aharon Katzir (1914-1972), noted physical-chemist, who was killed in the terrorist massacre at Lod airport in 1972.

received many awards including the Israel Prize for Exact Sciences in 1961. He was president of the Israel Academy of Arts and Sciences from 1962-68, and of the International Union of Pure and Applied Biophysics from 1963. He was one of the passengers killed in the Japanese terrorist attack at Lod (Ben Gurion) Airport in 1972. His brother Ephraim Katzir, a biophysicist, became the fourth president of Israel in 1973.

KATZIR, EPHRAIM (1916-   ), scientist and fourth president of the State of Israel (1973-1978). He was born in Kiev, Russia and was brought to Israel in 1922. In 1973 he changed his family name of Katchalski to Katzir, as had his late brother, Aharon.

Ephraim Katzir served in the *Haganah and studied at the Hebrew University where he received the degrees of M.Sc. (summa cum laude) in 1937 and Ph.D. in 1941. In 1948 he returned from study abroad to work in the fledgling scientific research force of Zahal, the army of the embattled State of Israel, and rose to the rank of Lt. Colonel. When the Weizmann Institute of Science was established in Rehovot in 1949, Katzir was invited to found and head its department of biophysics. In 1962 he was appointed Racoosin Professor of Biophysics. He earned an international reputation for pioneer research in the field of polyamino acids. He lectured at universities and conferences abroad, served on editorial boards of scientific journals and holds membership and honors in major scientific societies. In Israel he encouraged interest in popular science

and in science education. At the University, for the army and in public life he served on numerous committees, often as chairman, devoted to the development of science and its application. Professor Katzir stresses the moral responsibility of the scientist to society. He has expressed concern that Jewish values be taught in ways relevant to a technological era. The President of Israel, he believes, must represent all that is best and most enduring of the Jewish ethic and must symbolize the link between the Jews of Israel and of the Diaspora.

Ephraim Katzir is married to the former Nina Gottlieb. The President's older brother, the distinguished Professor Aharon Katzir, was a victim of the terrorist massacre at Lod airport in 1972.

KATZNELSON, BERL (1887-1944) was a leader of the Zionist labor movement and a central figure of the Second Aliyah.

Born in Bobrinsk, Belorussia, Katznelson was the son of a member of Hovevei Zion (see *Hibbat Zion), and from childhood grew up with dreams of *aliyah*. While in Belorussia, he was a librarian in a Hebrew-Yiddish library as well as a teacher of Hebrew literature and Jewish history. In both capacities he influenced many young people with his Zionist ideas.

In addition to his desire to settle in Israel, Katznelson was strongly imbued with the ideal of physical labor and when he arrived in Israel in 1909, he worked on farms and served on several labor councils. Together with Meir Rotberg, Katznelson helped found the consumer cooperatives for the sale of food, known as "Hamashbir." To meet with the health problems of workers, he helped initiate Kuppat Holim, the Sick Fund. (Both Hamashbir and Kuppat Holim are well-established institutions in Israel today.) After the founding of the *Histadrut, the General Federation of Jewish Labor, Katznelson became the editor of the Histadrut's newspaper *Davar*. In this position, he made the newspaper a spiritual guide for the labor class and attracted many attentive readers.

Katznelson was deeply committed to maintaining the influence of Jewish values, even though among his fellow labor idealists he often stood alone in his views. He was one of the few voices in non-religious labor circles to press for the observance of the Sabbath and festivals, dietary laws in Histadrut kitchens, and the circumcision of children in the kibbutzim.

1. Ephraim Katzir, president of Israel.
2. Mayor Teddy Kollek presenting President Efraim Katzir with an award upon his appointment as honorary citizen of Jerusalem.

In 1939, when Great Britain became increasingly hostile to Jewish immigration to Palestine, Katznelson was instrumental in pressing for *"illegal" immigration. Moreover, under his guidance, his disciples parachuted into Nazi-held territory to try to aid Jewish survivors. Interestingly, during World War II, Katznelson prophesied that the Jews would have to emerge from the war with a Jewish state. However, he died in 1944 before he could see his prophecy realized. Monuments to his memory were established at Bet Berl in Zofit, Oholo on Lake Kinneret and Kibbutz Be'eri.

KAUFMANN, ISIDOR (1853-1921) was a Hungarian Jewish painter, famous for his scenes of everyday Jewish life, especially in the *shtetl* (small Jewish town). During the early years of his career, Kaufmann traveled through Galicia, Poland and the Ukraine, from one village to another, making sketches. From these emerged a group of paintings and portraits which have considerable historical significance because they document the lifestyle of the *shtetl* and depict the *shtibl* (small synagogue) and Jewish ritual objects.

The charm and skill of Kaufmann's paintings were recognized in his lifetime. Emperor Franz Josef bought his painting *The Rabbi's Visit* and presented it to Vienna's Museum of Fine Art. Furthermore, honors were bestowed on Kaufmann by the German emperor and the Russian czar. His son Philip (1888-1969) also achieved renown as a painter.

KAUFMANN, YEHEZKEL (1889-1963) was a biblical scholar, historian and essayist. Born in the Ukraine, Kaufmann studied in the so-called "modern yeshivah" in Odessa and in 1918 received a Ph.D. from the University of Berne. Until 1928, when he emigrated to Erez Israel, he lived in Berlin, where he began his scholarly work. In Erez Israel he taught in the Re'ali School in Haifa and in 1949 he was appointed professor of Bible at Hebrew University, which post he held until his death.

Kaufmann's monumental eight-volume work *Toledot ha-Emmunah ha-Yisre'elit* (1937-57; condensed and translated into English under the title *The Religion of Israel*, 1960) puts forward the thesis in opposition to many modern Bible scholars — that Israelite monotheism was not a gradual development out of paganism but an entirely unique happening in religious history. He also disproved to a large degree many of the modern critical theories about the authorship of the books of the Bible. In other books, Kaufmann proclaimed his faith in the Jewish people. Whatever individual Jews may do, the Jewish people will continue to exist and must seek its salvation as a separate nation and not by assimilation.

In his many years of teaching in Israel and by his books, Kaufmann raised a whole generation of disciples and has had a major influence on modern Jewish scholarship.

KAYE, DANNY (1913-   ), U.S. actor and comedian. The son of a tailor, Jacob Kaminski, Danny Kaye was born and brought up in Brooklyn, New York. He turned to entertaining after a brief career as an insurance agent. In 1939 he played ten weeks on Broadway in *The Straw Hat Revue,* a show partly devised by Sylvia Fine, whom he married and who continued to write material for him.

His spectacular rise began in 1941, when Moss Hart wrote a part for him in the musical *Lady in the Dark.* Kaye scored an immediate success, and soon became a stage and screen favorite on both sides of the Atlantic. His many-sided gifts were fully displayed in the film *The Secret Life of Walter Mitty* (1947). Other films were *The Inspector General* (1949), *Hans Christian Andersen* (1952), and *Me and*

1. Berl Katznelson, Palestinian labor leader and founder of the Histadrut labor union.
2. The paintings of Isidor Kaufmann immortalized the lifestyle of 19th-century Polish Jewry.
3. American entertainer Danny Kaye in the film *Me and the Colonel,* 1958.

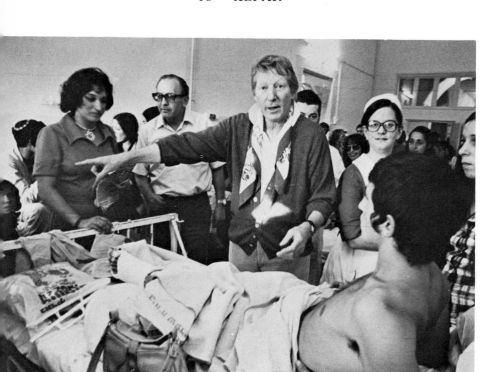

1. Kaye clowns his way through the wards, cheering up wounded soldiers during the Yom Kippur War, 1973.
2. Administrative office in Kefar Ezyon, 1943.

the Colonel (1958). Kaye developed a highly individual style which relied on mime, song, irony, and a sunny personality. In the theater, he was able to hold an audience with an hour-long act of song and monologue.

Danny Kaye serves as ambassador at large for the United Nations International Children's Fund, and visits Israel frequently.

KEFAR EZYON, a kibbutz in the Hebron hills about 14 miles south of Jerusalem, affiliated to the religious kibbutz movement. The first attempt at settlement in that location was made in 1926 by religious Jews from Iraq, but the site was abandoned during the Arab riots of 1929. In 1935 S. Z. Holzmann, a Jewish citrus grove owner, acquired the land and planned a village and country resort. He named the area Kefar Ezyon, a translation of his own name (*ez = holz =* wood). But work was brought to a standstill by the Arab rebellion of 1936-39. In 1943 a group of Polish immigrants founded the first of four villages in the area, again naming it Kefar Ezyon. The four villages were known as the Ezyon Bloc. Kibbutz members worked in farming and afforestation despite frequent Arab attacks from the end of 1947. During the War of Independence, the kibbutz harassed Arab communications on the Jerusalem front. A group of 35 members of the Palmaḥ and Haganah

(remembered as Ha-Lamed-He; the letter *lamed* = 30 and *heh* = 5) who attempted to reinforce the Bloc, was intercepted by Arabs and all its members killed on January 16, 1948. A relief convoy in May suffered severe losses and on May 14 the Bloc fell to the Arab Legion and vast numbers of Arab irregulars. Most of the defenders were massacred. The villages were totally obliterated and the Legion set up camp on the site.

In the *Six-Day War of 1967, the Bloc area together with the Hebron hills was recaptured by the Israel army. In September 1967, Kibbutz Kefar Ezyon was reestablished by a group which included children of those original settlers killed in 1948. The new kibbutz, in addition to farming, set up a number of industrial enterprises.

KENNEDY, JOHN FITZGERALD (1917-1963). Crowning a hill on the outskirts of western Jerusalem and constructed in the shape of a tree whose trunk was severed before it was fully grown is the John F. Kennedy Memorial. It was built with contributions by citizens from each of the 50 states of the U.S. in memory of the 35th American president, whose life ended tragically by assassination at the age of 46.

During his political career, Kennedy showed a strong belief in America's moral commitment to Israel and to Jews all over the world. As a senator, he proposed legislation easing immigration to America for Jewish refugees from Arab countries. When he ran successfully against Richard *Nixon for the presidency in 1960, he received the support of 80% of the Jewish voters. As president, he recognized the anti-Nasser government in Syria in 1961 and sold Hawk missiles to Israel for protection against air attack in 1962. During his administration, American economic and technical assistance to Israel were substantially increased. At the same time, in an unsuccessful effort to bring peace to the Middle East, he tried to

persuade Egyptian President Nasser to foster economic and social progress at home rather than concentrate on his foreign wars. In 1968, his younger brother, Senator Robert F. Kennedy, was assassinated in Los Angeles by an Arab extremist.

KEREN HAYESOD. The settlement of modern Israel would not have been possible without Keren Hayesod (the Palestine Foundation Fund), the financial arm of the World Zionist Organization, founded in 1920. Its purpose was to appeal to Zionists and non-Zionists alike for funds to finance immigration and colonization in Palestine and to encourage business enterprise in close cooperation with private capital. Contributions were to constitute an annual voluntary tax.

The head office was in London until 1926 when it was transferred to Jerusalem. From 1925, the fund operated in the United States with the *Jewish National Fund, as the United Palestine Appeal, and later combined with other groups to form the United Jewish Appeal. The UJA operates in the United States, while the Keren Hayesod head office in Jerusalem coordinates operations in 60 other countries including the State of Israel. Keren Hayesod and the United Jewish Appeal in the United States are based mainly on the work of volunteers. In almost every country with a Jewish population there is a central committee to collect contributions. The emergency campaign initiated just before the Six-Day War, 1967, increased twelvefold Keren Hayesod's normal annual income from countries other than the United States. This was achieved by an increase in both the size of individual contributions and the number of donors, which rose from 200,000 to 400,000. The income rose from $15m in 1966 to $150m in 1967. Keren Hayesod has helped establish 820 towns and villages since 1921; has cooperated in the support of the many activities of the *Jewish Agency; and has helped to finance such important

enterprises as the General Mortgage Bank, Israel Land Development Corporation, Mekorot Water Company, Israel Electric Corporation, Bank Leumi, Zim Navigation Company, El Al Airlines, and many others.

KHAZARS were a people who inhabited a region of southeast Europe between the seven and tenth centuries c.e. During part of this time some of the leading Khazars converted to Judaism.

Origin and Location of the Khazars. The origin of the Khazar people is not certain. It appears that they are descended from the Huns and Turks since in the fifth century c.e. their region belonged to the empire of the Huns, and later in the sixth century c.e., to the West Turkish Empire.

The extent of the Khazar empire is also questionable. From the sparse archaeological evidence, scholars assume the territory of the Khazars to have been in the area of the Crimea, the Volga and the Caucasus or in the general area between the Black Sea and Caspian Sea (also called Sea of the Khazars). However, there is additional evidence that the Khazar kingdom at one time reached as far west as the Danube River, and that Khazars even occupied Kiev at some time before 862 c.e.

Khazars and Judaism. In spite of the negligible information about the origin of the Khazars, the presence of Jewish groups and the impact of Jewish ideas in Eastern Europe during the Middle Ages attest to the probability of Khazar influence. Groups have been mentioned as migrating to Central Europe from the east or have been referred to as Khazars, thus making it possible to assume that they originated from the former Khazar Empire. Furthermore,

1.   John F. Kennedy at his inauguration as president of the United States, January 1961.
2.   The extent of the Khazar empire.

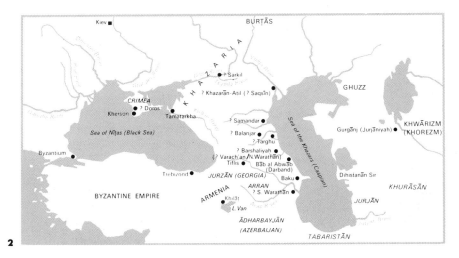

1. Letter from the Jew
Ḥisdai Ibn Shaprut to the
king of the Khazars, tenth
century.
2. Residential buildings of
Kibbutz En Ḥarod in
northern Israel.

although the 12th century traveler *Benjamin of Tudela did not mention Khazaria, he did mention Khazars living in Constantinople and Alexandria.

Conversion to Judaism. There is evidence from several sources that in approximately the late eighth century c.e. the king of the Khazars became a Jew. An account of the king's conversion to Judaism formed the basis of *Judah Halevi's famous philosophical work, the *Kuzari,* which presents the arguments in support of Jewish beliefs that persuaded the king to convert. However, the extent of the Khazars' observance of Jewish law is somewhat questionable. Some sources indicate that their adherence to Judaism was imperfect since they retained a number of pagan customs dating back to their Turkic origins. Moreover, it seems that while the Khazars were known by their neighbors as Jews, they had little or no contact with the central Jewish organizations in Iraq. There is also a tendency to associate the Khazars with the *Karaites (a Jewish sect which observed biblical tradition but denied talmudic-rabbinic laws); however there is no conclusive evidence to establish the Karaism of the Khazars.

An important source of information about the Khazars' observance of Judaism is the Khazar Correspondence. This was an interchange of letters in Hebrew between *Ḥisdai ibn Shaprut, a well-known Jewish personality of Muslim Spain in the tenth century, and Joseph, king of the Khazars. The authenticity of the correspondence is, however, questionable. Ḥisdai's first letter to Joseph is in the form of an enquiry; Ḥisdai heard that the Khazars were Jews and was interested to learn more about them, their kingdom and their conversion to Judaism. Joseph's reply to Ḥisdai relates the early history of the Khazars and deals at length with the story of the conversion to Judaism under the king Bulan. He relates Bulan's dream which initiated the desire to convert, and he describes the debate between the representatives of Judaism, Christianity and Islam, after which Bulan decides to accept Judaism. Joseph further mentions the reforms which took place under a later king, Obadiah, who built synagogues and schools and introduced the Khazars to Torah, Mishnah, Talmud and liturgy.

After this correspondence, which took place during the tenth century c.e., there is very little additional information about the Khazars as an independent people. Their territory was apparently invaded by Russian and later by Mongol armies, and the Khazars were scattered throughout Eastern Europe and parts of Asia. At one time, the Turkish-speaking Karaites of the Crimea and Poland claimed that they descended from the Khazars, and this connection was further reinforced by evidence from folklore, anthropology, and similar language. Moreover, there seems to be a connection between the Khazars of the Caucasus region and the *Mountain Jews of today.

KIBBUTZ. One of the original contributions that modern Jewish settlement in Ereẓ Israel and the State of Israel has made to the world is the kibbutz. A kibbutz is a group of people who choose to live and farm collectively. The idea started in 1909, when seven wage-earning pioneers working near the south of Lake Kinneret asked the Jewish National Fund to be allowed to farm a plot of its land on their own responsibility. The trial period of kibbutz *Deganyah was such a success that by 1969 Israel had 93,000 people living in 231 kibbutzim. Some are rugged border outposts newly settled by twenty-odd determined young Israelis as part of their army service. Some of the older-established kibbutzim have factories as well as farms, and have as many as 1,600 members, with swimming pools and air-conditioning.

One for All, All for One. The swimming pools, however, are no-one's private property. There is no private wealth whatever. Once a new member is accepted after a year's trial period, he gives everything he owns (apart from personal possessions) to the kibbutz. In addition, he is expected to put in his honest day's work in whatever field the kibbutz planning committee finds most useful for the kibbutz as a whole.

On the other hand, though he will never own a private swimming pool, the individual kibbutz member does not have to worry about paying his own

gas bills, nor does his wife do her own family's shopping. The kibbutz as a whole attends to their needs — housing, food, clothing, schooling, medical care, and so on. If their kibbutz can afford it, they will be allowed a certain degree of freedom in spending according to their individual taste — on clothing, cultural activities, hobbies and vacations. **Children**. Kibbutz children live very differently from their city friends. Firstly, they live in children's houses, where they eat, sleep, play and study together. In some ways they are a miniature kibbutz of their own, conducting their own affairs with the advice of teachers and trained group leaders. In some kibbutzim they even operate their own small farms.

Mothers (especially those with young babies) visit their children frequently during the day, and after work the children are with their parents. A few kibbutzim prefer to have the children sleep in their parents' homes. The school timetable includes certain hours on the farm, where teachers and pupils continue their work side by side.

1. Deganyah Alef in the Jordan Valley, first kibbutz established in Erez Israel.
2. Communal dining room at Kibbutz Kefar Blum.
3. Wedding on a religious kibbutz. The couple is conveyed on a flower-covered tractor, accompanied by the singing and dancing of friends.

The Community at Work. Each kibbutz strives to set up a society where there is fair play for every single member. It is governed by a weekly meeting of all its members, who from time to time elect committees to deal with farm management, education, and so on. There is a communal kitchen, laundry, and tailor shop.

Physical labor is respected, so that kibbutzim employ outsiders only when they have no alternative, such as at harvest time. (Nowadays the harvest is not necessarily the members' main concern, for many kibbutzim engage in secondary industries such as textiles and furniture production.) All kinds of work are considered as being of equal value, though being near nature is especially prized. In recent years, however, kibbutzim have had to face the fact that an increasing number of people want to work in nearby cities as university lecturers, doctors or lawyers, while still remaining members of the kibbutz.

Another problem is the position of the woman in the community. The kibbutz was intended, among other things, to free women from household chores so that they could tackle other tasks. In practice, however, as a kibbutz grows older, scores of hands are needed to care for its children and for household work of various kinds. Some women are therefore not

very sure that they have gained anything by the change. A further problem is that some members may have outside sources of income, such as gifts from overseas, and if some of this is kept, this leads to visible inequality.

Collective Cooperation. Kibbutzim with similar ways of thinking often group together in federations, which save their member-villages money by purchasing for them all in bulk, and arranging from one central office to sell all their crops. In addition, many kibbutzim cooperate with other kibbutzim in the same region, whether they share the same ideas or

1. Religious kibbutzniks take time out from guard duty during the tense times in 1948 to do some studying.
2. Cleaning the kibbutz chicken coops.
3. A member of Kibbutz Kefar Giladi in the Upper Galilee harvesting plums.

not, and together they are able to build central silos and arrange heavy transport. Likewise, the kibbutz associations have their own adult education courses, choirs, amateur orchestras, art collections, bulletins, publishing houses, and even their own teachers' training college. Thousands of members of certain older kibbutzim, after completing their three-year army service, volunteer a year's labor — unpaid, of course — in newer kibbutzim, in order to help them stand on their own feet.

Kibbutz Festivals. The kibbutzim have developed their own festive occasions, with pageants, song and dance, and have given them a connection with ancient festivals by using the biblical Hebrew names and dates. These festivals stress the farming side of ancient Israel's life — such as in the kibbutz festivals of first fruits, sheepshearing, vineyards, and the harvest. Others commemorate events in modern Israel history, or in the history of a particular kibbutz, or mark the day on which the young people of the kibbutz become full members.

Plow and Sword. From the beginning of Jewish resettlement in Ereẓ Israel, the kibbutzim have accepted a double challenge — resettling the most inhospitable regions of the homeland, and safeguarding all settlers against attack. Thus, between 1936 and 1947, in the face of difficulties from British officials and Arab marauders, many kibbutzim were established literally overnight: a watchtower was erected and barricades were set up around it. This was called the "Stockade and Watchtower" plan.

These farming strongholds served as bases for the Haganah defense force and later for the Palmaḥ, its commando section.

Manpower. The early kibbutzim were manned by volunteers from pioneering youth movements abroad. The newer kibbutzim, especially in the desolate Negev and, after the Six-Day War (1967), in the Golan Heights, have generally been founded by *sabras,* including the children and grandchildren of kibbutzniks, and graduates of Youth Aliyah and various Israel youth movements. The Jews from Muslim countries, however, and the survivors of the Holocaust, who arrived in enormous numbers during the early years of the state, were not used to the kibbutz style of life, and often preferred to settle in moshavim.

The kibbutzim nevertheless worked hard for the rescue and relief of European refugees smuggled ashore in the pre-state days of "illegal" immigration. Certain kibbutzim particularly seek to have migrants from a range of different countries, in order to contribute thereby to the harmonious mingling of the exiles.

The Religious Kibbutz. There are over a dozen religious kibbutzim, which combine the usual kibbutz principles — labor, pioneering, equality, and communal living — with a way of life organized according to the Torah. This means that they have to be familiar with its laws. These farmers therefore gather every day to study Torah with their friends. Every detail of Jewish observance is attended to. Cows, for example, must be milked seven days a week, so in order to safeguard the sanctity of the

1. This industrialized kibbutz has a milk processing and packaging plant.
2. Babies in the kibbutz children's house play while their parents work in the fields.

Sabbath they are milked on that day by automatically regulated milking machines.

In all their dealings with each other, in their kibbutz communities and in their youth villages, these settlers seek to bring into day-to-day action the ideals of social justice of which the prophets spoke. **Contribution to Israel Life.** The kibbutz way of life leaves an imprint throughout the country. Only four out of every 100 Israelis are kibbutzniks, yet they make up about 14% of army officers. A quarter of all the casualties in the Six-Day War were soldiers from kibbutzim. 12% of the nation's total wealth in the course of a year is produced by the kibbutzim, and in some of the Knessets one sixth of the members were kibbutz members.

KIDDUSH. The table is set for the festive meal, with the Sabbath candles glowing in polished holders. The family stands and the father raises the brimming silver cup to say *Kiddush,* the blessing and sanctification over wine. This age-old ceremony is in fulfillment of the biblical command, "Remember the Sabbath day to keep it holy" (Exodus 20:8). "Remember it," said the rabbis, "over wine," for *wine is the symbol of joy.

Kiddush is recited on the evening of the Sabbath, or the festival, before the start of the meal. Nothing may be eaten before *Kiddush.* On Sabbath eve, the first paragraph of *Kiddush* includes a phrase from the end of the first chapter of Genesis and the passage at the beginning of the second which describe God's completion of Creation and His sanctification of the seventh day as a day of rest. *Kiddush* continues with the benediction for wine, preceded by the word *savri* (Attention!) so that all present, men and women, may fulfill the requirement of *Kiddush* by listening carefully to the recital of the prayer and by responding "Amen" afterwards. When wine is not available, the blessing is said over **hallah,* the Sabbath loaves. Reform Judaism has retained the *Kiddush* ceremony, which is an integral part of Orthodox and Conservative practice. The festival *Kiddush* concludes with the *She-he-heyanu* blessing, ". . . who permitted us to reach this day." When the festival follows the Sabbath, *Kiddush* includes *Havdalah,* the benediction which terminates the Sabbath.

The proper recitation of *Kiddush* is just before the festive meal, at the place where the meal will be eaten. However, it is a custom among Ashkenazi Jews to say *Kiddush* in the synagogue just after the Sabbath

1. French *Kiddush* cup, 1835, inscribed with the blessing for wine.
2. Drawing by the 19th-century Dutch artist, Josef Israels, of an old Jew reciting the *Kiddush.*

2

services. Originally it was for the benefit of travelers who were lodged in the synagogue, to enable them to fulfill the precept. This custom is not followed in Israel.

The morning *Kiddush,* before the first meal on the Sabbath or festival day, was instituted by the rabbis. Beverages other than wine may also be used. In homes and in synagogues this *Kiddush* has become an occasion for visiting and socializing. See also **Sabbath.*

KIDNAPPING. Stealing a human being for gain is a capital offense in the Bible. One verse (Exodus 21:16) says that kidnapping is to be punished by death under all circumstances. Another (Deuteronomy 24:7) states that the kidnapper should be put to death if he enslaved or sold his victim. The rabbis interpreted the verses to mean that kidnapping either a Jew or non-Jew is forbidden under all circumstances. But the death penalty is only applicable if the kidnapper actually exploited his victim as a slave or sold him in slavery. Of course, in order to convict there has to be testimony of valid witnesses. The eighth of the Ten Commandments "Thou shalt not steal" is understood by the sages to refer to kidnapping and not to ordinary theft which is prohibited elsewhere in the Torah.

Since the prohibition against kidnapping applies to both Jews and non-Jews, slave-trading is aboutely forbidden according to Judaism. There can be no justification whatsoever for enslaving another person against his will. See also *Slavery.

KIEV, capital city of the Ukrainian S.S.R. and scene of Jewish persecution throughout most of the city's history. From as early as the eighth century c.e. Jews were living in Kiev, and were engaged in commercial business. And as the Jewish community increased in numbers, so did the number of Jewish scholars. By 1815 there were 1,500 Jews living in Kiev with two synagogues and other communal institutions. However, the Jewish community was constantly harassed by expulsion orders and anti-Semitic decrees (such as prohibitions against Jews owning property or engaging in trade). In 1835, Czar Nicholas I ordered all the Jews expelled from the city. When the restriction was lifted, Jews returned to the city and the Jewish community continued to grow. Jews achieved positions in the various professions, Jewish students attended Kiev University, and several Hebrew writers lived and wrote in the city (among them *Shalom Aleichem).

The development of the Jewish community by no means indicated the absence of persecution, however. Tensions between Christians and Jews continued to grow and, both in 1881 and 1905, sparked pogroms which raged in the streets of Kiev. Rioters ran uncontrolled through the city injuring many Jews, and laying waste to their homes and property. Between 1911 and 1913, Kiev was the center of the notorious *Beilis blood libel trial, and was again racked by the agitation of the masses.

During the first 20 years of the Soviet regime which began in 1917, Kiev became a center of Yiddish culture. Yiddish authors lived and wrote in Kiev and the city had a Yiddish state theater, as well as Yiddish newspapers and publishing houses.

The fall of the city to the Germans on September 21, 1941, marked the end of Kiev Jewry and the destruction of the archives of Kiev's Yiddish culture. Kiev was the setting of Babi Yar, the location of the infamous brutal massacre and a mass execution ground throughout the German occupation, the grave of 100,000 Jews. At the end of World War II, Jews returned to Kiev and within the next 15 years, the city's Jewish population grew to over 200,000. However, an anti-Semitic atmosphere has continued to prevail in the city. Kiev has only one synagogue and its congregants have been tormented by Soviet authorities, and have been forbidden to have contact with foreign visitors. Between 1960 and 1966, the baking of *mazzot* was prohibited and Jews were punished for baking them "illegally" in their homes.

After the *Six-Day War in 1967, Jewish national feeling reemerged publicly in Kiev. The anniversary of Babi Yar has become a rallying day for Jews, most of whom come to express their Jewish identification. However, Soviet oppression of Jews continues and many have been arrested and imprisoned on charges of "Zionist activities."

KING DAVID HOTEL. If you ever get lost in Jerusalem, you can probably find your way by sighting the King David Hotel, a golden-pinkish, six-storey stone building set off by pale green shutters, that overlooks the crenellated walls of the Old City.

Built in 1930, this 250-room landmark is the most famous hotel in Israel. Its roster of guests has included queens, prime ministers, diplomats, wealthy businessmen and ordinary tourists. The hotel met a unique challenge in 1977 with the housing of President Sadat of Egypt and his entourage.

But even an institution like the King David cannot

2

1

3

1. A handful of Kiev Jews braving Soviet repressions to pray at the city's only synagogue, 1964.
2. Tombstone in Kiev whose inscription makes reference to the Nazi victims who died between 1941 and 1943.
3. King David Hotel, Jerusalem.

1. Rescue workers bring out one of the victims of the *Irgun* explosion at the King David Hotel in 1946.
2. Remains of an ancient fortress amid the modern resort facilities of Lake Kinneret.

escape the troubles of the outside world. On July 22, 1946, 80 people died when the north wing housing British government and military offices was blown up, after warning, by the *Irgun Ẓevai Le'ummi,* a militant Jewish group opposed to British policy in Palestine. Twenty-one years later, during the Six-Day War, a dozen foreign journalists and guests remained safely in the hotel while fired upon by Jordanian soldiers.

KINGSHIP. In biblical times in the ancient Near East, the monarch was accepted as the sole ruler, with complete authority over his subjects. The status of kings varied from emperor to vassal as the kingdoms varied in size from a tribe like Midian to a vast empire such as Egypt. But the idea common to all was that the direct relationship between the king and the deity was part of the natural order.

Kingship in Israel was established later in the history of the nation and it developed with important differences from neighboring states. Early efforts to establish a monarchy were resisted as a contradiction of the direct rule of God over His people. This attitude existed even when *Saul was made Israel's first king, but it did not last. The king came to replace the judge and the prophet as the national leader, yet he was guided by them in his strong but not absolute rule in military, as well as political, matters.

The primary feature of the coronation was the *anointing of the king's head with oil by a priest or

prophet, the sign of the divine covenant — that is, he had been chosen as God's anointed. From its inception, the monarchy was in principle hereditary. In the northern kingdom of Israel there were many rebellions and frequent changes of dynasty. In the southern kingdom of Judea the monarchy remained in the house of *David. The ideal king was seen as a king of justice. Prophecies of the future declare that in the "end of days" the kingdom of the Jews will be returned to a descendant of the House of David.

KINNERET, LAKE. The Kinneret is a freshwater lake in northeast Israel. It covers an area of 64 square miles; its maximum length (north to south) is 15 miles and its maximum width (east to west) is 10 miles. The surface of the lake is approximately 696 feet below the level of the Mediterranean Sea and, at its deepest, the water is about 144 feet deep. The Kinneret is fed by a number of fresh water streams. There are also salty springs at the lake bottom and along its shores. These add to the salt content (salinity) of the water which is intensified by the high evaporation rate due to the hot climate. The amount of water in the lake varies a great deal with the shift from rainy to drought years. Until the winter of 1973/74 several years of drought had lowered the surface considerably but that exceedingly rainy winter restored it to its average. The river Jordan flows out of the southern end. In 1964 the National Water Carrier was completed to bring sweet water to the more southern sections of Israel; Lake Kinneret is the main reservoir from which the water is taken.

Because of its abundant water supply, warm climate and surrounding fertile area, Lake Kinneret has attracted man since prehistoric times. The most ancient human remains and artifacts found in Ereẓ Israel come from an area not far from Lake Kinneret's shores. In the Early Bronze Age some of

the largest cities of Canaan were situated nearby and the *Via Maris* ("Maritime Route") passed its shores contributing to the wealth of the cities. In fact, Egyptian documents mention the hot springs on the shores of Lake Kinneret and their beneficial effects. In Bible times, Kinneret served as a prominent boundary mark: in the Canaanite era, it was the border of Sidon, king of the Amorites, and after Israel's conquest of the land, it marked the boundary between the territories of Naphtali on its western shores and Manasseh on its eastern shores.

In the period of the Roman occupation, King Herod received the city of Hippus (Susitha), which bordered on the east of the lake, and Herod's sons, Antipas and Philip, founded the cities of *Tiberias and Julias (Bethsaida). (Subsequently the lake also became known as the Sea of Tiberias.) Moreover, it was also during the Roman period that the Lake Kinneret region served as the setting of Jesus' preaching, and later as the center of his apostles' activities. As a result, many churches were later built on these same shores. The crusaders fought to control the lake area because of its historic connections with Christianity. The New Testament refers to the lake as the Sea of Galilee and the Sea of Gennesareth.

Beginning with the 20th century, Jewish settlement was gradually revived on the lake's west and south shores, with the founding of such settlements as Deganyah and Kinneret, and later on the east shore with the establishment of Kibbutz Ein Gev. A fishing industry was developed and tourism promoted, and today the area is an important vacation center particularly in winter when it is very warm there. Every year there is a swimming contest across the Kinneret in which hundreds of people, both young and old, participate.

Until 1967, Lake Kinneret and a small strip on the eastern shore of the lake served as the border between Israel and Syria. However, Syria's aggression and its attempts to set up military positions on Israel territory near Ein Gev became increasing sources of friction and tension. This was one of the causes of the *Six-Day War which resulted in Israel's occupation of the Golan Heights (east of Lake Kinneret). Thus as of 1967, Lake Kinneret was no longer the border between Israel and Syria, and it is presently an inland lake of Israel.

KISHINEV is the capital city of the Moldavian S.S.R., formerly within Bessarabia. Except for a period of Rumanian annexation (1922-1940) it has always been part of Russia. In the 19th century it was a large commercial and industrial city and a flourishing center of Jewish communal activity. There were five schools with instruction in Hebrew and Yiddish, a yeshivah, and many printing presses for Hebrew and other books, where thousands of Jews were employed.

The Russian policy which limited the means of livelihood open to Jews left many of them poor and so a number of welfare organizations were established to help them. Kishnev was the headquarters of these and of many other Jewish institutions of Bessarabia, including the developing Zionist movement.

Kishinev exploded into the conscience of the world when two violent pogroms, encouraged by the Russian government, and by the local police chief, erupted at the turn of the century. At Easter 1903, the body of a Christian child was found abandoned and a Christian woman patient committed

1. Agricultural settlements bordering on Lake Kinneret provide a patchwork of lush green. In the background are the mountains of the Golan Heights.
2. Victims of the Kishinev pogrom of 1903 laid out in the yard of the cemetery.

suicide in a Jewish hospital. Although later investigation showed that neither death could be connected with Jews, the events sparked brutal mob violence. Students from Russian theological seminaries and universities were among the most violent. The local army garrison, which could have controlled them, took no action. Forty-nine persons were murdered, and 500 injured. In the destruction and looting, over 2,000 were left homeless. There was a public outcry throughout the world and demonstrations were held in major cities. Americans handed a letter to President Theodore Roosevelt for delivery to the Czar, but the latter refused to accept it. Public opinion compelled some official action, but it was only a token procedure. *Bialik described the pogrom in a moving poem. Tolstoy and other Russian writers expressed their sympathy. In 1905 another pogrom was met with resistance by a Jewish *self-defense unit. But Jews were beginning to leave Kishinev for the U.S. and Palestine. There was constant harassment, official and unofficial, which continued through the period of the Russian revolution, when Jews from the Ukraine streamed into Kishinev, and even during the period of Rumanian annexation, before World War II. Schools, newspapers and other institutions of Jewish culture were shut down. In 1941 there were about 70,000 Jews in Kishinev when German and Rumanian units entered the city. By 1947 there were 5,500 left, though Jews from surrounding areas later returned to settle again in Kishinev.

Like other Jewish communities in Russia, Kishinev now lives under the restrictive measures imposed by the government. All synagogues but one are closed, *mohalim* are warned not to perform circumcision, bar-mitzvah is forbidden. There is a Jewish dramatic group, however. The city's Jewish population today is estimated at about 60,000.

KISHON, EPHRAIM (1924-). Some people, in their hectic rush through life, are oblivious of the little things that can bring so much joy and fascination. Yet a few, like the Israel writer and director, Ephraim Kishon, are so acutely perceptive that almost nothing eludes them, or fails to amuse them. Kishon has verbally jousted with American parking lot attendants, Israel telephone operators, bungling government officials, his own shortcomings, and a thousand other subjects, and he has kept his audience reading, laughing, and thinking for many years.

1. Ephraim Kishon, Israel's most famous satirist.
2. Scene from Kishon's film *Sallah Shabbati,* starring Chaim Topol, 1964.

He was born in Budapest, Hungary, as Ferenc Kishont. (According to one of his satires, his name was changed a few hours after his ship landed in Israel by an impatient immigration clerk who preferred his own spelling.) At first, Kishon studied art, but his talent to amuse soon surfaced, and he began publishing humorous essays and sketches for the Hungarian stage.

After he arrived in Israel at the age of 25, he studied the Hebrew language diligently and began to contribute articles to *Omer,* the easy-Hebrew daily. Since 1952, he has written a column of political and social humor and satire that appears in *Ma'ariv* and is translated and reprinted in other newspapers as well.

His style is original and his characters are vivid and engaging. *Sallah Shabbati,* a comedy film written, directed, and produced by Kishon about the housing problem and the new immigrant in Israel, has enjoyed worldwide popularity. Among his satirical works in English are *Look Back, Mrs. Lot; The Sea-Sick Whale;* and *So Sorry We Won.*

KISSINGER, HENRY (1923-), U.S. political scientist and the first Jewish secretary of state. Born in Fuerth, Bavaria, to Orthodox parents, he emigrated to the United States with his family in 1938 and worked to support his parents while he studied accountancy. Kissinger was drafted into the U.S. Army in 1943 and there came under the influence of Fritz Kraemer, a fellow German refugee lawyer. For a period during World War II, Kissinger was military commander of the occupied town of Krefeld. He then spent eight years studying political science at Harvard University, where he came to know many future leaders of the emerging nations. In 1957 his book *A World Restored* won the Sumner Prize.

Kissinger favored the development of tactical nuclear weapons and the maintenance of a strong, conventional army. In the Kennedy and Johnson administrations he occasionally acted as an adviser. In 1962 he became a full professor at Harvard, and his reputation as a hard-thinking realist recommended him to Richard M. Nixon who, after his 1968 presidential victory, appointed Kissinger presidential adviser on foreign policy, with responsibility for directing the National Security Council. At 46, Kissinger was thus catapulted into one of the most influential positions in the world.

Nixon's own history as an anti-Communist secured Kissinger against attack from those in the U.S. who feared the administration's new policy of closer ties with the Communist bloc.

Kissinger negotiated the cessation of the Vietnam war and the withdrawal of U.S. troops. He also initiated a successful policy of friendship toward China, which resulted in the reestablishment of diplomatic relations between Peking and Washington. Following the Yom Kippur War of October 1973, Kissinger did everything to encourage some sort of negotiations between Israel and the Arab states. After weeks of personal diplomacy during which he shuttled back and forth between Jerusalem and Cairo, and Jerusalem and Damascus, he succeeded in bringing about a separation of forces, first with Egypt and then with Syria. After the successful completion of the separation with Egypt, the Geneva conference was convened to continue negotiations in the hope of reaching stable peace agreements.

Despite Kissinger's apparent diplomatic success in Vietnam (where the war did not end), for which he received a Nobel Peace Prize, and his spectacular tours of the world's trouble spots, there were still many in the United States and elsewhere who were critical of his policies. To the Jews especially, it appeared that Israel was being asked to make concessions affecting its security in order that the United States might enjoy the benefits of trade with the Arabs, the Russians, and the Chinese. With the election of Jimmy Carter as president Kissinger's appointment as secretary of state ended. He became a professor at Georgetown University and was appointed vice-chairman of Chase Manhattan Bank's international advisory committee. He is publishing his memoirs in a multi-volume work.

KITEL (Yiddish: "Gown"). In Ashkenazi tradition it is not just the bride who wears white on her wedding day. The groom, too, stands under the canopy wearing his white *kitel*, or robe, over his wedding finery. The day of their *marriage is a solemn one for the bride and groom. They pray that their past sins will be forgiven and they can start their life together afresh. The white of their clothing symbolizes the purity and the forgiveness of sin for which they are hoping. For this reason a similar garment is used to clothe the dead for *burial. The *kitel* therefore also serves to remind the wearer of how brief life is, and of the necessity for atonement.

The *kitel* is traditionally worn on those important occasions when the Jew is concerned with such thoughts. It is worn during prayer services on *Rosh Ha-Shanah and Yom Kippur; at the seder on *Passover eve; by the *ḥazzan* on the eighth day of *Sukkot when the prayer for rain is recited and the first day of Passover during the prayer for dew.

KLAUSNER, JOSEPH GEDALIAH (1874-1958), literary critic, historian, and Zionist. Klausner was born in Olkienik, near Vilna. In 1885 his family moved to Odessa where he attended a Hebrew day school. He showed great interest in the Hebrew language, which was to be one of the main interests of his life. He became a member of the *Sefatenu Ittanu,* a society for the revival of spoken Hebrew, established in Odessa in 1891. In 1897 he proceeded to Germany, where he studied at Heidelberg, and in the same year he strongly urged participation in, and he attended, the first Zionist Congress in Basle. At the age of 28 he moved to Warsaw to succeed *Ahad Ha-Am as editor of the Hebrew literary monthly, *Ha-Shilo'ah,* a position he held for 23 years. In February 1917, he was invited to lecture at Odessa University, but following the Bolshevik Revolution in October he immigrated to Palestine, settling in Jerusalem in 1919. He took an active part in the Va'ad ha-Lashon (later, the Academy of the Hebrew Language) and continued to act as editor of *Ha-Shilo'ah* when it was revived in Ereẓ Israel from 1921-26. When the Hebrew University was established, he was appointed to the chair of Hebrew literature. In 1944, at the age of 70, he was appointed to the chair of the History of the Second Temple. From 1950 until shortly before his death he acted as editor in chief of the *Encyclopaedia Hebraica.* He published his autobiography in 1946.

KLEMPERER, OTTO (1885-1973), conductor, was born in Breslau and started his career in 1907 in Prague. He was director of the opera in Cologne from 1917 to 1924, and in Wiesbaden from 1924 to 1927. As conductor of the Kroll Opera in Berlin from 1927

1. Henry Kissinger, standing beside the then President Richard Nixon, takes the oath of office as Secretary of State of the United States.
2. Joseph Klausner, Hebrew writer and historian.
3. Otto Klemperer, renowned conductor.

to 1931, he achieved renown for his stimulating interpretations of Mozart and his sponsorship of modern works. From 1931 to1933, he conducted the Berlin State Opera and Philharmonic Choir. Emigrating to the U.S. in 1933, Klemperer became director of the Los Angeles Philharmonic, later reorganized the Pittsburgh Symphony Orchestra, and undertook tours to various countries. Illness and accidents interrupted his career, but he returned to the podium in spite of increasing bodily handicaps which obliged him to conduct while seated. From 1947 to 1950 he was the musical director of the Budapest Opera and then for several seasons worked again in Berlin. Subsequently he conducted the newly formed Philharmonia Orchestra in London. He then returned to the U.S. Klemperer was considered the last of the great conductors in the grand German tradition. Klemperer became estranged from Judaism at an early age but toward the end of his life he became increasingly conscious of his Jewishness. He visited Israel several times and conducted the Israel Radio Orchestra in several concerts. Before he died he became an Israeli citizen.

KOHLER, KAUFMANN (1843-1926) was a U.S. Reform rabbi who exercised a significant influence on the trend of American Reform Judaism in his day. Born in Bavaria, Kohler grew up in an Orthodox home and pursued traditional rabbinic studies. However, despite his upbringing, his viewpoint diverged sharply from traditional Judaism. Kohler received a doctorate from the University of Berlin in 1867, and his thesis took such a radical viewpoint that no Orthodox rabbinic position was open to him.

He was warmly recommended by German Reform leader Abraham *Geiger, however, and under his guidance accepted the office of rabbi of Congregation Beth El, Detroit in 1869. In 1871 he moved to Sinai Congregation of Chicago, and in 1879 succeeded his father-in-law, David *Einhorn, at Temple Beth El, New York.

Kohler emerged as a national champion of Reform Judaism in 1885, when he published a series of sermons on the Reform position. The outcome of this was the convening of the Pittsburg Conference of Reform rabbis and its adoption of a new radical program known as the Pittsburg Platform (see also *Reform Judaism). In 1903, Kohler was appointed president of *Hebrew Union College and during his tenure there sought to improve its curriculum and faculty.

Throughout his career Kohler showed wide scholarly interests and distinguished himself as a researcher and writer. He was editor of the department of philosophy and theology of the *Jewish Encyclopaedia,* to which he contributed 300 articles, and was one of the editors of the JPS English translation of the Bible. Among the ideas which he advanced in his writings was his strong belief that the task of the Jew was to lead the world to a universal religion and that the messianic era was approaching in his own day.

KOLEL, the Hebrew word for "comprehensive" or "embracing all," has two different applications. The first use of the term originated in the 19th century when the Ashkenazi community in Ereẓ Israel broke up into *kolelim,* organizations based on countries of origin, whose purpose was to distribute funds from the Diaspora. The system of *kolelim* was an upshot of the *ḥalukkah* system in which the religious community in Palestine was supported by contributions of Diaspora Jews. (For more on this see *Ḥalukkah.) However, when this general *ḥalukkah* system did not provide for immigrants from a particular country to receive their incomes from donors in their country of origin, the system of *kolelim* was established, with a *kolel* for each settler community. By 1913 there were 26 such *kolelim* in Jerusalem, the most famous of which were *kolel Hod* (for immigrants from Holland and Germany), *kolel Varsha* (Warsaw) for members of Polish origin, and the largest, *kolel Hungarya* (Hungary), which supported about 2,500 people.

The second application of *kolel* evolved in the late 19th century when it was used to refer to institutions of advanced talmudic studies for married students. Since the yeshivot was confined to unmarried students, special provision had to be

1. Kaufmann Kohler, former leader of Reform Judaism.
2. These yeshivah students belong to a *kolel* which provides for the material needs of their families, leaving the men free to pursue their religious studies.

made for married students. The *kolelim* were often established by the yeshivot and provided funds for the support of the student, his wife and family. In recent years, the number of *kolelim* in Erez Israel has grown considerably and it has become quite common for married men to study, supported by monthly stipends sufficient for a livelihood. (See also *Yeshiva.)

KOOK, ABRAHAM ISAAC (1865-1935)

KOOK, ABRAHAM ISAAC (1865-1935), first Ashkenazi chief rabbi of modern Erez Israel, was a unique blend of the traditional and the modern — a deeply religious man who, unlike many of his contemporaries, also took an active interest in day-to-day life.

Born in Latvia, Kook took the initiative at a very early age to supplement his traditional Jewish education with broader studies of Jewish and philosophical subjects. By the age of 22 he was appointed rabbi of Zaumel and in 1895 became rabbi of Bausk.

In 1904, he emigrated to Erez Israel where he served as rabbi of Jaffa. It was here that he began to identify with the Zionist ideal and, in opposition to most other rabbis, joined the political movement. This combination of orthodoxy and political Zionism seemed almost a contradiction-in-terms in those days. The majority of religious leaders believed that there could be no return to Zion before the coming of the Messiah; and the active Zionists were mostly those who had abandoned their traditional religious roles and replaced them with secular, political activities. Rabbi Kook, on the other hand, believed that the return to Erez Israel marked the beginning of divine redemption *(athalta di-ge'ullah).*

In 1914 Kook went to Europe to urge traditional Jews to fulfill the Zionist ideal but, caught up in the outbreak of World War I, was unable to return to Palestine. He therefore took a temporary position as rabbi of a congregation in London. On returning to Palestine after the war, Kook was appointed chief rabbi of Jerusalem and, with the formation of the chief rabbinate in 1921, he was elected the first Ashkenazi chief rabbi of Palestine.

Rabbi Kook was very popular among all sections of the population both non-religious and religious (except for the extreme *Neturei Karta group). He felt that the irreligion of many of the settlers was a passing stage and found religious significance in even the most secular activity. He was outstanding for his *ahavat Yisra'el,* love of Jews, and once said

that just as the Temple had been destroyed, according to the Talmud, because of *sinat hinnam* (undeserved hatred) among Jews, it will be rebuilt only because of *ahavat hinnam*, i.e., love for Jews even if it is undeserved.

In 1924 Rabbi Kook set up a yeshivah in Jerusalem, known as *Merkaz ha-Rav* which carries on the spirit of his philosophy. It is one of the yeshivot whose students are drafted into the army and do regular service. The student body is very active in pioneer settlement. The head of the yeshivah is Rabbi Kook's son, Zevi Judah. When Abraham Isaac Kook died in 1935, thousands of Jews lined the streets of Jerusalem to mourn the passing of a great scholar, humanitarian, and religious leader.

KORAH

KORAH was a cousin of Moses who led a revolt against Moses' leadership during the time of the wanderings in the wilderness. The Bible relates that Korah, together with Dathan, Abiram and 250 followers, challenged Moses' authority, claiming that Moses had taken too much glory for his own family when he should have shared it with the other cousins. After all, they claimed, Moses' brother Aaron was the high priest and Moses himself was the leader. Yet they were not the only ones who were holy and who had heard God's voice on Mount Sinai. Why, therefore, should they be more honored than the rest of the congregation? Moreover, Korah was angered when Moses chose a younger cousin, Elizaphan ben Uzziel, for an office which Korah felt should be his since he was older. Not only did Korah challenge Moses' position but also tried to make him

1. *The Punishment of Korah,* from a 15th-century Latin Bible issued in Naples. The illustration shows Korah, Datham and Abiram complaining about Moses (left panel) and being swallowed up by the earth in punishment for their insolence (right panel).
2. Rabbi Abraham Isaac Kook, first Ashkenazi Chief Rabbi of Palestine.

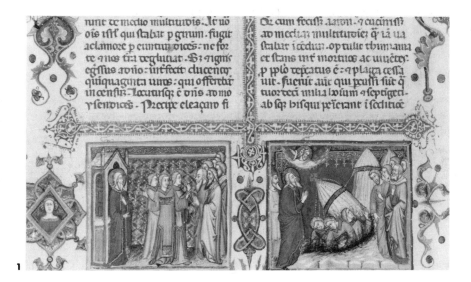

look ridiculous in the eyes of the people. According to the *aggadah, he asked Moses questions which mocked halakhah. For example, he asked Moses about the necessity of affixing a mezuzah to the doorpost of a room filled with Torah scrolls which already contain in them the passage written in the mezuzah. When Moses answered that a mezuzah was necessary, Korah and his followers ridiculed his answer.

In a similar fashion, Korah tried to demonstrate the injustice of Torah laws and tried to negate their importance. Moses desperately tried to appease Korah and his followers, but they continued to oppose him. Finally, when the very integrity of the Torah was at stake, when Korah and his followers denied that the Torah was given by God, Moses made a public stand against them. Moses told the people of Israel to separate themselves from these wicked men and then spoke out: "Hereby you shall know that the Lord hath sent me to do all these works and I have not done them of my own mind. If these men die the common death of all men . . . then the Lord hath not sent me. But if the Lord make a new thing, and the ground open its mouth and swallow them up and all that belongs to them, and they go down alive in the pit, then you shall understand that these men have despised the Lord."

When Moses finished speaking, the earth opened its mouth and swallowed Korah, Dathan, Abiram and their families together with all their belongings, while all Israel stood and watched. Then the 250 followers were consumed by a fire from Heaven. The Talmud relates the legend that on the place of Korah's engulfment voices could be heard saying: "Moses and his Torah are true, and we are liars."

KORCZAK, JANUSZ (born Henryk Goldszmidt; 1878?-1942), Polish author, educator, and social worker, whose devotion to children turned him into a legendary hero. Korczak was born into a wealthy and assimilated Warsaw Jewish family and became a physician. He grew interested in the poor while working as a volunteer in summer camps for underprivileged children and in 1911 became the head of a new Jewish orphanage in Warsaw. Korczak had a revolutionary educational approach which gave children a system of self-government and the opportunity of producing their own newspaper. After the Nazi invasion of Poland, Korczak tried to protect the orphanage and rescued many other youngsters. When the Nazi deportation order was served in 1942,

Korczak told his children that they were going on a picnic in the country. When he and some 200 orphans at last reached the cattle trucks waiting to ship them to the extermination camps, Korczak was offered his freedom. He refused to abandon the children and went with them to his death.

On the basis of his experience with children Korczak published works, such as *How to Love a Child,* and *The Child's Right to Respect.* He also wrote stories for children which were translated into many languages, including Hebrew. They are very popular in Israel.

KOTLER, RABBI AARON (1892-1962) was one of the leading rabbinic personalities of the post-World War II period. He was a descendant of renowned rabbis and a dynamic and articulate spokesman for Orthodox Judaism.

He received his early education from his father, Shneur Zalman Pines, the rabbi of Sislowitz. Due to his exceptional talents, he was admitted to yeshivah even before his bar mitzvah. At 14 he entered the famous Slobodka yeshivah in Russia and soon gained prominence as one of its outstanding students.

Rabbi Kotler became assistant to his father-in-law, Rabbi Isser Zalman Meltzer, head of the Eẓ Ḥayyim Yeshivah in Slutsk. After the yeshivah moved to Kletsk and his father-in-law emigrated to Ereẓ Israel, Rabbi Kotler directed the yeshivah. His original teaching methods attracted many students from all over the world.

Rabbi Kotler distinguished himself as a forceful communal leader, particularly in matters relating to Jewish education. On a visit to the United States, he established an institute of higher rabbinical learning at Spring Valley, New York.

During World War II Rabbi Kotler fled Europe with a number of students, finally reaching Japan. They then continued to the United States where he established the Va'ad Haẓẓalah (Rescue Committee) in in aid of war refugees. He established the Beth Midrash Gavo'ah in Lakewood, New Jersey for advanced talmudic studies, a yeshivah of world renown which numbered 250 students at the time of his death. He became president of the Supreme Council of Agudat Israel in 1954 and held the post until his death. He was active in the Union of Orthodox Rabbis and helped found Israel's independent Orthodox educational system *(Ḥinnukh Aẓma'i).* Twenty-five thousand people attended his funeral.

The achievements of Janusz Korczak in working with orphans and his heroism during World War II have inspired numerous studies, plays and books and a movie released in 1974. He gave his life for the sake of his young charges.

KOTSK, MENAHEM MENDEL OF (1787-1859) was one of the outstanding and most original leaders of the hasidic movement in Poland. Although born into a non-hasidic family, he was attracted to the hasidic movement in his youth. However, his brand of *Hasidism was different from that of Israel ben Eliezer *Ba'al Shem Tov; in fact his teachings caused a revolution within hasidic thought. For Rabbi Menahem Mendel the truth was the ultimate goal in life, the ultimate in the worship of God. To achieve this truth he was ready to sacrifice everything else. Accordingly, he taught that sometimes to reach this truth man must go against himself and society; he must not give in to outside pressures, nor conform, nor try to please himself or anyone else. This teaching was actually practiced by Menahem Mendel's followers, mostly scholarly young men who flocked to Kotsk to search for the truth, leaving their wives and children behind.

Menahem Mendel's search for the truth was often harsh and fiery. Contrary to the Ba'al Shem Tov who approached everyone with love and kindness, Rabbi Menahem Mendel approached the world with a furious, uncompromising zeal. Leaning more toward the teachings of Elijah ben Solomon, the *Gaon of Vilna, the main opponent of Hasidism, he too emphasized the study of Torah as the supreme duty of the Jew and the safest path to follow in the search for the truth.

Menahem Mendel's willingness to abandon worldly life reached a climax when, about 20 years before his death, he decided to "leave this world." He locked himself up in a room near the study house where his disciples were learning. Food was passed to him through a window and he was rarely seen by anyone except the close members of his family. Nevertheless, his seclusion did not cause the ranks of his followers to dwindle. Moreover, after his death the impact of his teachings and his fiery approach to Torah and truth continued to be felt among Polish Hasidim.

KOUFAX, SANFORD (Sandy; 1935-), U.S. baseball player and sportscaster, was born in Brooklyn, New York. He entered professional baseball in 1954, and in 1955 joined the Brooklyn Dodgers. It was not until 1959 that he demonstrated the form that was to make him famous. In a game that year between the Dodgers (who had been transferred to Los Angeles) and the San Francisco Giants, he struck out 18 batters in a nine-inning game

to equal a major league record. Koufax led the Dodgers to three National League championships and two World Series triumphs. He won two games in both the 1963 and 1965 World Series and set a one-game mark of 15 strikeouts against the New York Yankees in the 1963 Series. He established other modern major league records and was the first pitcher to average more than one strikeout per inning in his career. Troubled by arthritis, he retired from baseball at the close of the 1966 season. Koufax would never play on Rosh Ha-Shanah and Yom Kippur. On his retirement he became a national television sports broadcaster. His autobiography, *Koufax*, was published in 1966.

KOVNO (Kaunas), a city in Lithuanian S.S.R. By the middle of the 19th century Kovno had become a center of Jewish cultural activity and learning in Lithuania. In that period Kovno was the home of Isaac Elhanan *Spektor (known as the Kovner Rav) and Abraham Mapu the writer. The great yeshivot, Or Hayyim and Slobodka, were situated there.

Jews took part in the trade between the cities of Kovno and Danzig as early as the 16th century. Their competition aroused opposition from the Christian merchants whose influence caused the banning of Jews from Kovno on many occasions. After the partition of Poland in 1795 Kovno became part of Russia. Under Russian rule the Jewish population increased. After World War I Kovno became the capital of independent Lithuania and the center of its Jewish commercial and industrial enterprises. A Jewish cooperative bank was established there. Kovno was also the seat of other central Lithuanian Jewish

2

1

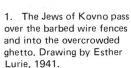

1. The Jews of Kovno pass over the barbed wire fences and into the overcrowded ghetto. Drawing by Esther Lurie, 1941.
2. Baseball star Sandy Koufax.

organizations and institutions. By the beginning of the 1930s five Jewish daily newspapers were published in Kovno and there were many Jewish schools. Most of the youth belonged to the Zionist groups, especially *He-Ḥalutz.* Under Soviet rule from June 1940 to June 1941, the Jewish institutions were closed down.

During World War II, Lithuanians actively joined the Germans in killing Jews in Kovno. A Jewish underground was formed and joined the partisan resistance against the Germans. Most of the survivors from Kovno eventually settled in Israel. Today there is a small Jewish community in Kovno and anti-Semitism is still active. Several incidents in which Jews were beaten in the streets were reported in 1968.

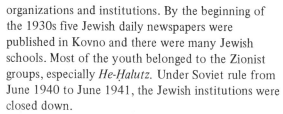

1. Girl in the Kovno ghetto wearing the yellow badge of the Jews.
2. Home of Nachman Krochmal in Zolkiew, Poland.

KRANZ, JACOB (1741-1804), known as the *maggid,* the traveling preacher, was probably the most loved of his profession. All who heard him were captivated by the wonderful stories he made up to illustrate the points he wanted to make. He was barely 20 when he became the *darshan,* the official preacher, in his own city of Zietil near Vilna, and he traveled also to bring his message to the towns nearby. Rich and poor; scholar, layman and simpleton — all found something of interest in his discourses. For the *maggid* was himself a learned man. He drew on the vast treasury of sacred Jewish works and taught his lessons for living in words everyone could understand. For 18 years Rabbi Jacob preached in the town of Dubno where he achieved his greatest fame. His reputation grew among scholars and learned rabbis. When the *Gaon of Vilna, the great rabbi Elijah ben Solomon Zalman fell ill and was too weak to study, he asked the Dubno *maggid* to visit him and read him his stories, parables and biblical interpretations. Once the *maggid* was asked, "How is it that for every moral lesson you have a beautiful story to teach it with?" The *maggid* smiled. "To answer that I can tell another story. I was once walking in the woods and saw a boy shooting arrows at targets. There were targets on every tree and each one had an arrow dead center. 'How expert you are!' I said. 'How did you manage so many exactly at the bull's-eye?' 'It's easy,' the boy answered. 'First I shoot the arrow and then I draw the target around it.' I do the same," said the *maggid.* "First I decide on the lesson, and the story — it always comes out just right!"

All of his works were printed after his death by his son, Isaac, and his pupil Baer Plahm.

KROCHMAL, NACHMAN (1785-1840) was a philosopher and historian, a leader of the *Haskalah movement and one of the founders of the "Science of Judaism," the *Wissenschaft des Judentums* of the 19th century. He was born in Brody, Galicia and acquired his extensive education entirely on his own. He attracted great figures of the Haskalah who came to settle in his town. His chief inspirations in Jewish thought were from *Maimonides and *Ibn Ezra, and in general philosophy from Kant, Schelling and Hegel. His central preoccupation was to understand Judaism in its historical development. Each nation, Krochmal believed, has its own spiritual principle which is the foundation of its life; its national continuity is determined by the extent of its faithfulness to that principle. Israel differs from other nations because of its special relation to God, but still it requires the continuous renewal of national life. In teaching this philosophy he was a forerunner of modern Zionism. In his studies of Jewish literature, especially of *halakhah* and *aggadah,* Krochmal applied his method of historical analysis and made important contributions to the study of their development. Krochmal believed in teaching and discussion, face to face, as the best method of communication, but his friends insisted that he put his ideas into writing. His chief book is *Moreh Nevukhei ha-Zeman* ("Guide for the Perplexed of the Time"). Its title reflects his debt to Maimonides' "Guide of the Perplexed."

KURDISTAN is a region in the Middle East which spans Turkey, Iran and Iraq. *Onkelos, the Bible commentator, translates *Ararat,* the mountain of Noah's ark, as "Kardu." Most of the Jews of Kurdistan lived in northern Iraq. They produced many rabbis, scholars and poets. Among the best

known were those of the *Barazani family.

Before the establishment of the State of Israel, there were between 20,000 and 30,000 Kurdish Jews living in 140 communities. Ancient tradition holds that they are descended from the *Ten Lost Tribes and date from the Assyrian exile of the eighth century b.c.e. The first to mention this was *Benjamin of Tudela, the 12th century traveler. Another tradition states that among Assyrians of northern Iraq are families of Jewish origin who were forcibly converted to Christianity 500 years ago. They still observe certain Jewish customs and have not assimilated. Little is known of the Kurdish Jews before the 16th century. Thereafter, reports of emissaries and travelers show frequent and great changes in the Jewish populations of every village and town. Pogroms and economic instability forced residents to flee to neighboring communities for short or long periods until the danger was past. Some were farmers who produced grains and tobacco. In the cities the Jews were tradesmen, including peddlers, or craftsmen — dyers, weavers, gold- and silversmiths, carpenters etc. Drought and famine added to the problems and many people lived in extreme poverty. The feudal lord considered himself owner of the Jews and their possessions. Robbery and murder were common. For protection, Jews paid tax to an *agha*, a tribal chief, who exploited as much as he protected them. When persecutions increased in the 20th century and reached a peak with the revolt of Rashid Ali in 1941, many fled to Palestine.

Community life in Kurdistan centered around the synagogue and its school. The *hakham* performed all of the services. He was the *hazzan, teacher, *scribe and the writer of *amulets. He performed *circumcision and *shehitah*. Before the 19th century, the community leader was the *nasi* who collected taxes and to whom the *hakham* was subordinate. In the 19th century this was abolished and the *hakham* became leader. Smaller communities were governed by larger ones. For legal and religious questions they turned to the rabbis of Baghdad. Early in the 20th century, the *Alliance Israelite Universelle opened schools in two towns. The language of these Jews, expecially of the mountain region, was Aramaic with many words from Turkish, Persian, Kurdish and Hebrew. They called it *lishna yehudiyya*, language of the Jews. Throughout the centuries, the emissaries who came from Erez Israel made note of the fact that the Kurdish Jews were sympathetic and generous.

Aliyah began in the 16th century, usually to the city of Safed. Significant immigration began in the 1920's. When the State of Israel was established Jews traveled to Baghdad and began a mass immigration. In 1950-51 "Operation Ezra and Nehemiah" was organized by the Jewish Agency to return to Israel Jews from the lands of the ancient Babylonian exile. They are now scattered in towns and settlements and many live in and around Jerusalem. The older ones maintain contact with others from their old communities through committees established for this purpose. In 1973 the Hebrew University organized a folklore outing for elderly Kurdish people, who described and recorded their customs, legends, recipes, costumes, dances, songs and stories so they would be preserved.

1. A Kurdish family raises the Passover platter during the traditional *Seder* ceremony.
2. Immigrants from Kurdistan arriving in Israel in the 1950s.

K. ZETNIK is the penname of Jehiel Dinur (born Feiner; 1917-   ), writer on the Holocaust who believes that he has survived the concentration camp for the sole purpose of telling future generations the

"... This is actually the history of the Auschwitz planet — the chronicles of Auschwitz. I, myself, was at Auschwitz camp for two years. The time there is not a concept as it is here in our planet. Every fraction of a second passed there was at a different rate of time. And the inhabitants of that planet had no names. They had no parents, and they had no children. They were not clothed as we are clothed here. They were not born there and they did not conceive there. They breathed and lived according to different laws of Nature. They did not live according to the laws of this world of ours, and they did not die. Their name was a number, K. Zetnik number so-and-so... And I believe wholeheartedly that I must carry this name as long as the world will not awaken after the crucifying of the nation to erase this evil, as humanity has risen after the crucifixion of one man..."

(Testimony of Jehiel Dinur at the Eichmann Trial, 7th of June, 1961)

horrors experienced by six million Jews. He chose that penname because *kazetnik* is a Yiddish term derived from K. Z., the German abbreviation for concentration camp.

K. Zetnik was born into a ḥasidic family in Poland, and was active in the youth movement of the Orthodox Agudat Israel which published his first poems, in Yiddish, in its newspapers. During World War II he suffered all the torments and tortures of the Holocaust, yet managed to survive. In 1954 he emigrated to Israel and settled in Tel Aviv. He was invited to testify at the Eichmann trial in 1961 where he was asked why he used that name. He explained, "I must carry this name as long as the world has not awakened after crucifying this [Jewish] nation, to erase this evil. . . ." K. Zetnik's works, written in Yiddish and Hebrew and translated into many languages, deal with different aspects of the Holocaust. *House of Dolls* (1956) is about Nazi degradation of Jewish women, and *Piepel* (1961) tells of the terrors experienced by children in Auschwitz.

LABOR. The Bible regards labor as an aspect of world order. In the story of Creation, man working the soil is the important element in the development of vegetation (Genesis 2:5). Work is praised not only for purposes of earning one's bread but also for the contentment which results. Idleness, on the other hand, is condemned as a social evil. The sages declared, "He who does not teach his son a trade is as though he had taught him to be a thief." Rabbinic literature stresses the dignity of labor and refers with pride to its great scholars who did work that might be thought menial to avoid being dependent on others. Rabbi Johanan the shoemaker is only one example. The ideal suggested and followed by most of the sages is to combine learning and work. *Maimonides proposed that the day be divided into thirds, with equal time for learning, labor and other matters.

Labor Relations. Two basic principles helped shape biblical labor policy. First, the employer's duty to pay his worker on time (Leviticus 19:13; Deuteronomy 24:15). Second, the right of the worker to eat from the produce of the field while he is working (Deuteronomy 23:25,26). The worker's duty is to do his work in a faithful manner. Throughout the ages, rabbinic interpretation of these biblical precepts has developed the labor relations that are a model of social justice. Recent rabbinic decisions have upheld the right of workers to organize and, where unavoidable, to strike. In the modern state of Israel, labor, especially a return to agriculture, is regarded as a basic political philosophy. (See *Israel, Economic Life.)

LACHISH is a development area in southern Israel which has served as a blueprint for regional planning for Israel and for other developing countries. It stretches from the Mediterranean coastal plain north of Gaza eastward to the Hebron hills of the pre-1967 border. The area includes over 40 villages, most of them moshavim, in its 275 square miles. The western portion has settlements dating from the period of 1939-47, but development of the dry central and eastern sections became possible only when the construction in 1954 of the Yarkon-Negev water conduit made irrigation possible. Before 1967 the Lachish area performed a very important defense function, since it separated the Gaza strip, which was held by Egypt, from Jordan.

In addition to its economic and military roles, the area was also the testing ground for sociological principles. The State of Israel had found that putting new immigrants from different places together in the same town or village was not very successful. Each ethnic group had its own customs and folkways, and the change was too abrupt. The theory developed — and was successfully tested at Lachish — that each

1. Israelite labor used in the building of the two Egyptian treasury cities Pithom and Ramses, depicted in the 14th-century Spanish *Barcelona Haggadah.*
2. Figurine of a horse and rider found at Lachish, dating from 1000-586 b.c.e.

group should occupy its own village and meet the other groups in a central service town in which the children would go to school, in which people would have entertainment facilities, and in which the main marketing would be done. The plan provided for the establishment of four or five farm villages with some community services grouped around a rural town with broader economic, social, educational and cultural facilities. These clusters are in turn connected with a larger urban center with a still higher order of community facilities. Kiryat Gat serves as the urban center for the Lachish region. The population is about 20,000.

LAG BA-OMER (Hebrew: לַ״ג בָּעוֹמֶר) is a minor festival celebrated on the 33rd day of the counting of the *Omer, the 18th day of Iyyar. (The Hebrew term ל״ג is made up of ל = 30 + ג = 3 = 33.)

In contrast to the preceding days of the Omer period on which activities like being married, listening to music, having one's hair cut, and shaving are prohibited to observant Jews, Lag ba-Omer is the day on which all forms of mourning are suspended. It is a day of weddings and bonfires, a day on which children have a holiday from school in order to play with bows and arrows in the open fields and woods, a day on which thousands visit the grave of Simeon bar Yoḥai, in Meron or the grave of Simeon ha-Ẓaddik in Jerusalem.

History of Lag ba-Omer. The origins of this holiday are wrapped in mystery. No mention is made of it in the Torah and only a hint is to be found in the Talmud. According to this tradition, 24,000 (some texts say 12,000) students of Rabbi *Akiva died in a plague because they "did not properly respect one another." The plague is said to have lasted from Passover to Shavuot (hence the custom of

mourning during this period). However, a certain version of this text reads that the plague lasted from Passover *ad peros aẓeret* ("until the start of Shavuot"). The word *peros* is then interpreted to mean 15 and the text as a whole is then understood to mean that the plague stopped 15 days before Shavuot or, approximately on the 33rd day after Passover. We therefore mourn their deaths until Lag ba-Omer, on which we celebrate the end of the plague by suspending all mourning and observing a joyous holiday.

Rebellion against Rome. Many scholars reinterpret this tradition, suggesting that Rabbi Akiva's "students" were actually soldiers who died in one of the rebellions against Rome. Some of these scholars, basing themselves on *Josephus, suggest that Lag ba-Omer commemorates the day on which the great rebellion (66 c.e.) against Rome began. Others believe that the holiday originated in celebration of a dramatic victory won by the armies of *Bar Kokhba during the rebellion he and Rabbi Akiva led against Rome. This interpretation explains why Lag ba-Omer is a scholars' holiday (Rabbi Akiva's valiant "students"), why bows and arrows are part of the celebration, and why the period of mourning is suspended. It may also explain the origin of the bonfires which typify the holiday — they were

1. First haircut of a three-year-old boy on Lag ba-Omer, 1970, at Meron.
2. Ḥasidim gathered in Meron to celebrate Lag ba-Omer, the anniversary of the death of Simeon bar Yoḥai.
3. Bonfires are lit on Lag ba-Omer in memory of the "victory fires" kindled after Bar Kokhba's successful campaign.

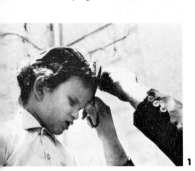

"victory fires" kindled after Bar Kokhba's successful campaign.

Simeon Bar Yoḥai. Another approach to the origins of Lag ba-Omer is found among the kabbalists. According to their traditions, *Simeon bar Yoḥai, a student of Rabbi Akiva, and the author of the *Zohar* died on Lag ba-Omer. The anniversary of his death is "celebrated" not by mourning, but rather by rejoicing. The celebration is called *hillula de-Rabbi Simeon bar Yoḥai,* a term which means "wedding" and probably symbolizes the "wedding" of the earthly and heavenly spheres which took place when he ascended to heaven. Loyal followers visit the rabbi's grave in *Meron; they shoot bows and arrows because Simeon was so righteous, no *rainbow (the 'reminder' of God's promise not to destroy the world even if there is no righteousness) appeared during his lifetime. Bonfires are lit, according to one tradition, in memory of the brilliant, supernatural flame which illuminated his home until shortly before his death. Another aspect of the celebration is the first haircut given to three-year-old boys on Lag ba-Omer at Meron *(ḥalaka).*

Lag ba-Omer and May Day. Some modern scholars have drawn attention to the similarities between Lag ba-Omer and the way spring holidays (May Day) were celebrated in western Europe. It was common practice in Germany to shoot arrows at evil spirits on May Day; in England "every man . . . would walk in the sweet meadows and green woods"; in many parts of Europe bonfires were lit at the end of April or the beginning of May. The scholars believe that during the Middle Ages, Europe's Jewish communities incorporated many May Day customs into the celebration of Lag ba-Omer.

Whatever its origins, Lag ba-Omer, especially in Ereẓ Israel, has evolved into a day when young children celebrate their holiday from school by setting huge bonfires and young men and women, who have been waiting patiently for the Omer period of mourning to end, are joined in marriage.

LA GUARDIA, FIORELLO HENRY (1882-1947), U.S. congressman and mayor of New York City, known as "Little Flower," a translation of his Italian first name. Raised as a Protestant, although his mother was of Jewish descent, La Guardia was appointed U.S. consul in Fiume, Italy at the age of 20. In 1907 he returned to the U.S. to work as an interpreter at the Ellis Island immigrant reception center while attending law school. He thus became intimately acquainted with the needs of the immigrants, many of whose languages he mastered, including Yiddish. His career was built on immigrant support. From 1916 La Guardia was congressman for a Manhattan district of New York, composed chiefly of Jews and Italians. After a brief period in the army, in 1918 he returned to Congress, where he sponsored a resolution calling for a U.S. protest at the Paris Peace Conference against anti-Semitic outbreaks in Poland and Eastern Europe.

Reelected several times to the New York Board of Aldermen, La Guardia was a consistent supporter of the poor. He was elected mayor of New York in 1933 and again in 1937 and 1941, becoming famous for his earthy and flamboyant manner. He greatly improved municipal services and fought corruption in politics. A 1937 speech of his depicted Hitler as deserving a place in the "World's Fair Chamber of Horrors." Official State Department apologies to the German Embassy followed. In 1946 La Guardia briefly held the post of director general of the UN Relief and Rehabilitation Administration. He wrote *The Making of an Insurgent, An Autobiography, 1882-1919* (1948). A successful Broadway musical "Fiorello!" was based on his career.

LAMENTATIONS, BOOK OF is one of the five *megillot* (scrolls) in the Hagiographa section of the *Bible. The book consists of five poetic chapters which lament the destruction of the *Temple and Jerusalem, which took place in 586 b.c.e. Lamentations is read to a distinctive mournful chant in the synagogue every year on the Ninth of Av, the anniversary of the destruction of both Temples.

The English title, Lamentations, is a translation of

1. North African women dancing at the tomb of Simeon bar Yoḥai in the traditional celebration of Lag ba-Omer at Meron.
2. Fiorello La Guardia, the mayor of New York City who fought corruption in politics.

the Hebrew word *kinot*, and the book is referred to in the Talmud as *Sefer Kinot,* or *Megillat Kinot.* However, the title more frequently used in Hebrew manuscripts and printings is *Eikhah* אֵיכָה, after the book's opening word "How [does the city sit solitary . . .] ."

Each chapter of *Eikhah* is an independent elegy and each of the first four is written in the form of an alphabetical *acrostic, as if to express sorrow which runs the gamut from A to Z. The third chapter is a triple acrostic, having three verses for each letter of the alphabet.

The image depicted in the first chapter is that of the city of Jerusalem, desolate, lonely, her inhabitants in exile. Her former allies have abandoned her. The second chapter stresses God's role in this destruction and refers particularly to the destruction of various parts of the city (Temple, walls, gates). The third chapter reflects on the meaning of suffering and attributes the catastrophe to Israel's sins. Its conclusion is that only repentance will bring an end to the suffering and that God, in His kindness and mercy, will forgive. Chapter four vividly describes the suffering of Jerusalem's inhabitants; according to the tradition, however, this chapter is an elegy for *Josiah, king of Judah, who died in the battle of Megiddo, and whose death marked the virtual end of Judah's independence. The fifth chapter is an impassioned plea to God not to forsake His people.

Lamentations itself contains no statement of its authorship but it is traditionally believed that it was written by the prophet *Jeremiah, the dominant personality who lived through this disaster. However, due to the noticeably different styles of the chapters, modern scholars argue that the book had several authors. In the same way they argue that each chapter was written at a different time or stage of the siege of Jerusalem and the Babylonian exile. Nevertheless, it is generally accepted that all parts of the book were composed before 538 b.c.e., the date of King Cyrus' proclamation permitting the return from exile, since no reference to hopes of return are made in the book.

LANDAU, EZEKIEL BEN JUDAH (1713-1793) was a halakhic authority of the 18th century, known as the *Noda bi-Yehudah,* after the name of one of his works. Landau is considered one of the most famous rabbis of the close of the classical Ashkenazi rabbinic era. Descended from a wealthy and distinguished family which traced its ancestry back to Rashi, he was endowed with rare intellectual ability and a strong character which loved truth and honored his fellow man. His main interest lay in the study and teaching of Torah and he was regarded as the prototype of the ideal Jew. At age 21 he was already a *dayyan* (judge in rabbinic court of law) and at 30, the rabbi of Yampol. In 1754 he was named

1. Opening page of the Book of Lamentations from a 14th-century German manuscript. The opening word of the book *Eikhah* ("how") is printed in bold letters across the center of the page and the actual text and commentaries begin beneath it.
2. A sketch of Rabbi Ezekiel Landau, one of the outstanding rabbis of the 18th century.

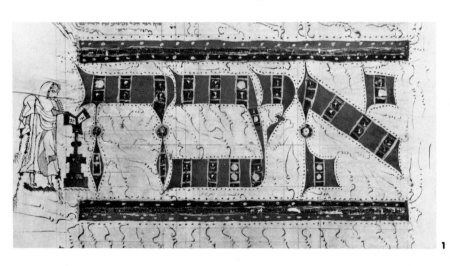

rabbi of Prague and the whole of Bohemia, one of the highest positions of that time.

Landau is known for his attempt to put an end to the *Emden- *Eybeschuetz controversy which had split the Jewish world. His strong commitment to preserving traditional Judaism led him to denounce the false messianic movements, the Shabbateans and Frankists (see *Shabbetai Zevi and *Frank, Jacob) and even to oppose *Hasidism which he feared might be another false messianic movement. However, he supported the traditional elements in the *Haskalah movement, at the same time opposing those with anti-rabbinic tendencies.

Landau's diplomatic skill, his active role in the Jewish social and religious events of the time and brilliant halakhic works earned him a reputation throughout Europe. The social climate of Landau's time, the opening of the gates of the ghetto and the entry of Jews into general non-Jewish society posed many problems which demanded halakhic rulings. Landau distinguished himself in his attitude to the new situation and toiled with sincerity for the establishment of a correct relationship between Jews and non-Jews and the development of feelings of patriotism for the country. Some of his halakhic decisions on timely crucial issues aroused a storm in the rabbinic world at the time, but later became significant guidelines for succeeding generations. He was the first rabbi to give a decision on the permissibility of *autopsies and his opinion is still considered basic in any halakhic discussion of the subject. His most famous work *Noda bi-Yehudah* contains some 860 responsa on halakhic problems.

LASKI, HAROLD (1893-1950), the British left-wing socialist and political theorist, was born into a prominent Manchester Jewish family, and began his career as a lecturer at McGill University in Canada in 1914. Two years later he taught at Harvard, where he became a close friend of the U.S. Supreme Court Justice Oliver Wendell Holmes. Laski lectured at the London School of Economics from 1920 and in 1926 was made professor of political science.

In the years between the World Wars, Laski was a member of the industrial court, the departmental committee on local government, and the committee on legal education. From 1936 he was also a member of the executive of the British Labor Party, becoming its chairman in 1945 and the chief target of Conservative propaganda during that election year.

Laski's influence waned after the Labor victory,

but nonetheless had a profound effect on the development of British socialism. He was an outstanding member of the British Fabian Society of left-wing intellectuals. Nazi persecutions aroused his interest in the Jewish question and he began to take a deep interest in Zionism. He declared himself in favor of a Jewish state in Palestine.

Harold's brother, Neville Jonas (1890-1969), achieved distinction as a lawyer, becoming eventually judge of the crown court of Liverpool. He was president of the Board of Deputies of British Jews (1933-39), vice-president of the Anglo-Jewish Associations, and in 1934 chairman of the administrative committee of the Jewish Agency for Palestine. The novelist Marghanita Laski (1915-   ) is his daughter.

LASKOV, HAYYIM (1919-   ), Israel's fifth chief of staff, was born in Belorussia and moved to Palestine in 1925. His father was killed by Arabs in 1930 and ten years later he joined the Palestinian Jewish units of the British army. In 1944 he commanded a mechanized machine-gun platoon of the Jewish Brigade in Italy. He joined the *Haganah permanent staff in 1947 and the following year commanded the first mechanized battalion of the Israel army in the battles of Latrun, Nazareth, and Galilee. During the War of Independence, he was promoted to *alluf* (brigadier general) and director of training. In 1951 he became commander of the Israel Air Force. In 1953 Laskov went to study at Oxford University, but was recalled in 1955 and appointed deputy chief of general staff. He was commanding officer of the armored corps in 1956. During the Sinai Campaign of that year he led a divisional task force on the northern axis. Appointed commanding officer of southern command after the fighting, he became chief of the general staff in 1958. In 1961 he retired from the army to become director general of the ports authority. He resigned in 1970, and thereafter participated in various public bodies. He is the ombudsman of the army, that is the person to whom soldiers' complaints against the army authorities are addressed for investigation.

LAW, JEWISH. The Hebrew term *halakhah* which we shall use as the equivalent of "Jewish Law" is derived from the root *halakh* ("to go"). Some scholars believe that originally the term may have meant a property tax or regulation and was applied to particular laws; now, however, it has come to include

1. British statesman, Harold Laski.
2. Hayyim Laskov, Israel military leader.

2

1

1. Title page of *Shulḥan Arukh,* a comprehensive code of Jewish Law compiled in the 16th century by Joseph Caro. It is framed with portraits of six famous Jewish commentators and surmounted by the crown of the Torah, basis for the entire Jewish legal system. Printed in Mantua, Italy, 1722.

2. Illustration of Moses, "Giver of the Law," with the Ten Commandments. From a 13th-century French manuscript.

the whole body of laws by which an observant Jew is commanded to regulate his life.

Written Law. Traditionally, the source of *halakhah* is God who revealed Himself to Moses on Mt. Sinai. The written record of this revelation is contained in the Torah (see *Bible). According to rabbinic tradition, the Torah contains 613 commandments. The commandments encompass all aspects of life from Sabbath and Holy Days to Divorce and Damages. The Torah, and therefore *halakhah,* makes little distinction between "ritual" and "civil" law.

The problem, however, is that human beings may find it difficult to understand God's law. Sometimes laws in the Torah seem to conflict with one another (Numbers 18:20-32 vs. Deuteronomy 14:22-26; see *Tithe). Sometimes they are presented too briefly for the average man: what, for example is the exact definition of "work" which is prohibited on the Sabbath (Exodus 20:10)? As a result, the Torah, or the "Written Law" (*Torah she-bi khetav*) must be interpreted.

Oral Law. Tradition says that Moses received the techniques for interpreting the Torah (as well as the Torah itself) from God on Mt. Sinai. Moses then conveyed these principles of interpretation to the leaders of the Jewish people.(For more on these principles, see *Hermeneutics.) They, in turn, handed them down orally from generation to generation. Whenever a new situation arose or whenever there was a dispute, these principles of interpretation were applied to the Torah text and a "new" law was expounded. This new *halakhah* was then conveyed orally to succeeding generations. Thus, alongside the written law there grew an oral law to explain, interpret, and apply the written law to changing social and economic and political conditions. Even critical scholars recognize the antiquity of much of the oral law. Surely someone must have explained at a very early stage what the Torah meant by "work"!

Rabbinic Courts. The Torah itself granted to "the magistrate in charge at the time" the power to interpret the law (Deuteronomy 17:8-13 and see *Courts). For centuries magistrates, scribes and rabbinic scholars studied every letter of the Torah as they applied it to new situations. Their influence grew with the passing years. The power to interpret the written law soon evolved into the power to re-interpret it and even in an emergency, to circumvent it. The rabbinic courts of the first two centuries c.e. sometimes suspended or abolished laws, sometimes they enacted new laws without specific authorization for that law in the Torah. The rabbis, for example, authorized the celebration of *Hanukkah, even though no mention of this holiday could possibly have been made in the Torah. Nevertheless, the blessing recited over the Hanukkah candles contains the words, "who has sanctified us by His commandments," thus endowing the observance of a holiday created by the rabbis with the status of one actually commanded in the Torah.

So great was the authority assumed by rabbinic courts that, according to tradition, even God could not overturn their majority decision. Once Rabbi Eliezer ben Hyrcanus summoned a heavenly voice *(*bat kol)* to support his arguments against those of the majority. Rabbi Joshua rejected the divine intercession, quoting the verse in Deuteronomy 30:12 to the effect that the Torah "is not in the heavens," and the verse in Exodus 23:2 to the effect that majority decisions must be followed. The rabbinic account goes on to say that God accepted the majority view and "rejoiced that His children had vanquished Him." (See *Democracy.)

Disagreements. Inevitably, however, different human beings began to interpret the Torah in different ways and so disagreements arose as to what a given *halakhah* was. Sects developed, each with its own *customs (minhag)* and each with its own approach to the written law. Even among the predominant sect, the *Pharisees, there developed different 'schools' of *halakhah* (see Rabbi *Akiva and *Hillel).

During the period of Jewish independence (till approximately 70 c.e.) the resulting conflicts were usually solved by the *Sanhedrin, whose decisions were widely accepted. When, however, the Sanhedrin's power diminished, there was no longer any authoritative decision-making body. The Oral Law, which was always expanding in response to changing social, political and domestic situations now became ridden with unresolved conflicts. It had become imperative to organize the Oral Law and to determine an authoritative basis for resolving differences.

Mishnah. Finally (about 200 c.e.), Rabbi *Judah ha-Nasi succeeded in arranging most of the Oral Law into a six-volume code called the *Mishnah*. Rabbi Judah, however, did not include every law and every opinion. On the other hand, there were many instances in which he did convey more than one view on a given *halakhah*. Of the 523 chapters in the *Mishnah*, only six are free from conflicting opinions.

Talmud. The *Mishnah*, therefore, very much like the Torah itself quickly became the basis for a new round of discussions on what the *halakhah* should be. [Not all scholars agreed with Rabbi Judah's method of selection. Some favored opinions rejected by him or not included in his *Mishnah*. Other scholars sought to apply the principles of the *Mishnah* to the rapidly changing economic and social circumstances in which the Jewish people found themselves after the *Bar Kokhba revolution.] These discussions, which took place both in Erez Israel and in Babylonia over a period of approximately 300 years (200-500 c.e.) were recorded in volumes known as the *Talmud. The Talmud then constituted the authoritative interpretation of the written Torah. It became the new source for all further Jewish Law. For a detailed description of the Mishnah and Talmud, see *Talmud.

The style of the Talmud, however, made it difficult for the average student to locate and determine any given *halakhah*. Very often the Talmud recorded differing interpretations of the *Mishnah*. Very often these differences themselves were reinterpreted or modified by scholars of later generations. [The new interpretation was then debated as though it was the accepted *halakhah*. But was it? Or was the whole discussion merely an attempt to clarify an opinion which never became normative?] The Talmud records these arguments; it seldom decides what the *halakhah* should be.

Another problem for the student seeking to locate

The French Sanhedrin, created in 1807 to make decisions on religious law for the Jewish community.

Page from a manuscript of the Mishnah, one of the earliest attempts at codifying Jewish law. This copy dates back to the Middle Ages.

any given *halakhah* is the type of "logic" employed in the Talmud. The rabbis might start off with a discussion of the proper *time* for reciting the evening *Shema. This may lead them to a discussion of priests and the timetable which regulated their lives. This in turn might lead to a discussion of ritual purity, a criterion for priests. Thus, the Talmud might discuss some laws of ritual purity within the section dealing with prayer. No wonder then that the Talmud has been referred to as a sea *(yam)*, vast, all-embracing and exceedingly fluid.

THE CODIFICATION OF TALMUDIC LAW

Geonic Period (589-1100). The stylistic problems found in the Talmud, plus ever-changing historical conditions, led to the creation of what is called Responsa literature. Observant Jews, incapable of finding the *halakhah* in the Talmud, referred questions *(she'elot)* to great scholars *(Geonim)* whose responsa *(teshuvot)* then became law. Often the same problems were of concern to a number of different communities, therefore it became desirable to collect these responsa and make them available to Jews everywhere. This need led to the development and dissemination of books of laws. These books were based on the Talmud, but also included legal decisions made during the Geonic period. See also *Gaon.

The Rif (1013-1103). During the 11th century c.e., the center of Jewish life moved from Babylonia to North Africa and Western Europe. Once again, the differing economic and social practices of the new host countries created more problems for Jewish law, necessitating the development of an updated code. Rabbi Isaac ben Jacob ha-Kohen Alfasi "of Fez," (North Africa) known in Jewish history as the Rif, sought to meet this challenge. In his book *Sefer ha-Halakhot*, the Rif summarizes talmudic arguments, eliminating irrelevant discussions and assembling pertinent material from all over the Talmud. Following the order of the *Mishnah*, he first summarizes the talmudic discussions most relevant to it, then those somewhat related to it and finally those only loosely connected to the subject matter of the *Mishnah*. Alfasi then summarizes relevant responsa literature and concludes with his opinion of what the *halakhah* should be.

Unlike some earlier Babylonian authorities, Alfasi makes frequent use of the Jerusalem Talmud and is often guided by the arguments of Palestinian authorities. In cases of conflict between the two Talmuds, Alfasi follows the principle of *hilkheta ke-vatra'i* (the law is according to the later scholar) and decides according to the Babylonian Talmud because, he reasons, it was compiled at a later date and, therefore, Babylonian scholars were aware of the material in the Jerusalem Talmud and rejected it.

The Rif confined himself to those portions of the *halakhah* which were practiced in his time. He omitted those sections dealing with sacrifices and other matters not then relevant. On the other hand, he included material from the *aggadah* which taught moral conduct not easily reducable to codification. For more on the Rif, see *Alfasi, Isaac ben Jacob.

Moses Maimonides (1135-1204). The Rif's work suffered from at least two shortcomings: 1) it was organized on the pattern of the Talmud and so it was not always easy to find any given *halakhah;* 2) it contained the talmudic arguments and so it was not always simple to determine what the law should be. Rabbi Moses ben Maimon (known, after the acronym of his name, as the Rambam) sought to overcome these difficulties. He spent most of his life in Cairo. There Maimonides and his fellow Jews were challenged by the *Karaites, the proponents of Aristotelian philosophy, and forces in the Muslim world which sought the forceful conversion of Jews. He was especially sensitive to the need for a clear, well-organized statement of the *halakhah*. Maimonides spent at least ten years producing a work whose purpose was to make the entire Oral Law, from Moses to his time, known to all without difficulties and differences of view. To attain this objective, Maimonides set for himself four guiding principles: 1) to locate and assemble all material relevant to the *halakhah* from the written Torah to his own day; 2) to classify and subdivide the material according to subject matter; 3) to determine what the *halakhah* should be and to state his conclusion without quoting sources and without presenting contrary opinions; 4) to present his conclusions in clear, easily understood Hebrew.

The result was a 14-volume masterpiece *Ha-Yad ha-Hazakah* ("The Strong Hand", see Deuteronomy 34:12; *Yad* is the Hebrew equivalent of 14: *Yod* = 10, *Dalet* = 4) which fulfilled all of the author's goals. The work is also known as the *Mishneh Torah* ("The Repetition of the Torah"). Maimonides' work embraced the whole spectrum of Jewish life including philosophy, morals, ethics, the principles of faith and even those laws omitted by the Rif because they were considered not relevant at the time. The 14 volumes

THE DEVELOPMENT OF JEWISH LAW

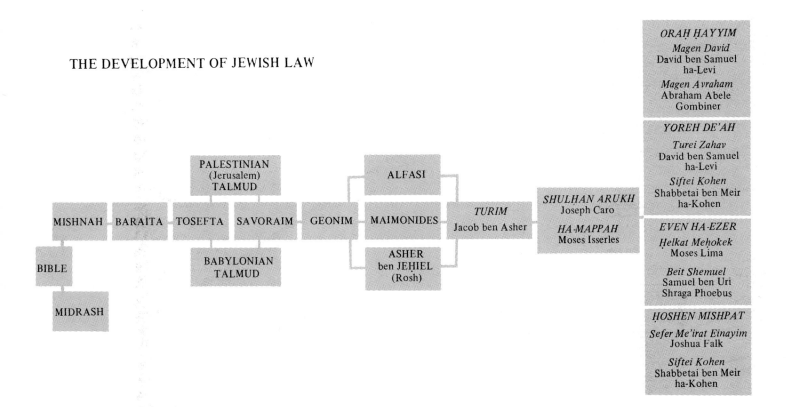

were divided into 83 different areas of Jewish life. Each of these was subdivided into chapters (1,000); each chapter was subdivided into individual laws (approximately 15,000). The laws were stated in magnificent Hebrew and, in almost all cases, without reference to the sources and arguments on which his decisions were based. Maimonides disagreed with the Rif approximately 30 times, he added some 120 halakhic rules (often prefaced by words such as "it seems to me") and he even dared to call talmudic laws concerning witchcraft and enchantment "lies and falsehoods . . . not fitting for Jews who are intelligent and wise."

Reactions to Maimonides. The wisdom of Maimonides' decision to omit talmudic sources and give only the *halakhah* without stating the requirements leading up to his decision was severely criticized by many scholars. Some attacked him personally, implying that his goal was to have his work replace the Talmud as the source of Jewish law. His sharpest critic, Abraham Ibn Daud, feared that Maimonides' work would inhibit the study of talmudic sources and thus deprive contemporary judges of a choice between differing opinions. Maimonides himself recognized this potential

weakness and spoke of his intention of indicating his sources in a separate work. This task was never accomplished by him. Other scholars rose to his defense and wrote commentaries in which they sought to uncover his sources. Some of these commentaries are now published along with most editions of the *Mishneh Torah.* For the personal history of the Rambam, see *Maimonides.

Asher ben Jehiel (c. 1250-1327). Maimonides' work and the controversy which surrounded it, stimulated many scholars to try their hand at writing codes of *halakhah.* One of the most successful was produced by Asher ben Jehiel. His work, *Piskei Ha-Rosh* (c. 1300) was modeled on that of the Rif. It too was arranged according to the order of the Mishnah, and it too sought to summarize talmudic arguments before rendering decisions. Asher had lived in France and Germany before settling in Spain. He added the customs and traditions of Western European Jewry to those of Babylonian, North African and Spanish Jewry. There is a separate entry on *Asher ben Jehiel.

Jacob ben Asher (1270? -1340). Asher ben Jehiel's third son, Jacob, sought to combine the advantages of the work of the Rif with those of Maimonides. He organized the *halakhah* into a logical order and stated the essence of individual laws briefly without indicating talmudic sources (following Maimonides' system). He then appended a digest of the opinions on which he based his decision (after the style of the Rif). He generally followed the opinions of the Rif, but when these were disputed, he employed the principle of *hilkheta ke-vatra'i* (the law follows the latest authority) and accepted the decisions of his father. His work was divided into four sections or rows *(turim* – hence the title *Arba'ah Turim): Tur Oraḥ Ḥayyim* containing laws of prayers, blessings, Sabbath and festivals; *Tur Yoreh De'ah* containing dietary laws, laws of ritual purity, circumcision, mourning and even some aspects of business law; *Tur Even ha-Ezer* covering all aspects of family relationships; and *Tur Ḥoshen Mishpat* embracing the rest of civil and criminal law. Like the Rif, Jacob ben Asher omitted laws not relevant in his time. See also *Jacob ben Asher.

The Shulḥan Arukh. During the next two hundred years many Jews were forced to leave France, Germany and Spain. They resettled in Poland, Turkey and especially Ereẓ Israel. The intermingling of Jews from different areas with different customs, when combined with the religious revival associated with the coming of many to Ereẓ Israel, aroused new yearning for an authoritative guide which would explain exactly what the law should be. Rabbi Joseph Caro (1488-1575), who came to Ereẓ Israel in 1536 and settled in Safed, sought to meet this need. He spent over 20 years (1522-42) working on a commentary, *Beit Yosef* which updated the *Turim* of Jacob ben Asher. He then combined the basic organizational structure of the four *Turim* with Maimonides' idea of stating only the law and produced an independent work called the *Shulḥan Arukh* ("The Set Table," 1563). Scholars interested in tracing the law from the Torah through the 16th century could consult the *Beit Yosef.* Ordinary people wanting to know what the law required, could consult the *Shulḥan Arukh.* Caro had thus fulfilled Maimonides' aim (unfulfilled) of writing two independent works.

Caro's *Shulḥan Arukh* was even more concise than Maimonides' *Mishneh Torah.* He omitted scriptural references, moral, ethical and philosophical concepts, legendary (aggadic) material, and laws not relevant to his time. It was also more up to date in that Caro had before him the work of Asher ben Jehiel as well as the Rif and the *Mishneh Torah.* In cases of

disagreement amongst the three, he generally followed the majority opinion. In deciding on issues not covered by any of them, he took into account the opinions of 32 different post-talmudic scholars. Finally, in cases where local custom *(minhag)* ran counter to his decisions, he generally gave the *minhag* precedence.

Moses Isserles (1525?-1572). At the very time when Caro was writing the *Beit Yosef* in Safed, Moses Isserles was working on his own commentary to the *Turim* in Cracow, Poland. After the publication of Caro's work, Isserles decided to write a supplement to the *Shulḥan Arukh.* Caro's system of deciding by majority opinion among the Rif (North Africa), Maimonides (Cairo), Jacob ben Jehiel (Germany and Spain) definitely favored the Sephardi customs. Isserles' comments, known as the *Mapah* ("Table Cloth") reflected the *halakhah* and customs of Jews living in Germany, France, and Poland. Isserles also rejected Caro's method of deciding by majority. Instead he leaned heavily on the principle of *hilkheta ke-vatra'i* and brought to his work the latest opinions of Ashkenazi scholars. He also gave great weight to custom *(minhag)* as a factor in determining the *halakhah.*

Later Commentaries. Despite some strong opposition, Caro's *Shulḥan Arukh,* when supplemented by Isserles' *Mapah,* became the major source book for Jewish law. Naturally, commentaries abounded. Some of them, which sought to explain the reasons behind decisions cited in the *Shulḥan Arukh,* were published along with the text itself. Thus the student found, in one volume, both the *halakhah* and a summary of the arguments tracing its development from the Torah.

Other commentators sought to apply the principles of the *Shulḥan Arukh* to new situations. One of the most widely accepted was written by Israel Meir (Ha-Kohen) Kagan, better known, by the title of one of his books, as the *Ḥafeẓ Ḥayyim.* His six-volume work, called the *Mishnah Berurah* (Vilna, 1907) has become an almost indispensible guide to the *Oraḥ Ḥayyim* section of the *Shulḥan Arukh.*

An abridged version of the *Shulḥan Arukh (Kiẓẓur Shulḥan Arukh)* was published in 1894 by Solomon Ganzfried. It encompassed all the laws relating to the mode of life of the ordinary Jew living outside of Ereẓ Israel including etiquette, hygiene, and ethical norms, but omitted details which were not common practice or were not deemed necessary for the ordinary man. The *Kiẓẓur Shulḥan Arukh,* despite its obvious scholarly deficiencies, was accepted as an important handbook for Ashkenazi Jewry. It has been translated into English by H. E. Goldin (1928) under the title "Code of Jewish Law."

We have seen that fresh attempts to codify the *halakhah* were made at crucial periods of Jewish history. Each new code brought relevance and vitality to an age-old system. 400 years have passed since Caro produced the *Shulḥan Arukh.* Jewish life has confronted the emancipation, the mass migration of Jews to the United States, the division of world Jewry into differing religious movements (Reform, Conservative, Reconstructionism), the Holocaust, and the establishment of the State of Israel. In the light of these events, some Jewish leaders have called for a complete revision and updating of the *Shulḥan Arukh.* Others have questioned the binding nature of *halakhah* and have suggested a guide in place of a code. Still, the vast majority of observant Jews continue to consider the *Shulḥan Arukh* as the most authoritative source of God's word as revealed to Moses and as interpreted by His disciples ever since.

LAW OF RETURN is a law of the State of Israel which gives every Jew the right to settle in Israel as an *oleh* (Jew immigrating to Israel). Passed by the Knesset on July 5, 1950, the Law of Return is one of the earliest and most significant of the basic laws of the State of Israel. Indeed, the Law of Return is the closest document to a constitution that the State of Israel has. It guarantees that every Jew, by virtue of his being a Jew, has the right to "return" and settle in the Jewish homeland, and immediately receive Israel citizenship should he so desire. In keeping with the purposes of the law, the status of *oleh* is also accorded to all Jews who entered the country before the law was passed, as well as to any Jew who goes to Israel other than as an immigrant and subsequently expresses his desire to stay and settle in Israel. Moreover, the Israel government has in certain cases even granted Israel citizenship to Jews outside Israel who wish to return and be Israel citizens but who, for reasons beyond their control, are unable to (for example, Russian Jews).

The Law of Return has certain restrictions however, and provides that entry to Israel may be denied to a person who is seen as likely to endanger the public welfare (i.e. a person with a criminal record or dangerous illness).

Legal Problems. The provisions of the Law of Return have given rise to a number of legal problems, in particular the definition of a Jew for the purposes of the law. Accordingly, the Israel courts have had several significant cases where the law has been challenged. Should the definition of *halakhah* apply, according to which a Jew is anyone born of a Jewish mother or properly converted to Judaism? Or does the term include any person who declares himself to

3

1

2

1. "Operation Magic Carpet" which brought the Jews of Yemen to Israel where they were guaranteed citizenship under the Law of Return, 1949.
2. Casablanca Jews en route to Israel in the 1950s.
3. An Iraqi woman in an Israel immigrants' camp, 1951.

1. The Statue of Liberty, on which is inscribed the famous poem by Emma Lazarus, is the first American landmark seen by shiploads of new immigrants.
2. Emma Lazarus' poem on a plaque at the foot of the Statue of Liberty in New York harbor.
3. New immigrants to Israel joyfully return to the soil of their ancient homeland.

requirements, it has aroused a great deal of controversy, and the National Religious Party refused in 1974 to join the coalition government over this issue.

Although the amendment does not consider the non-Jewish partners and children of Jewish *olim* as Jews, it does provide that they be granted full material rights and privileges of *olim*. Moreover, the Israel law with regard to a non-Jew who wishes to become an Israel citizen is the same as the American law with regard to non-Americans wishing citizenship: after a period of residence in the country, they may apply for naturalization. (See also *Conversion to Judaism; *Jew.)

LAZARUS, EMMA (1849-87), U.S. poetess, best remembered for her sonnet engraved on the Statue of Liberty at the entrance to New York. Her first verse appeared in 1866 and attracted the attention of the poet Ralph Waldo Emerson, to whom she dedicated her second volume *Admetus and Other Poems* (1871). Her interest in Jewish problems was awakened by George Eliot's novel *Daniel Deronda*, with its call for a Jewish national revival, and by the Russian pogroms of 1881-82. She began translating the great medieval Spanish-Jewish poets such as *Judah Halevi and Solomon ibn *Gabirol. She joined immigrant relief workers on Ward's Island and publicly opposed anti-Semitism. More poems on specifically Jewish themes appeared in her *Songs of a Semite* (1882). *An Epistle to the Hebrews* (1883) set forth her ideas on a national and cultural revival of Jewish life in the U.S. and Erez Israel. After her death, her sister prohibited "anything Jewish" from inclusion in the collected edition of Emma's works, which appeared in 1899.

LEBANON, a country situated north of Israel. In ancient times the mountains of Lebanon, parallel to the Mediterranean coast, were considered the home of a God. From their white *(lavan* or *lbn* in Semitic languages) snow-covered peaks the name of the whole mountain range derived and eventually of the country itself.

Lebanon is mentioned often in the Bible as the northern-most boundary of the Promised Land. It was well-known in ancient times for its rich forests, which supplied cedar, pine and fir to the surrounding areas. In the tenth century b.c.e. Hiram, king of *Tyre sent cedarwood on floats to the harbor near Jaffa for the building of Solomon's Temple in

be a *bona fide* Jew? The case of Oswald Rufeisen, a monk who was born a Jew but converted to Christianity, questioned the applicability of the halakhic definition of Jew. Although Rufeisen was born a Jew, the Court ruled that the Law of Return did not apply since he had converted to another religion.

Another leading issue was the Shalit case in 1968 which raised the problem of the status of children born in Israel of a Jewish father and non-Jewish mother. The court ruled that for the purpose of entry in the identity cards, the Shalit children should be registered as Jews, since their father had declared that they were Jews and the clerk who registers the information has no right to question it. The court, however, pointed out that the rabbinic courts are not bound by this registration and will consider the children as non-Jews for the purpose of marriage.

However, in the wake of the political controversy which followed the Shalit decision, and upon the initiative of the religious circles of the country, the government decided to propose an amendment to clarify the definition of Jew in the Law of Return. This amendment adopts the halakhic definition of a Jew as anyone born of a Jewish mother or converted to Judaism. However, since the law does not stipulate that the conversion must satisfy halakhic

Jerusalem and again, in the time of Ezra (fifth century c.e.), Lebanese wood was provided for the second Temple, this time by the king of Persia. Wood from Tyre was often accompanied by workmen from Sidon, a leading Lebanese port and commerical city, famous for its carpenters and woodcraftsmen.

In pre-historic times, Lebanon was inhabited by a number of different peoples, and eventually by a West-Semitic population. When the 12 Tribes of Israel invaded the area, they drove the Lebanese out of the hills of Israel. But the history of the two nations remained linked, even after Lebanon was taken over by the Phoenicians in the third century b.c.e. The prophets of Israel often mentioned Tyre and Sidon and during the Maccabean wars (second century c.e.) when Israel and Lebanon were under Roman rule, these two cities attacked the Jews of Galilee, only to be repulsed by the Jewish bands. This period was followed by Byzantine occupation, during which time the population became mainly Christian. Islam arrived with the Arab conquest in the seventh century, and has remained the major religion of Lebanon until today.

Little is known about early Jewish communities in Lebanon, but in 1071 the Palestinian academy of talmudic scholars chose Tyre as its center. *Benjamin of Tudela mentions Jews who lived in the area and traded with the Druze in the 12th century. In the 18th and 19th centuries there were many Jews living in villages and outlying districts — almost all in association with Druze. Sephardi migrants arrived from Greece and Turkey in the early 20th century, and by 1929 there were 5,000 Jews in the country.

Lebanon is the only Arab country where Jews increased in number after the establishment of the State of Israel in 1948, because the Lebanese government protected Jews from attack and allowed Jewish refugees from Syria and Iraq to settle there. In 1951 there were 9,000 Jews in the area, many with Lebanese citizenship.

In 1958 a large exodus of Jews began, mostly to the Americas and Israel, as a result of political unrest. By 1967 only 5,000 Jews remained. Further emigration caused by the Six-Day War and its aftermath left about 1,500 in 1970 and in 1981 there were about 400 Jews in Lebanon.

For 20 years after the signing of an armistice agreement with Lebanon on March 23, 1949, Israel's relationship with its northern neighbor had been peaceful. Lebanon did not engage in military actions during the Six-Day War. But a gradual deterioration

of the situation began in 1968 when Palestinian terrorists initiated armed attacks from Lebanon on Israel. Thousands of members of Al Fataḥ and other terrorist organizations concentrated on the slopes of Mount Hermon on the Lebanese-Israel border and the area, together with most of south-eastern Lebanon, became known as "Fataḥland." Lebanon was caught between the terrorists' demands for freedom of movement and Israel's insistence that, by harboring them, Lebanon shared equally in the blame for their actions. The conflict of interests brought about the resignation of the Lebanese government in April 1969, and in November of that year, the signing of an agreement with the terrorists, allowing them to remain in the area. Israel has retaliated by bombing and attacking the terrorist bases in Lebanon, for which she has been censured by the United Nations. Israel has helped the Christian Lebanese in the southern region of the country in their battle against the PLO.

Israel forces heading for the Lebanese shore to attack terrorist bases there.

LEEDS, in Yorkshire, in the northeast of England, is the city with the third largest Jewish population in Great Britain. Its Jewish population of 18,000 (out of a total of 508,000) also represents the highest proportion of Jews in any city population in the country.

The growth of Leeds as a Jewish community took place slowly. The Jewish cemetery was acquired only

1. A bazaar in the market of Leeds, 1884.
2. A poem of thanksgiving which was composed and recited in the Jewish community of Leghorn after an outbreak of cholera from which the city was spared, 1876.
3. A Jewish pageant in Leghorn, which included an elaborate procession with horses and a large chariot. The illustration is from a manuscript dated 1766.

in 1837, and until 1846 a small room served as the synagogue. As the clothing industry in Leeds grew, the Jewish population increased. Many of the Russian and Polish immigrants who settled in Leeds at the end of the 19th century worked as tailors. Leeds University established a Hebrew education department and during the 1940s and again in the 1960s, Jews served as lord mayors of the city.

In 1980 there were eight synagogues in the city; three of these were combined in the United Hebrew Congregation with a total of nearly 2,000 members. The Leeds Jewish Representative Council was organized in 1938 and includes almost every local synagogue, Zionist group, charitable organization and Friendly Society.

LEGHORN. The main port of Tuscany in central Italy, Leghorn was once little more than a miserable, malaria-infested village. Its rulers, the Medicis, attempted to turn it into an important port, and Ferdinand I in 1593 issued an invitation directed at the Jews of Europe, to settle there in return for full religious liberty, amnesty for crimes previously committed, the opportunity for *Marranos to return to Judaism unmolested, and the right to receive Tuscan citizenship. Settlers would be allowed to own houses and would be exempted from wearing the Jewish *badge.

In 1675 the expanded town received the status of a free port. It became an important junction for trade between the Atlantic and North Sea ports and those of the Mediterranean and Near East. There were only 114 Jews in Leghorn in 1601 but roughly 3,000 by

1689. Most were either of Spanish or North African origin. The original promises given by the Medici were on the whole adhered to, and the community enjoyed their protection. The Jews benefited from the enlightened reforms of Leopold I of the House of Lorraine and in 1780 obtained the right to representation on the municipal council. At the end of the 18th century there were 5,000 Jews in the port. They were the only Italian Jewish community living without a closed ghetto. In 1765 one-third of Leghorn's 150 commercial houses were owned by Jews. Jews also owned shops in the town and were generally prosperous; they engaged in the working of coral, which they exported as far as Russia and India, and in soap and paper making.

The situation deteriorated, however, after the French occupation of the port in 1796, and a subsequent British blockade. When Tuscany was annexed to Sardinia in 1859 (both becoming the kingdom of Italy in 1861), Leghorn's commercial importance began to wane in the face of competition from other ports. By the end of the 19th century the Jewish population was half what it had been a century earlier.

Jewish organized life in the city included a number of charitable institutions, including one providing for the ransom of Jewish prisoners. There were also a number of yeshivot, and a much-admired synagogue. Ḥayyim *Azulai spent his last 30 years in Leghorn, and the family of Sir Moses *Montefiore originated there. Leghorn also became a center of Hebrew printing.

During World War II at least 90 Jews of Leghorn were sent to concentration camps, and others were killed in the surrounding mountains by the German army. The synagogue was destroyed by the Nazis. At the end of the war, about a thousand Jews remained in the port. A new synagogue was dedicated in 1962, but the Jewish population declined.

LEHMAN, HERBERT HENRY (1878-1963), U.S. banker, politician and statesman. Lehman began his public career during World War I when he became a member of the War Claims Board and rose to the rank of full colonel. Following several tours of Europe, during which he was moved by the plight of the devastated Jewish communities, he helped found the American Jewish Joint Distribution Committee. From 1924 until 1928 he involved himself in campaigns to elect his friend Alfred E. Smith to the governorship of New York State and to the Democratic presidential nomination. Later he became right hand man of Franklin D. Roosevelt and when Roosevelt went on to become president in 1932, Lehman won the governorship of New York by a million-vote majority. He was reelected for four more terms in office, and many of his reforms helped make New York one of the most socially progressive states in the Union.

Lehman resigned the governorship in 1946 to become head of the newly formed UN Relief and Rehabilitation Administration. He resigned from this position shortly thereafter, and turned his attention to the plight of Jewish refugees and their right to immigrate to Palestine. In the early 1950s, he was one of a small number of senators who outspokenly fought against the witch-hunts of Joseph McCarthy and his followers. He also headed the opposition to a discriminatory immigration bill. He was an internationalist in foreign policy and a staunch supporter of Israel.

LEIVICK, HALPERN (1886-1962), Yiddish poet and dramatist, was born in Belorussia, the eldest of a poor family of nine children. Leivick became active in the Jewish revolutionary Bund and was arrested several times. His early espousal of the cause of those who suffered was to become a lifelong theme. He refused a defense counsel at his trial, which took place after he had been in prison in Minsk for two years. In the court he expressed the basic motif of his later writings: "I want no one to plead my cause, because I do not want to defend myself. All that I have done I did with an unflinching will to help destroy the autocratic regime." After serving a sentence of four years' hard labor, he was exiled to Siberia for life.

With the help of money and documents from Communist Party friends who had emigrated to America, Leivick succeeded in escaping from Siberia. Traveling 1,000 miles along the frozen Lena river on a horse-drawn sledge, he reached European Russia, and made his way to the U.S. in 1913, where he began working in a sweatshop as a paperhanger.

Leivick wrote many plays and poems on his varied experiences both in Siberia and in America. All his work is very powerful. Some of his most beautiful lyric poetry was produced during four years in a sanatorium where he underwent treatment for tuberculosis. He visited Russia again after his recovery, and in 1937 spent a few months in Erez Israel. After World War II he visited the remnant of German Jewry and later depicted the suffering of the camps with terrible realism. A visit to Dachau inspired his greatest dramatic poem, *Di Khasene in Fernvald* (1949).

LENIN, VLADIMIR ILYICH ULYANOV (1870-1924), the revolutionary leader of the Communist movement and founder of the Soviet state. Lenin was, from the outset, confronted with the problem of how to treat the Jews of Russia, many of whom were themselves revolutionaries. A group of Jewish Social Democrats known as the Bund, at times opposed Lenin but he never attacked them for being Jews. Indeed, throughout his life Lenin vigorously opposed anti-Semitism and refused to exploit the deep-seated hatred of Jews common among the Russian masses. However, Lenin did regard the Jews as an anachronism and thought that their assimilation into a future Communist society was inevitable. He considered that the Jews only retained their Jewish identities under persecution, and that once this had been removed they would cease to be Jews. Thus, as well as denouncing anti-Semitism, he also attacked all forms of Jewish nationalism and separatism, which he thought deflected Jewish workers from solidarity with their non-Jewish brethren.

After Lenin had assumed power in 1917, he endorsed the setting up of special departments for Jewish affairs in both the ruling Communist Party and in the various ministries. He accepted Yiddish as the national language of Russia's Jews, for he realized the importance of communicating with them in the language they understood. Soon after the revolution, Lenin initiated decrees outlawing pogroms and their instigators and courageously opposed demagogic Russian nationalist forces.

Nonetheless, Lenin did not oppose the persecution

1. Herbert H. Lehman, champion of Jewish refugees.
2. Halpern Leivick, Yiddish poet whose adventurous life included an escape from imprisonment in Siberia.

of Zionists and the suppression of the Hebrew language and Jewish religion in the Soviet state. Still, many arrested Zionists and rabbis were, during his rule, allowed to emigrate to Palestine. Even an attempt by a Jewish woman, Fanya Kaplan, to assassinate him, did not in the least change Lenin's approach to the Jews.

Of eight speeches recorded by Lenin in 1919, seven were rerecorded and marketed in the Soviet Union in 1961. The missing speech was the one which attacked anti-Semitism.

LENINGRAD, capital of Russia until 1918. Whether known by the name of St. Petersburg or Petrograd, Leningrad (its name since 1924) has been a center of Jewish life and culture. As with almost all cities in the Soviet Union, Leningrad has also had its share of anti-Semitism.

The city was established as St. Petersburg in 1703, and Jews settled there shortly after. Anton Divier, a Portuguese Jew, was appointed first police minister of the city in 1718. Throughout most of the 18th century Jews worked at various professions under the careful eye of city officials. At the end of the 18th century the city became part of the Russian Empire. In 1798 and 1800-1801, Shneur Zalman, the founder of *Ḥabad Ḥasidism, was imprisoned in St. Petersburg. After this, conditions worsened for Jews as Czar Nicholas I ordered that all Jews living in the city "without doing anything" be expelled. The residence restrictions against Jews were rigidly enforced.

Later in the 19th century the situation changed and Jewish culture flourished. Jews entered the universities and served in important positions throughout St. Petersburg. In 1881 there were 17,253 Jews (2% of the population) in the city. The Jewish community continued to grow, and became the center of Russian Jewish life. Jewish newspapers and a Russian Jewish encyclopedia appeared.

The city remained a center of Jewish life after the revolution of 1917. The Jewish population grew rapidly and by 1926 there were 84,505 Jews living in Leningrad. However, organized Jewish life was obstructed by the Soviet government. In 1980 there were 165,000 Jews listed in Leningrad, though the true number was probably nearer 200,000. There is one large synagogue, and it is full on the High Holy Days. Its chairman, Gedaliah Pecherski, was sentenced to seven years' imprisonment in 1961 for having "maintained contact with a foreign embassy."

Priests inspecting leprous wounds, copperplate engraving from the title page of *Negaim*, the mishnaic tractate dealing with the laws of leprosy. From a Hebrew-Latin edition of the Mishnah, Amsterdam, 1700-04.

Several Hebrew study groups have been established and identification with Israel is strong. A trial of suspected plane hijackers, Jews and non-Jews, in Leningrad attracted world attention in 1970. By 1981 all the Jews in the group had been released.

LEPROSY. The Hebrew word צָרַעַת, *zara'at*, which has been translated as leprosy is not actually the physiological disease of leprosy as we know it today (i.e. Hansen's disease). Rather it is a general biblical term to describe an affliction which strikes in one of three ways: on one's person, one's clothing or one's house. Several chapters in the Book of Leviticus and the entire talmudic tractate of *Nega'im* are devoted to a discussion of the disease. They explain the system of diagnosis of skin, garments and home, and enumerate the symptoms of the disease. These are generally a discoloration and deterioration of the flesh, the cloth or the stones. It was the priest who made the inspection; if he diagnosed the disease as *ẓara'at*, he then imposed a quarantine. At the end of the quarantine period, he made another examination. If no further degeneration was apparent, the patient was isolated for another week, after which he could be pronounced healed. The priest played no part in the healing, however, and only performed rituals after the person was cured.

How, then, was the cure effected? It was the responsibility of the afflicted person himself to pray and fast in order to win God's favor. *Ẓara'at* was seen as a disease inflicted by God and cured by God. The *aggadah* explains that *ẓara'at* was inflicted as a punishment for slander. Thus, according to the *aggadah*, the Hebrew word for leper, *meẓora*, is a play on words of the Hebrew *moẓi shem ra*, meaning to slander a person's reputation. The Midrash cites the case of Miriam who was stricken with leprosy after she had spoken ill of her brother, Moses. Then, after Moses had prayed for her, she was healed by God.

Another case of *ẓara'at* mentioned in the Bible is that of King Uzziah of Judah, in whose case haughtiness and rebelliousness were seen as causes of the affliction. Despite the warning of the priests, King Uzziah had entered the Temple and burned incense on the altar, a privilege granted only to priests. As a result, he was immediately stricken with *ẓara'at*.

Purification Ritual. After a person was cured of *ẓara'at* he went through a purification ritual conducted by the priest, which lasted eight days. On the first day, the priest performed the ritual outside the city or camp. He took cedar wood, crimson cloth and a live bird and dipped them in an earthen vessel containing a mixture of fresh water and the blood of another bird. The leper was sprinkled with this mixture seven times, after which the live bird was set free. The leper was then admitted to the camp after washing his clothes, shaving his hair, and bathing. After the seventh day, he repeated this washing process again, and then was allowed to enter his residence. On the eighth day he brought an offering to the Temple.

Leprosy as a Physical Disease. Leprosy as it is known today is a physical desease and those who suffer from it must be isolated. In 1887 a leper hospital was built in Talbiyyeh, Jerusalem. For many years of the hospital's existence, the famous Rabbi Aryeh *Levin acted as chaplain of the hospital, and despite the quarantine on lepers, continued to visit the hospital and extend his kindness to the patients.

LETTERS AND LETTER-WRITERS. The letter holds an honored place in Jewish history and literature. Since the form includes earliest diplomatic and state correspondence, business and private mail, discussions and arguments between communities on local or religious questions, polemics and controversial issues, letters have also provided invaluable material for scholarly research. Letters were often written to leading rabbis on questions of Jewish law, a practice that prevails even today. Collections of the answers, authoritative rabbinic opinions, are in a body of literature called Responsa (see *Law, Jewish). Jewish letters were written mainly in Hebrew, even after Jews adopted the languages of the countries of their exile. Hebrew was the language common to all Jews and remained the vehicle of all scholarly communication. The form of the letters included the date in Hebrew and the *sedra* of the coming week. At a later stage, Yiddish occupied a similar position for European Jews.

The Bible has many references to letters. The first was King *David's in the case of Uriah. The correspondence referring to *Nebuchadnezzar's second campaign against Judea in 589 b.c.e., the Lachish Letters, are the oldest Jewish letters still in existence.

Writing usually required a professional to execute it. In ancient times a royal court officer, the *sofer* (scribe), was undoubtedly the letter-writer as well. The professional letter-writer was an important post even into the 20th century. *Seals which were used to sign and close the documents of antiquity as well as letters, are displayed in the Israel Museum, and in other collections. Throughout the Middle Ages letters served as a major Jewish literary form. They were widely used as a means of publishing the writers' statements and views and were not necessarily private communications. They were delivered by a messenger whose errand was often interrupted on the journey so that the letter could be read to the public. Messages of importance were copied for reference and often read aloud in the synagogue or other gathering place. These letters were quite impersonal, usually formal and stylized, and there was often little difference between a letter and what we would describe today as an essay or treatise. Much of the ethical literature and some of the more important works of the Middle Ages were written originally as letters. An inquiry and an answer on the laws of prayer led to *Amram Gaon's compilation of the first prayerbook. Maimonides' *Guide of the Perplexed,* a message to his student, is another celebrated example. Maimonides' wide influence at that time, indeed, was due to his extensive correspondence with Jewish communities in all parts of the world. The expulsion of the Jews from Spain in 1492 produced letters from the exiles reporting their experiences in their new homes. These

1

1. Letter written by Mendele Mokher Seforim, probably to the literary critic and historian, Joseph Klausner, apologizing for not being able to fulfill the latter's request to send him biographical details about himself. Among the reasons for this inability he reports that his beloved grandson has been critically ill. He conveys regards to Bialik, to whom he refers as "our lazy and silent friend."
2. Leone Modena, the early 18th century rabbi and scholar whose numerous letters to Christian Hebraists have been published.

2

were eargerly received by Jews of the Diaspora, particularly the missives which came from Erez Israel. Letters of this period and later ones, and also from Italy and Germany, contributed greatly to Jewish scholarship. In the 19th century, thinkers often wrote books as though they were collections of letters. *The Nineteen Letters*, a philosophic work of Samson Raphael *Hirsch, had wide influence. In more recent times the letters of great religious and Zionist thinkers have been collected and published, among them Chief Rabbi A. I. *Kook, Theodor *Herzl and H.N. *Bialik. Experiences of the World Wars, the Holocaust and the wars in Israel, related in published letters, provide poignant human footnotes to history.

Among the enactments attributed to Rabbenu *Gershom in the 11th century was one protecting the privacy of letters with a threat of *herem, excommunication.

LEVIATHAN, an ancient outsized sea animal mentioned in biblical and talmudic literature, sometimes as real, sometimes as legendary. It is referred to in Isaiah, Psalms and Job. In modern Hebrew *leviathan* means a whale. The word "leviathan" seems to come from a root meaning "to coil" which indicates that its form was snake-like. In some references it is multi-headed. According to the *aggadah,* the Leviathan was one of the creatures which rebelled against the Creator, who thereupon destroyed them. The struggle between Leviathan and Behemoth, the monster which symbolizes land animals, is vividly described in *Akdamuth,* the Aramaic poem recited on Shavuot. Among the rewards in store for the righteous in the World to Come, according to the Midrash, is a feast prepared from the flesh of the Leviathan. The hide is mentioned in a special prayer at the end of the *Sukkot festival. "May I be privileged," the Jew prays, "to dwell in the *sukkah* made of the hide of Leviathan" in the world to come. Samson Raphael *Hirsch, a German scholar of the 19th century, interprets this as the symbol of all mankind united in a tabernacle of universal peace that encompasses the whole world.

LEVI ISAAC OF BERDICHEV (1740-1810) was a hasidic *zaddik* and rabbi; one of the most famous personalities in the third generation of the hasidic movement.

Levi Isaac was born into a distinguished rabbinic family in Galicia. After his marriage, he moved to Poland where he became acquainted with the *Hasidism of Israel ben Eliezer *Ba'al Shem Tov. In 1766, he went to study under Dov Baer, the Maggid of Mezhirech and became one of the intimate circle of his Hasidim. Later, Levi Isaac served as rabbi of Richwal and afterwards as rabbi of Zelechow where he first emerged as a hasidic *zaddik.* However, he encountered strong opposition from the *mitnaggedim* whose pressure caused his dismissal from Zelechow and later from Pinsk. In 1785, Levi Isaac moved to Berdichev where he remained a distinguished hasidic leader and rabbi until his death. Even the *mitnaggedim* finally acknowledged his Torah scholarship.

Levi Isaac's leadership in Berdichev was marked by active participation in public affairs. In 1801, he convened a meeting of leaders to discuss the government's oppressive measures against Jewish settlements, and in 1807, the name of Levi Isaac headed a list of Jewish contributors to the Russian war effort against the French.

Levi Isaac was instrumental in founding Hasidism in central Poland and in consolidating the movement in Lithuania and the Ukraine. In his teachings, he stressed the element of joy in Hasidism, the principle of *devekut* (cleaving) to God, and the necessity of devoted and fervent prayer where the spirit delights in the worship of God. He stressed the good in every man and believed in preaching to the Jewish people with kind words rather than harsh reproach. Above all, he shared in the distress of the Jewish people, and always pleaded their cause, and praised their righteousness.

Although he did not found a hasidic dynasty, Levi Isaac had many pupils and left an indelible mark on Hasidism. As a dearly beloved *zaddik,* he occasionally traveled through the land, inspiring people with the joy of worship and winning many over to Hasidism. His immense popularity made him a hero in much Hebrew and Yiddish literature, and particularly in hasidic folktales.

LEVIN, ARYEH (affectionately referred to as "Reb Aryeh"; 1885-1969), one of the most saintly figures in modern Israel. Aryeh Levin was born in Orla, near Grodno, Belorussia, to poverty-stricken parents. At the age of nine he left home to study at various yeshivot, notably the yeshivah of Slutsk, then headed by Isser Zalman Meltzer, and subsequently the great yeshivah in Volozhin. He emigrated to Erez Israel in 1905, continuing his studies in the Ez Hayyim

One of the Lachish ostraca, a collection of inscribed shards. This one is a letter indicating that a message sent by the commander Jaush to his subordinate Hoshaiah has apparently not been received.

Levi Isaac of Berdichev

yeshivah in Jerusalem. From 1915 until his death his official position was spiritual mentor *(mashgiaḥ)* to the junior department of the Eẓ Ḥayyim yeshivah.

He was a fine talmudic scholar, receiving *semikhah* from the greatest rabbis of the time, Ḥayyim Berlin, Samuel *Salant, and Abraham Isaac Ha-Kohen *Kook, whose faithful follower he was. From 1949 he conducted a yeshivah in the upper rooms of his modest home. But Reb Aryeh's fame and the widespread and boundless esteem in which he was held sprang not from his learning but from his good works. For nearly 50 years he devoted his life unwearyingly and without thought of self, to acts of charity and love. He undertook to visit hospitals, especially the Leper Hospital, and prisons; to comfort mourners; to bring a message of love and hope to the distressed and the unfortunate, radiating kindliness just by the touch of his hand.

In the turbulent years before Israel's War of Independence, Reb Aryeh regarded it as his special mission to attend to the needs of the Jewish political prisoners who had been jailed by the British Mandatory Government, particularly those sentenced to death. He acted as an intermediary between them and their families and remained with them in their last moments. He was widely known as "the rabbi of the prisoners." Reb Aryeh refused all honors, including the Freedom of Jerusalem, and always kept his home in the poor quarter of Mishkenot in Jerusalem.

Tens of thousands, including the most notable personalities in the country, attended his funeral.

LEVIN, MEYER (1905-1981), U.S. novelist, born and raised in the Chicago slums. Levin became a reporter for the Chicago *Daily News* and in 1925 was sent to cover the opening of the Hebrew University of Jerusalem. In 1928 he returned to Palestine to spend a year on a kibbutz. He had already written short stories of Jewish life, but *Yehudah* (1931) was one of the first novels about kibbutz life. Levin's writings covered a wide field — from Jewish mysticism to the modern American scene which he depicted with realism and vitality.

In *The Golden Mountain,* reissued in 1966 as *Classic Ḥasidic Tales,* Levin retold stories of the Ḥasidim, and in *The Old Bunch* portrayed his own generation of Chicago Jews. Levin was a correspondent in Spain during the Civil War, and later reported the Palestine disorders for the Jewish Telegraphic Agency. In 1946 he made the first

feature film of the *yishuv, My Father's House,* and a documentary, *The Illegals,* in 1947. His autobiography, *In Search,* appeared in 1950. *Compulsion* (1956), a best seller, was a study of the *Loeb-Leopold murder case of the 1920s. Levin also published a Passover *Haggadah,* various histories of Israel for juveniles, and books on the synagogue and the Jewish way of life. In 1952, Levin wrote the first dramatization of *The Diary of Anne Frank.* The work was not accepted and a literary scandal took place following Levin's claim that it had been rejected for anti-Semitic reasons. From 1958 Levin lived in Israel and in 1972 published *The Settlers.*

LEVITA, ELIJAH (1468/9-1549), Hebrew grammarian and lexicographer. Elijah Levita, who is also known as Elijah ha-Baḥur, was born in Germany but spent most of his life in Italy, teaching in Padua, Venice and Rome. He spent 13 years living in the home of Cardinal Egidius da Viterbo and many of his pupils were leading Christian Humanists and Hebraists. His early secular writings in Yiddish include *Bovo d'Antona* (based on an Anglo-French romance about knights and chivalry) and *Paris un Viene* (based on a medieval Provençal romance). He adapted these and others into Yiddish and also gave a Jewish flavor to the plot, often converting a meeting in a church to a synagogue. The former came to be known as *Bove Bukh,* and the expression *bobbe ma'aseh* (an unlikely tale) derives from that name.

Though invited in the name of King Francis I to

1. "Reb Aryeh" Levin, known as "the rabbi of the prisoners."
2. Double page of a Hebrew-Latin edition of *Sefer ha-Dikduk* by Elijah Levita, a work on Hebrew language and grammar.

lecture in Hebrew at the Collège Royal in Paris, he declined the offer, not wishing to be the only Jew allowed to live in France.

Elijah lost his property in 1527 when Rome was sacked by the armies of Charles V. He returned to Venice and there earned a livelihood as a proofreader in the printing house of Daniel *Bomberg. Elijah had to defend his teaching Torah to Christians against criticism from the rabbis; he claimed that such work led Christians to greater sympathy and understanding of Jews and to their defending Jews from attack. (However, two of Elijah's grandchildren converted to Christianity, and one of them helped those who calumniated the Torah.)

Elijah wrote many Hebrew grammar works and Hebrew and Aramaic dictionaries. He was the first to point out that the Hebrew vowel and accent system did not originate in the Sinai period but in post-talmudic times. His *Shemot Davarim* is the first known Yiddish-Hebrew dictionary.

LEVY, URIAH PHILLIPS (1792-1862) was a U.S. naval officer born into a distinguished Philadelphia family. He ran away to sea at ten, and by the age of 24 had become a midshipman. In 1859 he served for six months as commodore of the U.S. Mediterranean fleet.

Most of what is known about Levy comes from the records of six courts-martial and the proceedings relating to his fight against an order in 1855 dropping him and 200 fellow officers from the navy lists. An excellent and patriotic officer, he was very pugnacious and extremely sensitive about his Jewishness. His career undoubtedly suffered from anti-Semitism, as the proceedings established. His greatest liability, so far as popularity among the officer-class was concerned, was his active support of a law to prohibit corporal punishment in the navy. The S. S. *Vandila,* of which he was captain, became the first ship to sail without the use of the lash to maintain discipline. Levy was a member of Congregation Shearith Israel in New York and a charter member of Washington Hebrew Congregation. In 1854 he sponsored the new Seminary of the Bnai Jeshurun Educational Institute in New York.

Uriah's brother Jonas (1807-1883) was also a naval officer, and reached the rank of commander. In 1847, during the Mexican War, he participated in the naval battle for Veracruz, commanding the troop steamer *America*. He was appointed captain of the captured city.

Jonas Levy, like his brother, was active in Jewish life. He succeeded in altering a U.S.-Swiss treaty which discriminated against Jews in Switzerland. Under his leadership an act of Congress was passed giving full rights to the Washington Hebrew Congregation in 1855.

LIBRARIES. In ancient times, when most people could neither read nor write, there were relatively few books. Scrolls of the Torah and whatever other books existed were greatly valued and were kept in temples or in royal palaces. The Temple had a library, established by Nehemiah, containing books about the kings and prophets, royal letters and the books of Psalms, and the Qumran sect on the Dead Sea also had a library. The famous library of Alexandria contained the Septuagint and other Judeo-Hellenistic works.

Since Judaism has always valued education and literacy, anyone who could afford them owned books, at least a prayerbook, a book of Psalms and other books of scholarly or secular interest. The library of the Ibn *Tibbon family, physicians and scholars of the 11th and 12th centuries, was large and varied.

As the centuries passed, and as education became more widespread, Jewish communities and synagogues all over the world built up their own libraries. The invention of printing in the 15th century greatly increased the number of books available and in the long run significantly contributed to literacy and so to the growth of libraries. In Italy, almost every Hebrew school contained a library. By the end of the 18th century, the first of the modern Jewish communal libraries had been established in Mantua,

1. Commodore Uriah P. Levy, of the United States Navy.
2. Storage room at the Jewish National and University Library, Jerusalem.

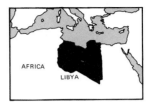

Italy, and many others sprang up soon after, intended mainly for the use of teachers and young people.

Jewish libraries have been established and developed by individuals, by various Jewish organizations and by other voluntary bodies interested in Jewish cultural work. Rabbinical seminaries too often built up fine libraries, such as that of the Breslau Jewish Theological Seminary. Private libraries were also founded, which later grew into public institutions; an example was that of Mathias Strashun in Vilna, which began with 5,700 books in 1892 and eventually had over 35,000.

In Germany under the Nazi regime, Jewish libraries, both public and private, were either looted or destroyed. Many of the confiscated books were recovered after the war and returned to the heirs of their owners or distributed to Jewish libraries and organizations, but the manuscripts and ancient handwritten volumes of the German libraries vanished. The Bodleian Library at Oxford and the British Museum contain rare collections of Hebrew books and *illuminated manuscripts. The Cambridge University Library has the largest collection of Cairo *genizah* treasures in the world. The largest collection of Judaica outside Israel is housed in the library of the Jewish Theological Seminary of America (which lost 70,000 volumes in a fire in 1966).

The Jewish National and University Library. It is only fitting that Israel, the homeland of the Jews, should have a library containing books on every aspect of Jewish life. In 1892, B'nai B'rith founded a library in Jerusalem which, with the help of private donations of books, grew rapidly. The library is situated today in the Hebrew University at Givat Ram in Jerusalem, and with over 1.5 million books, thousands of manuscripts and microfilms, serves both as the national library of Israel and as a reference library for students of the Hebrew University. Israel also has 280 specialized libraries, with 2,700,000 volumes; these include the Knesset library, and the Yad Vashem (Holocaust) library, as well as many non-specialist public libraries and, for isolated areas, mobile libraries which travel from place to place.

LIBYA, a country in North Africa consisting of the regions of Tripolitania, Cyrenaica (Cyrene) and Fezzan. There is no reliable evidence of Jewish settlement in these areas before the time of Ptolemy Lagos (ruler of Egypt 323-282 b.c.e.). He is reported to have settled Jews who served in his army around Pentapolis in Cyrene in 312 b.c.e. in order to strengthen his regime.

Under the later Maccabees, commerce between Cyrene and Erez Israel appears to have increased. A fresh wave of Jewish settlers reached Cyrene under Ptolemy Euergetes II who united the region with Egypt in 145 b.c.e. Cyrene became a Roman province in 74 b.c.e. Under the reigns of emperors Augustus, Tiberius, and Nero, the Jewish community flourished, and had its own synagogue and an amphitheater. Although Cyrenean Jewry under Augustus was forced to defend its right to send the half-*shekel (for census) per person to Jerusalem, its privileges were confirmed by Rome.

In 73 c.e. a desert prophet and Zealot exile of Erez Israel, Jonathan the Weaver, incited the Cyrenean Jews to revolt, leading them into the desert with promises of miraculous deliverance. He was captured and his followers massacred. At the same time, the Roman governor L. Valerius Catullus took the opportunity to execute some 3,000 wealthy Hellenized Jews and seize their property. Under Vespasian (69-79 c.e.) Cyrenean state lands were redistributed and conflict arose with Libyan nomads. It seems that some Jews were forcibly settled on the Transpolitanian shore at this time.

1. Modern honeycombed structure of the Zalman Aranne Library at the Ben Gurion University of the Negev, Beersheba, Israel.
2. Libyan Jews give thanks in public prayer after the British forces liberated their country from Fascist rule during World War II, May 20, 1943.

Jew from Tripolitania,
Libya.

In 115 c.e., under Trajan, a Jewish revolt broke out in Cyrene, Egypt and Cyprus under the leadership of one Lukuas, called by gentile historians "King of the Jews." Roman temples were destroyed and very large numbers of gentiles were massacred. The revolt was crushed and Lukuas is thought to have been killed in Judea.

By the third century Jews may again have been living in Cyrene. There was certainly a Jewish population on the eve of the Arab conquest of 642. Little is known of the Jews of Libya after this time until the 16th century. Apparently in 1510 some 800 Jewish families fled inland from Tripoli following the Spanish invasion. After a Turkish invasion the Jews again prospered. The Spanish refugee, Rabbi Simeon Lavi, settled in Tripoli and introduced Jewish scholarship there. In 1588-89 it appears that many Jews were forced to convert to Islam during a revolt against the Turks. In 1663 Abraham Cardozo arrived in Tripoli and conducted a Shabbatean campaign there. (See *Shabbetai Ẓevi.) In 1784-85, Libyan Jewry suffered famine, and were later threatened by the appointment of Ali Gurzi ("Burgul") as pasha. His banishment was celebrated by Tripoli's Jews as the "Purim of Burgul" every 29th of Tevet. There were no important incidents in the history of Libyan Jewry at the end of Ottoman rule.

Libya fell to the Italians in 1911 and the next 25 years passed peacefully, the Jews continuing their traditional occupations as artisans and peddlers. They attained equal rights, served in government positions and benefited from schooling. Zionist activity went unhindered. Then in 1936 the Italians began enforcing anti-Jewish legislation. Occupation of the area by Axis forces during World War II led to Jews being deported to labor camps, where they died of overwork or disease, or from heavy Royal Air Force bombing. During this period relations with the rural Muslim community did not generally worsen and some Muslims gave Jews sanctuary. Under British occupation Jews were again able to open their schools, but were subject to violence at the hands of young Arab extremists in 1945 and in 1948. Many were massacred.

Jewish emigration from Libya to Palestine began after the first pogroms and greatly increased following the establishment of the State of Israel. About 8,000 Jews remained in Libya under King Idris, but after the Six-Day War of 1967, 17 Jews were murdered in Arab riots and most of the remainder left when they could. Under the regime of Colonel Gaddafi which seized power in September 1969, the 400 or so remaining Jews were imprisoned in a concentration camp in Tripoli. Most were later released and some left the country. Their property was nationalized along with that of Italians in 1970. Only a handful of Jews remained in Libya in 1981. **Libya's Attitude to Israel**. In 1952 Israel, a new state itself, voted in favor of the UN resolution granting Libya independence. This gesture of goodwill was not reciprocated. The announcement of impending independence instead provoked anti-Jewish riots. Libya joined the Arab League and adopted a hostile attitude to Israel, which intensified under Gaddafi's rule. Gaddafi announced that his regime did not believe in the possibility of a peaceful solution of the region's conflicts and promised to apply his country's vast oil wealth to the confrontation with Israel. A "holy war fund" was established out of state grants, special taxes, and private donations. Selected Palestinians were allowed to live in Libya, collections were made for terrorist organizations and a military school for al-Fatah orphans was opened.

Libya came under increasing influence from Colonel Nasser's Egypt. Nasser exploited the situation to deepen Egyptian military and economic penetration of the country. (Egypt's 36 million people suffered from urban overcrowding while Libya, with only two millions, offered open spaces and vast oil wealth.) Many Egyptians were settled in Libya, British and U.S. military bases were taken over and their personnel expelled. An attempted union between Libya, Egypt and Syria proved a fiasco when Colonel Gaddafi tried to "march on Cairo" in 1973 and was halted by Egyptian President Sadat's forces at the border. In 1974 there were reports that Gaddafi had organized an attempted assassination of the Egyptian president, following Egypt's disengagement of forces negotiations with Israel after the Yom Kippur War.

LIEBMANN, JOST (Judah Berlin; c. 1640-1702) was a *court Jew who settled in Berlin and originally traded in precious stones and metals. His second wife, Esther Schulhoff, whom he married in 1677, was the widow of Israel Aron, founder of the Berlin Jewish community and Brandenburg court supplier. In 1678 Liebmann began supplying Frederick William, the elector of Brandenburg, with gemstones. From then on he was court jeweler in Berlin. Toward the end of the century he was considered one of the richest Jews in Prussia. King Frederick I owed him large sums of money. Liebmann had helped him build a considerable collection of gems, and in 1684 he was released from payment of the body tax which applied to all other Jews; in 1694 his business records were recognized as legal evidence in court.

Liebmann was influential in the Jewish community also, and secured rabbinic positions for his sons and other members of his family. He owned the only synagogue in Berlin.

After Liebmann's death his wife continued to supply stones to the court. As part of her payment, she was granted a license to mint and issue coinage. She was placed under house arrest by King Frederick William I, the frugal soldier king, on his accession in 1713 and released only after she had paid him large sums. Her sons were also purveyors of jewelry to the court, but on a smaller scale than their parents.

LIFE AND AFTERLIFE. The preservation of human life is one of the highest principles of Judaism, and Jewish law, both biblical and rabbinic, is exceedingly strict when human life in involved. It is a *mitzvah* for a person to look after his physical well-being and absolutely forbidden for him to do anything that might impair his health. When a human life is in danger everything possible must be done to save it and for this purpose all prohibitions except three, are suspended. Those three are murder, adultery and idolatry, which may not be performed even to save a person's life. Otherwise, however, all the prohibitions are permitted on condition that there is no other way to save the life. Thus, for example, if the only cure

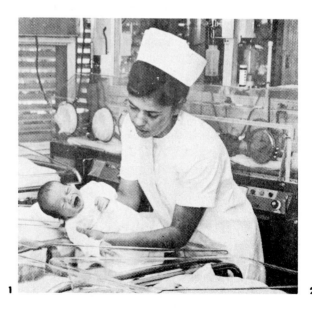

1. A newborn child, one of the greatest miracles of creation.
2. The Garden of Eden, where all life began and where some believe the soul returns after death. By the early Renaissance Flemish painter Hieronymus Bosch.

available is forbidden food, then the patient must eat it. Just as the preservation of life is a *mitzvah,* putting an end to life is absolutely prohibited. This applies not only to murder but any action which for any reason may cut short a person's life is forbidden. Mercy killing (euthanasia) is therefore unthinkable in Judaism, and if a person is close to death nothing should be done which might speed the end. For more on this see *Death and Mourning. This concern for life also applies to an unborn child; abortion is only permitted if the life of the mother is in danger.

Judaism's regard for human life is a direct result of the belief that life is a gift from God and that only He who gave it can take it away. Furthermore, all God's creation has a purpose and a value — "God saw everything He had made and behold it was very good" (Genesis 1:31) — and man has no right to interfere. This applies to everything and as such Judaism condemns wanton destruction for no purpose — "You shall not destroy" (Deuteronomy 20:19) is a biblical commandment.

Afterlife. The sages of the Talmud saw life as a prelude to life in the world to come. "This world is like a vestibule before the world to come; prepare yourself in the vestibule that you may enter into the hall" (Mishnah, Avot 4:21). In other words, according to rabbinic theology, the physical life a person has is a kind of trial period for his "real" life which comes after death. Indeed, in rabbinic parlance, the life after death is known as "the world of truth."

The exact nature of this afterlife is the subject of great discussion in classical Jewish sources. All agree that after death the soul continues to live. The souls of the righteous enter paradise, or *Gan Eden* (Garden

of Eden) as it is generally called. In that state "there is no eating or drinking . . . no envy, hatred or competition but only this: that the righteous sit with crowns on their heads and delight in the splendor of God's presence" (Talmud). The souls of the wicked enter hell, or *Gehinnom,* as it is known, where they undergo purification before they too can enter paradise. The general view is that the stay in *Gehinnom* is not longer than 11 months and can only be permanent in the case of exceedingly wicked persons.

Resurrection. Some rabbis believed in resurrection. That is that at a certain point in time God will bring everybody back to life and then the world will be a perfect place and physical life will go on indefinitely. This doctrine poses some obvious difficulties: the body actually decomposes after burial so how can it be reconstituted; furthermore what about overpopulation of the world? Those who believe in resurrection claim that anyway the whole process will be miraculous and the miracle will solve all the problems. Other rabbis however denied physical resurrection entirely and understood the afterlife to be a completely spiritual experience.

The argument about resurrection lasted well into the Middle Ages, and was one of the reasons for the sharp attacks against *Maimonides. Many believed that he denied the doctrine and his views started a controversy that lasted for hundreds of years. In modern times most Jewish theologians do not subscribe to the doctrine of physical resurrection and movements such as Reform Judaism do not consider it to be a necessary belief for the Jew.

The whole subject of afterlife is not explicitly stated in the Bible and many scholars are of the opinion that belief in afterlife was adopted by Jews during the Babylonian exile after the destruction of the First Temple when they came into contact with eastern religions such as Zoroastrianism. Traditional believers claim that there are "hints" to future life in the Torah, such as the verse "Then Moses and the Israelites sang this song" (Exodus 15:1). The Hebrew word for "sang" is in the future tense and the sages took this to mean that Moses and the Israelites will sing in the future, that is, in the world to come.

LIFSHITZ, NEHAMAH (1927-   ). At first glance, the concert held in Tel Aviv one cloudless April night in 1969 seemed quite ordinary. But the slender woman with the fine-featured face who was about to perform was received with thunderous applause and

Death which comes in the prime of life often seems unjust, as in the case of this young Israeli pilot being brought for burial. He was killed in the Six-Day War of 1967.

unconcealed emotion. It was the debut performance of Neḥamah Lifshitz, the Jewish folksinger who had escaped from the Soviet Union and had arrived in Israel only a few weeks before. After singing "Jerusalem of Gold," she told the assembled, "I, too, shall be thy harp, Jerusalem."

Neḥamah Lifshitz was born in Lithuania, where she graduated from the town's Hebrew high school. During World War II, the family escaped to Uzbekistan, the southernmost republic of the Soviet Union, and they returned to Lithuania in 1946. She received her musical training at the Vilna Conservatoire and gave her first performance in 1951. At an all-Soviet vocal competition in 1958, she was awarded the title of laureate of *estrada* (folk) artists. Because she was the first Russian to perform Yiddish and Hebrew songs publicly in 40 years, and since her concerts drew large and enthusiastic crowds, she has been named "the voice of the Jews of silence."

Since settling in Israel, she has made many public protests against the persecution of the Jews in the Soviet Union.

LINCOLN, ABRAHAM (1809-65), the 16th president of the United States, was the first to become officially involved in questions of anti-Jewish discrimination. After efforts by Lincoln, a law was passed in 1862 enabling Jews to serve as military chaplains (in this case rabbis) alongside their Protestant and Catholic colleagues. In December of the same year General Ulysses S. Grant issued an order expelling all Jews from the area of his command, on the alleged ground that Jews were engaged in illegal trading. Cesar Kaskel, a Jew from Kentucky, brought the matter to Lincoln's attention and the President issued an immediate cancellation of the order. The President told a delegation of Jews "I do not like to hear a class or nationality condemned on account of a few sinners."

Lincoln was a close friend of Abraham Jonas, a Jew from Illinois, and their correspondence reveals a warm mutual appreciation and common political loyalties.

American Jews have felt particularly attracted to Lincoln as the emancipator of the Negro slaves, and as spokesman for a way of life "with malice towards none, with charity for all."

LIPCHITZ, JACQUES (1891-1973), U.S. sculptor, was born in Lithuania and in 1909 went to Paris, where he studied and became a French citizen in

1925. In 1930 he held a large retrospective exhibition from which he gained an international reputation. He was forced to flee Paris in 1940 and the following year went to the U.S. and settled in Hastings-on-Hudson, New York.

Lipchitz was one of the foremost cubist sculptors and was influenced by the painters Picasso, Braque and El Greco, and by African art, which he collected. His style changed in the 1930s to the baroque — one of his most celebrated pieces from this period being that based on the Prometheus myth. Lipchitz often derived inspiration from biblical themes, as in his "Jacob Wrestling with the Angel," and "David and Goliath." "The Miracle," an exultant figure facing the Tablets of the Law, was inspired by the creation of the State of Israel. Lipchitz works are widely represented in important museums, particularly in the U.S. and Israel. He left all his casts to the Israel Museum, Jerusalem.

LIPKIN, ISRAEL BEN ZE'EV WOLF (Salanter; 1810-83) was the founder of the *Musar Movement. He studied at the yeshivah of Ẓevi Hirsch Broida in Salant, where he was called "the little *Alfasi." He was much influenced by Rabbi Zundel who stressed the ethical content of Judaism.

Throughout his life Lipkin sought the best way of influencing his community. He refused rabbinic office and decided to become a preacher and head of a yeshivah in Vilna. Soon he established his own yeshivah there and began preaching sermons expounding the doctrine of *musar,* a morality based on the study of traditional ethical literature. During a

1. American sculptor Jacques Lipchitz visiting Israel Museum's Youth Wing, February, 1971.
2. Neḥamah Lifshitz performing in Israel, 1970.
3. Copper cut-out of Abraham Lincoln, on the base of a monument in Cleveland, Ohio.

cholera epidemic which swept Vilna in 1848, Lipkin
was at the head of the most dangerous relief work. He
ordered the community to continue working during
the Sabbath, and on Yom Kippur during the
epidemic, mounted the pulpit and, ordering the
people to eat, set an example in public. Later he went
to Kovno and founded a yeshivah there.

In 1857 Lipkin moved to Germany, where he
lectured on Judaism to students of Koenigsberg
University. In Memel he published the periodical
Tevunah, to which all the outstanding Lithuanian and
Galician scholars contributed; there, too, he took
German citizenship. He moved to France in 1880 in
order to further disseminate his vision of Judaism.
From Paris he returned to Koenigsberg, where he
died.

Lipkin was a revolutionary in his ideas. He
proposed the compiling of an Aramaic-Hebrew
dictionary, and the translation of the Talmud into
Hebrew and European languages, its teaching in
universities, and the provision of religious books in
Russian. His *musar* system spread throughout
Lithuania. Among his sons was Yom Tov Lipman
Lipkin, a scientist of international repute.

LISBON, capital city of *Portugal. From the 12th
until the 14th century Jews lived peacefully and
prosperously in Lisbon, many being prominent in
court circles as tax farmers, physicians and
astronomers. A magnificent synagogue was
constructed in 1260, and Lisbon became the seat of
the Portuguese chief rabbinate. Under Ferdinand I
(1367-83), however, the Jewish quarter was sacked
and many Jews massacred. Jewish involvement in
collection of taxes for the greedy monarchy led to
extreme hostility toward the Jews after the king's
death. There were pogroms in 1449 and 1482. After
the expulsion from Spain in 1492, some Jews were
allowed to enter Lisbon by John II. Their crowded
living conditions led to an outbreak of plague and
they were driven beyond the city walls. When in
1496-97 the Jews were also expelled from Portugal,
their port of embarkation was Lisbon. Herded
together there from all parts of the country, they
were forcibly converted to Christianity, in many
cases children being parted from their parents forever.

In April 1503, between 2,000 and 4,000 "New
Christians" were massacred after one of them had
scoffed at a reported miracle. Although the New
Christians made every effort to prevent the
*Inquisition reaching Portugal, they failed and Lisbon

The Arraby Moor, leader of
Portuguese Jewry during the
Middle Ages. This painting is
part of a triple panel painted
in lifesize proportions in the
15th century.

became the seat of a tribunal of the Holy Office. For two centuries from 1540, a long series of public burnings and forced conversions took place. Many of those who perished were men of importance. Following a theft from a Lisbon church in 1630, a New Christian youth was put to death and many others fled the city. After the turn of the 18th century it became the custom to send to Lisbon for punishment all those found guilty by other inquisitorial tribunals of the realm. An earthquake in the city in 1755 allowed many Marranos to escape from prisons and prompted others to make their way overseas. Juridical differences between Old and New Christians were ended in 1773 and the latter thereafter disappeared as a separate class.

Jews from Gibraltar, under British protection, founded a community in Lisbon in 1813. Several synagogues were founded and a cemetery leased. The community received official recognition in 1868. However, complete equality was attained only with the 1910 revolution. Following World War I there was a very large influx of refugees from Eastern Europe. During World War II about 45,000 refugees fleeing the Nazis arrived in Portugal, mainly through Lisbon. There were 400 Jews settled in the city in 1947, and about 600 in 1981.

LITHUANIA, the southernmost of the Baltic states of northeast Europe, contained a unique Jewish community whose influence on Russian Jewry and on world Jewry in general extended beyond the boundaries of historic Lithuania. Both economic and historical factors were responsible for the unique character of the Litvaks, as Lithuanian Jews were known by their brethren the world over, of whom there were 1.5 million at the end of the 19th century. Lithuania was a poor country and most of its inhabitants were peasants. The local Jews, known for their unemotional, sharp-witted and pugnacious nature, concentrated in towns such as Vilna, Minsk, Bialystok, Vitebsk, Dvinsk, Brest-Litovsk, Kovno, Grodno and Pinsk; they generally formed the majority in these towns and were contractors, merchants, shopkeepers, innkeepers and craftsmen who regarded themselves as superior to their rural neighbors in every respect.

There were relatively few pogroms and massacres, which gave the Lithuanian Jews a feeling of security, as a result of which they felt free to openly retain their Jewish way of life. They spoke a special Yiddish which differed from the Yiddish spoken in Poland

and Volhynia, and their way of life was based on the Written and Oral Law. The *Shulhan Arukh* and its commentaries guided them in all aspects of their daily life. Torah learning flourished everywhere. Lithuanian Jews were considered the best examples of *Mitnaggedim*, i.e., opponents of *Hasidism. The personality which symbolized the supremacy of Torah learning within Lithuanian Jewry was that of the *Gaon of Vilna, Elijah ben Solomon Zalman, who lived during the second half of the 18th century. In his time Ḥasidism blazed a trail in the south and the *Haskalah invaded the country. Elijah's disciples fought against these new forces, and yeshivot became their fortresses. Ḥayyim Volozhiner established a yeshivah in Volozhin and during the 19th century

1 and 2. Two typical scenes of small-town life in Lithuania in the early part of this century.

2

1. Jewish newspaper seller in Lithuania, 1937.
2. Children in primary school in the Lithuanian district of Telz, 1937.

large yeshivot were established in Mir, Telz, Slobodka, and other townlets. Israel Meir ha-Kohen (Ḥafez Ḥayyim) started his yeshivah in Radun, and Isaac Jacob Reines, a founder of the Mizrachi organization, tried to adapt to the modern era and in 1904 established a yeshivah in Lida where secular subjects were taught. During the middle of the 19th century, the *Musar movement emerged. Under Rabbi Israel (Salanter) *Lipkin it tried to strengthen traditional Judaism.

The yeshivot of Lithuania attracted young men throughout Russia who became the rabbis of Jewish communities all over the world: Isaac Elhanan *Spektor, Joseph Baer *Soloveichik, Ḥayyim Ozer *Grodzenski, and many others.

Ḥasidism did not spread through Lithuania to the same extent as it did in the other parts of Eastern Europe. Only one branch, Ḥabad Ḥasidism, took root in Belorussia.

An important cultural factor in Lithuania from the close of the 18th century was the Hebrew press. During the 19th century Vilna became one of the world's leading centers for the printing of Hebrew books. It was here that the famous Romm edition of the Talmud was printed.

Although Lithuania played an important role in the preservation of traditional Judaism, it also contributed considerably to the movements which shook the Jewish world and brought many changes in it – Haskalah, Zionism, and Jewish Socialism. The development of Hebrew literature in Lithuania and the activities of Hebrew authors and poets were closely connected with Zionism.

Lithuanian Jewry was severely affected by World War I. The area was divided among several states – independent Lithuania, Belorussian S.S.R. and Poland. In Belorussian Lithuania, Judaism was suppressed. In Poland, Lithuanian Jews flourished until the German invasion of June 1941 brought physical annihilation. There was a degree of Jewish self-government in independent Lithuania and the educational system set up was one of its most important achievements. Many Jews emigrated nonetheless because of economic hardship.

When the Soviet Union gained control over Lithuania (1940-1941) many Jews were given important positions in the administration. At the same time some Jews – Bund leaders, Zionists, and other "counter-revolutionaries" – were deported to Siberian forced labor camps.

1

The entire country was occupied by the Germans in one week in 1941, so that only a handful of Jews managed to escape into Russia. The local Lithuanian population enthusiastically helped the Germans in their program of mass murder, only a few brave individuals extended a helping hand to the Jews.

Lithuania was liberated by the Soviet army in the summer of 1944. The Jewish survivors consisted of several hundred Jewish partisan fighters and a few families and children who had been hidden by gentiles. Lithuania was one of the centers from which pressures came to establish a revival of Jewish cultural life after the war; an amateur Yiddish theater group was established there. In 1959 the census gave Lithuania's Jewish population as 24,672.

LIVERPOOL. A synagogue existed in Liverpool, a major seaport in northwest England, as early as 1752. Local records show that there were at least 20 Jews there in 1790 (mostly peddlers and traders) and excellent relations existed between them and their gentile neighbors. Benjamin Goetz (called Yates), a seal engraver, officiated at synagogue services.

The first cemetery was consecrated in 1789, and the regulations of the community were drawn up in 1799 – in Yiddish. Land for a synagogue, built in 1808, was a gift from the city. The present synagogue of this Hebrew congregation is in Princes Road.

The first Jewish sermons to be given in English in Britain were preached in Liverpool by Tobias Goodman, a schoolmaster who was born in Bohemia.

Russian and Polish refugees arrived at the end of the 19th century, and so did a Levantine Sephardi community. A rabbinate was set up in 1904, and the first two men to hold positions were the Lithuanian rabbi Samuel Jacob Rabinowitz, an early Zionist leader, and Yehuda Unterman, who later became chief rabbi of Israel.

Hebrew schools existed in the city from 1840. A Jewish welfare board was founded in 1875, and a yeshivah was opened in 1915. A local monthly newspaper, the *Liverpool Jewish Gazette,* first printed in 1947, was still in circulation in the 1970s.

British Jewry's first Hebrew day school — in the higher grade — was founded in Liverpool by Jacob Samuel Fox, journalist and educator from Bialystok in Russia, who was educated at the Berlin Rabbinical Seminary. Lord Cohen of Birkenhead (1900-1976), professor of medicine at Liverpool University (1934-1965), a founder of Britain's National Health Service, a president of the British Medical Association and of the Royal Soviety of Medicine, and a governor of the Hebrew University of Jerusalem was from Liverpool. In 1981 there were about 6,500 Jews in Liverpool and five mayors since 1863 have been Jewish.

LODZ, a city in central Poland, and center of the textile industry. It contained only 11 Jews in 1793

1. "The Market at the Lodz Ghetto," by artist Szymon Szerman.
2. The Old Hebrew Congregation Synagogue on Princes Road, Liverpool, England, built in 1874.

but after 1820 its importance as an industrial center grew and with it the Jewish population, which eventually became the second largest in independent Poland. From 1827 Jews were allowed to acquire building sites, to build and to live in two streets and in the market area. German textile workers, anxious to avert competition from Jewish weavers, pressed for their expulsion.

In 1848 the Czar abolished the limitations on Jewish settlement in Polish cities. The restriction of a Jewish quarter in Lodz was finally abolished in 1862. A synagogue was erected outside the old ghetto and Jews settled all over the city. They were particularly active in supplying raw materials for the textile industry.

During World War I the city was very heavily damaged, German residents collaborating with the German invaders. When Poland became independent of Russia, the Polish government did not grant Jewish industry aid for reconstruction. In the 1920s anti-Jewish fiscal policies further inhibited the recovery of Jewish industry, which also had to cope with the general economic depression of the time. Several Jewish unions were organized to fight Polish worker hostility, but many Jews were forced out of employment.

Throughout these difficult times the Jewish community maintained its autonomy. It had a kosher slaughterhouse, a *mikveh,* and a *talmud torah* for its poor, and a number of charitable organizations. A lodge of B'nai B'rith was established in 1926. There were yeshivot and various schools. A number of poets, scholars, musicians and actors lived in Lodz. Zionist societies were active and ran several newspapers. With the rise of Nazism in Europe the situation deteriorated rapidly from 1933. Organized murders occurred in 1934 and 1935. The local fascists, on a platform of purging Lodz of Jews, won an overwhelming majority in municipal elections of 1934, though the socialist parties were victorious two years later. In 1938 rich Jews were arrested and imprisoned.

At the outbreak of World War II Lodz had 233,000 Jews, about one-third of the city's population. Many immediately fled to Warsaw or into the Soviet Union. The German army entered Lodz on September 8, 1939. The great synagogue was burned down in November and the deportation of Jews to concentration camps began. A ghetto was established and a pogrom specially organized to speed Jews into it; 164,000 people were crammed into less than two square miles. A planned policy of starvation was carried out. Jewish property was stolen by Germans and 15,000 Jews deported to labor camps. The death rate due to tuberculosis increased to 26 times what it had been in 1936. The Jews in the ghetto made brave efforts to organize food kitchens, hospitals, factories and schools. There were even secret political parties, some of which tried to sabotage production. In early 1942, 55,000 Jews were sent to their deaths in concentration camps. There followed the mass murder of 16,000 others — all children up to ten years of age, persons above 60, and the sick. The ghetto then itself became a labor camp. By September 1944 the whole remaining population of 76,701 was deported to Auschwitz. (See *Concentration Camps.)

When the liberating Soviet forces entered Lodz, there were only 870 surviving Jews. But by the end of 1946 over 50,000 had resettled, mostly from the Soviet Union. Jewish cultural life was revived and Zionist activity was intense. In 1950 the Sovietization of Poland was completed and these activities were stopped. In three waves of *aliyah,* almost all Jews had left Poland by 1970.

LOEB-LEOPOLD CASE. One of the most sensational murder cases of the 20th century involved Richard Loeb (1905-1936), aged 18, a graduate of the University of Michigan, and Nathan Freuenthal Leopold (1904-1971), aged 19, a graduate of the University of Chicago. Both were the sons of wealthy Jewish families. As they said at their trial in 1924, they had attempted the "perfect crime" when they kidnapped and killed a 14-year-old neighbor, Bobby Franks. After a highly publicized trial, in which they were defended by the famous attorney Clarence Darrow, they were sentenced to life imprisonment plus 99 years, and the court recommended that they never be released.

In jail the young men developed a correspondence school, teaching a wide range of subjects to the inmates of 19 penitentiaries. In 1936 Loeb was murdered by another prisoner. Leopold, who possessed an amazing intellect, worked ceaselessly at his prison activities. He participated in wartime malaria experiments, and mastered no fewer than 27 languages. After much effort he was finally paroled in 1958 and sent to Puerto Rico, where he worked at the Castaner General Hospital. He took a master's degree and published a book on birds, as well as his autobiography *Life Plus 99 Years* (1958). The sensational case was described by Meyer Levin in the novel *Compulsion* (1956), which Leopold declared was an unwarranted invasion of his privacy.

LOGIC is the study of the rules and principles of correct reasoning. The term logic, according to Maimonides (1135-1240), refers to that which is intelligible in the mind, and its verbal expression. Since logic is concerned with clear expression, grammar often forms a part of logical writings. Shem Tov *Falaquera, for example, prefaces one of his works with an account of the origin of language, its nature, and its parts, a classification which was very important in the philosophic analysis of the Bible in the Middle Ages. The two mental acts which are basic to logic are conception, involved in the understanding of the essence of things, and judgment, to decide whether propositions are true or false. Maimonides does not consider logic a part of philosophy. He views it as a tool to be used with all the other sciences. Some of the methods of biblical analysis and legal interpretation employed by the rabbis of the Talmud do rest on the rules of logic (see *Hermeneutics) but it is doubtful that the rabbis had a formal knowledge of the subject. However, beginning with Saadiah Gaon (died 942 c.e.), who refers to Aristotle's categories and proves that they are not applicable to God, Jewish thinkers have been acquainted with the treatises of Aristotle which formed the basis of logic.

The first work on logic that we know of, written by a Jew, is Maimonides' essay in Arabic. It was translated three times into Hebrew and was published in English in 1966 under the title *Maimonides' Treatise on Logic.* After the 13th century when Jewish scholarly activity shifted to Christian countries and Arabic was no longer the language of the Jews, many basic writings on logic were translated into Hebrew and a greater number of Hebrew works on logic were written by Jews.

Maimonides' work was extremely useful and popular. It served not only as a handbook of logic, but, until comparatively recent times, also as an introduction to general philosophy. The Jews were also familiar with other logical writings of the Islamic period (about the 10th-13th centuries) which had been translated from Arabic into Hebrew. These translations are of great importance because in many instances the original Arabic texts were lost. Moreover, many of these texts were translated from the Hebrew into Latin and were used by later gentile scholars.

LOHAMEI ḤERUT ISRAEL. Known as Leḥi, or the Stern Gang, this armed underground organization was founded in Palestine by Avraham Stern as a splinter group of the Irgun Ẓeva'i Le'ummi (IẒL), which had decided in 1941 on a truce of underground armed activities during World War II. The Stern Gang opposed this policy and declared a continuation of the war against the British. It opposed voluntary enlistment of Jews in the British army and even tried to make contact with representatives of the fascist powers. The British Palestine police and secret service were therefore mobilized against the group. The conflict between the British and the Stern Gang reached a peak in February 1942, and the British reacted by killing members of the gang. On February 12, Stern was himself caught in his hiding place and killed on the spot by British police officers.

Considerably weakened, the group was on the verge of collapse when some of its members managed to escape from prison and reorganize. They then renamed themselves Loḥamei Ḥerut Israel (Freedom Fighters of Israel) and continued operations until the end of the Mandate in 1948. Members were now continually armed, when arrested admitted membership, denounced the authority of courts trying them and made political statements. In November 1944 two members of the group assassinated Lord Moyne, British Minister of State for

Public notice given by the Palestinian government promising rewards for information leading to the arrest of seven I.Ẓ.L. members responsible for anti-British activities, January 1942.

the Middle East, in Cairo. They were caught and hanged.

In July 1945 Leḥi and IẒL agreed to cooperate in their struggle against the British. Leḥi carried out sabotage operations and armed attacks on military and government installations while also attacking individual members of the British police and army. Its secret radio waged a constant propaganda campaign and it distributed leaflets and posters.

The British authorities arrested anyone in any way connected with the group and imposed very severe sentences. On March 17, 1947 Moshe Barazani was sentenced to death for having a hand-grenade in his possession. Before the sentence could be carried out, he and Meir Feinstein, an IẒL member, blew themselves up in prison. Following the UN resolution on partition of Palestine, Leḥi took part in attacks on Arab forces, including the massacre of Arabs in Deir Yasin, which it captured with IẒL cooperation.

On May 29, 1948, two weeks after the establishment of the State of Israel, Leḥi members joined the Israel army. In Jerusalem, however, members of Leḥi continued to operate independently for a time and were suspected of the assassination of Count Folke Bernadotte on September 17, 1948. Thereafter leading Leḥi members were arrested by the Israel authorities and the group was disbanded. Leḥi leaders took part in the elections to the first Knesset. Annual memorials to Avraham Stern are held by ex-members.

LONDON, capital of the United Kingdom and seat of Britain's largest Jewish community. The earliest record of a London Jewish community dates from the reign of William Rufus (1087-1100). In 1130 the Jews of the city were accused of killing a sick man (possibly a *blood libel) and were forced to pay the then enormous sum of 2,000 pounds sterling as a fine. The anti-Jewish riots which broke out at the coronation of Richard I at Westminster on September 3, 1189, soon spread to London, where the Jewish quarter was burned and 30 people killed. Under both John (1199-1216) and his son Henry III (1216-72) further ill-feeling was expressed against the Jews, many of whom were involved in tax collection for the monarchy. A baronial attack on London Jewry was organized in 1215. In 1244 London Jews were accused of the ritual murder of a child; as a result a 60,000 mark levy was imposed on the Jews of the

realm. In 1263, following a petty argument between a Jew and a debtor concerning interest, the Jewish quarter was again sacked and several Jews murdered. Simon de Montfort made several attacks on the Jews of London and in 1266 they sought refuge in the Tower of London.

Edward I's prohibition on Jewish moneylending drove some inevitably into dishonest ways. Some 300 were said to have been hanged in 1278 for clipping the coinage. In 1232 Henry III confiscated the principal London synagogue and opened an institution for conversion. In 1281, following another ritual murder charge, the Jews were confined to their own quarter. In 1283 the Bishop of London ordered all synagogues closed; and finally in 1290 the Jews were expelled *en masse* from the country.

A very few Jews returned to the city during the period of the expulsion, usually to attend on royalty. A few *Marranos settled after the expulsion from Spain and Portugal. Roderigo *Lopez, Elizabeth I's physician was a member of a crypto-Jewish group. By the mid-17th century the small secret community of practicing Jews was sufficiently emboldened to petition Oliver *Cromwell for official protection. Under Charles II the community enjoyed *de facto* recognition. Its original synagogue in Creechurch

Jewish clothing merchants in London's East End. Sketch from a 19th-century English journal.

Lane was remodeled in 1674 and in 1701 a new one was erected in Bevis Marks. A considerable number of refugees from Spain and Portugal and from Holland came to swell the ranks of London's Jewry, which now included brokers, importers and wholesale merchants, with a sprinkling of physicians.

Ashkenazim arrived from Amsterdam and Hamburg in the 1690s and organized their own congregation. They eventually became the most numerous and influential element of the city's Jewish community, but many were poor peddlers and rag traders. An eventual merging of representatives of the Ashkenazi and Sephardi communities led to the creation of the Board of Deputies of British Jews. A Jews' Free School was founded in 1817. In 1831 Jews were admitted to the freedom of the city, and henceforth were allowed the privilege of entering the retail trade. The first Jewish Lord Mayor of London was David Salomons, appointed in 1855. Jews were admitted to Parliament in 1858.

A Reform congregation was created in 1840 and branch synagogues of both Ashkenazi and Sephardi communities were established in the fashionable West End. Jews' College was founded in 1855 and four years later the Board of Guardians for the Relief of the Jewish Poor. A United Synagogue came into being in 1870, merging all Ashkenazi congregations of the city, and a Liberal synagogue in 1910.

With the influx of Russian and East European Jews in the last quarter of the 19th century, the population rose from 47,000 to around 150,000, two-thirds of them living in the poor and cramped East End. Most of these people worked as tailors, shoemakers and carpenters. A Yiddish press and an active trade union movement grew up. In 1889 a six-

week strike of 10,000 Jewish tailors ended a period of exploitation of Jewish immigrant labor. As the Jews grew more prosperous, so they tended to move to the suburbs, such as Stamford Hill in the northeast and Golders Green in the northwest. Orthodox London Jewry received a new impetus from a wave of immigrants from Germany following the rise of Hitler in 1933. British fascists, under Sir Oswald Mosley's leadership, caused deep concern among London Jewry in the years before World War II and were finally banned by the government.

The move to the suburbs was stimulated during World War II by heavy bombing of London, especially the East End and its dockland. During the post-war period Jewish prosperity increased rapidly and Jews settled in ever increasing numbers on the northern edges of the city. London's total Jewish population dispersed throughout the suburbs to some extent it ceased to be a closeknit community and this led to a weakening of Jewish identity.

By the 1980s there were about 200 synagogues belonging to five major religious organizations in London. Jewish day schools were under control of the London Board of Jewish Religious Education, the Zionist Federation, the Jewish Secondary School movement and other such bodies. The London Jewish Welfare Board ran some 19 homes for the aged, and in addition there were Jewish Blind and Deaf Associations, various charitable institutions and a number of youth clubs, a major center being Hillel House, built by B'nai B'rith, in Euston in 1970. There were ten libraries of Jewish collections open to the public, and a Jewish Museum at Woburn Place. The chief rabbinate was centered in the capital.

LOPEZ RODERIGO (1525-94), Portuguese Marrano physician. Lopez settled in London early in the reign of Queen Elizabeth I, became a member of the College of Physicians and was the first house physician at St. Bartholomew's hospital. He later became physician to the Earl of Leicester and then to Elizabeth herself. Lopez worked closely with the Queen's favorite, the Earl of Essex, and took part in an intrigue to secure English intervention on behalf of Dom Antonio, pretender to the Portuguese throne. He later broke with Dom Antonio and began to work for an understanding with Spain. The Spanish court secretly negotiated with him and offered a heavy bribe if he would murder the pretender. Early in 1594 he was arrested and accused of plotting to poison Queen Elizabeth, was found guilty and

1. The Ben Uri Art Gallery in London which exhibits works by Jewish artists.
2. Caricature of Herman Adler, Chief Rabbi of the Ashkenazi congregation of Great Britain at the turn of the century.

Quid dabitis

Proditorum fini fini.

1. A depiction showing Rodrigo Lopez supposedly planning to poison Queen Elizabeth I.
2. Street scene in Los Angeles, California.

LORKI, JOSHUA (died about 1419) of Lorca, Spain, was a physician and writer who converted to Christianity and became an active enemy of Judaism. Lorki's teacher had converted to Christianity and this influenced him profoundly. He was very young at the time and it was to this teacher that he confided his questions and his doubts. In time Lorki too converted, taking the name of Géronimo de Santa Fé. Immediately after his conversion he initiated the Tortosa *disputation, one of the longest and most important of the debates forced on the Jews of the Middle Ages. The Christian attack was based on Lorki's essay which claimed to prove the authenticity of Jesus from Jewish sources. The disputation, which lasted nearly two years, caused great hardship for the Jews. It kept the Jewish representatives away from their homes and communities for long periods. Missionaries were very active and the Jews without their leaders were demoralized. The debaters themselves experienced great difficulty. They were unable to earn for their families' needs and unable to help their communities in distress. The debates were frustrating and confusing since Lorki was always given the last word. The disputation ended badly for the Jews. Portions of the Talmud were censured by the Christians and many Jews were forced to convert. After the disputation, some important

executed at Tyburn on June 7, 1594. The case attracted much attention and it is generally believed that Lopez was the basis for Shylock in Shakespeare's *The Merchant of Venice*.

Jewish philosophic works appeared, among them Joseph *Albo's *Sefer Ha-Ikkarim*.

Probably when still a Jew, Lorki wrote a book on the therapeutic qualities of certain plants and herbs.

LOS ANGELES, a city in southern California with about four million inhabitants, occupying 455 square miles of territory. It is the third most populous city in the U.S. and the largest city in area, in the world. In 1981, Los Angeles was the home of an estimated 503,000 Jews, second only to New York.

In 1841, the first party of pioneers traveling overland from the Middle West included Jacob Frankfort, the first Jewish resident of Los Angeles. When California joined the U.S. in 1850, following the Mexican War, and gold was discovered in the north of the state, Jews came from Western Europe and the eastern U.S. seeking to make their fortunes. Some of them opened stores or bought carts and wagons to begin trading with the wealthy Spanish rancheros of southern California. A Los Angeles census of 1850 revealed a total of 1,610 inhabitants, eight of whom had recognizably Jewish names. Seven of these were merchants and one a tailor.

Jewish religious services were formally established in 1854 with the arrival of Joseph Newmark, who served as patriarch of the Jewish community until his death in 1881. The first synagogue was built in 1873 at 273 N. Fort Street (now Broadway).

Jews participated freely in every facet of social, economic and communal life in Los Angeles. In 1873 they took the initiative to form the first Chamber of Commerce. Jewish business, concentrating on wholesale and retail merchandising, was among the largest. I. W. Hellman (1843-1920), a Jewish banker, became one of the dominant financial powers in the state.

In the early 20th century, large numbers of Eastern European Jews began to migrate to Los Angeles, sent by the Industrial Removal Office in New York. By 1920, the Jews numbered 70,000 out of a population of 1,200,000. The rapidly increasing Jewish population created, for the first time, distinctively Jewish neighborhoods and numerous congregations. By the 1980s there were over 150 Jewish congregations in Los Angeles, with institutions of higher learning for the Orthodox, Conservative and Reform trends of Judaism. Los Angeles was also the home of the film-making industry, through which many Jews have risen to international fame. (See *Motion Pictures.)

LOST PROPERTY. We often hear little children chanting: "Finders keepers, losers weepers," but in Jewish law, this is not the rule. Returning lost property is a *mitzvah;* keeping it is considered theft.

The Torah commands: "You shall not see your fellow's ox or sheep gone astray, do not ignore it; you must take it back to your fellow . . . You shall do the same . . . with anything your fellow loses and you find . . ." (Deuteronomy 22:1-3).

If someone sees a lost object and knows he cannot keep it, he might be tempted to walk away and not get involved, but "do not ignore it," says the Torah; the finder must try to restore the article to its owner. Of course there are sometimes difficulties in trying to return property, and the Talmud outlines the steps the finder should take in such cases. For instance, he may not know who the owner is, especially if there is no name on the lost article. In most cases the finder must publicly proclaim the find. The person who can identify the object by describing any identifying signs on it, is considered to be the owner. But if, after the find has been announced, no one comes to claim it,

then "you shall bring it home and it shall remain with you until your fellow claims it " (Deuteronomy 22:2). That is, if the article is not immediately claimed, the finder remains responsible for it. He must continue to publicize it until three festivals (Passover, Shavuot and Sukkot) have passed, and must keep it until the owner claims it. There are, however, exceptions to these rules. A finder does not have to be the one to return lost property if to do so would be undignified, such as when an elderly man finds something soiled or heavy. Nor must he take time off from a paid job. In the case of a lost animal, if the cost of upkeep is too great, the finder may sell the animal after a certain period and save the money for the owner.

But if you find a ten-dollar bill in a department store (the money has no identifying sign and since hundreds or thousands of people pass through there every day the location of the loss is no proof of ownership), or a utensil in the trash heap — that is, if the object's owner cannot be identified, or if it was obviously thrown away, or lost a long time ago so that the finder can assume, or may even have heard, that the owner does not expect ever to find it again — that is called *ye-ush,* the owner's right to that object is given up and the finder can keep it.

The *mitzvah* of returning lost property has wider ramifications. It includes preventing other loss as well. Thus, man has a duty to help prevent damage, if he can, from flood or fire, or by an animal destroying something. It includes the idea of helping someone to find his way. "Every man for himself!" and "Finders keepers!" are not legitimate doctrines according to Judaism. Each man is his brother's keeper and Jewish law insists that everyone has the responsibility of helping prevent loss to another.

LOTS. The Bible records the practice of casting lots as an impartial way of arriving at decisions on a variety of problems. When there was a question of choosing a person or persons from a group, lots were drawn to determine the choice. The *aggadah* states that lots were drawn when Moses chose the 70 elders. The Mishnah describes the use of lots in the allocation of duties in the Temple, and in the choosing of the "scapegoat" for the atonement ritual in the Temple (see *Day of Atonement). Another example of lots in the Bible is found in the story of *Jonah, where the seamen on Jonah's ship determined that he was the cause of the storm by drawing lots. At *Masada, when the Jewish defenders chose to martyr themselves rather than die at the

North Main Street, Los Angeles, in the late 19th century, showing the stores of Jewish merchants Harris and Jacoby, M. Kremer, S. Lazard and Co., and M.W. Hellman.

Potsherd, found at Masada, believed to have been used in the casting of lots. The shard, one of 11 such pieces, bears the name Ben Jair, probably referring to Eleazar ben Jair, commander of the Zealots at Masada.

hands of the Roman enemy, thay cast lots to choose who would be slain and who would commit suicide. The selection of a date for some future action was also determined by the casting of lots. Thus, the holiday of Purim, whose meaning is "lots," was so called because lots were cast by Haman to decide on a day for killing the Jews. The Bible also mentions lots in connection with decisions on the distribution of goods or the allocation of land. For example, it was lot-casting which determined the apportionment of Canaanite territory and the apportionment of the levitical cities.

The technique of casting lots usually involved picking out a piece of wood, paper or stone from an urn or some other receptacle. On this piece was written the "lot" of the person or property chosen. Another method was to throw objects to the ground and then interpret the way they fell according to some pre-arranged understanding.

The fact that the casting of lots is mentioned in the Bible as taking place "before the Lord" reflects the belief that divine guidance influenced which lot was chosen. Thus, it was believed that while man cast lots, it was God's will that determined how they fell. However, the Torah expressly warns against divination and the use of lots to reveal hidden meanings (see *Magic). Moreover, the use of lots in gambling was also prohibited.

In the State of Israel today, games of chance are forbidden, but the government sponsors a weekly national lottery known as Mifal ha-Payis, the proceeds of which go to hospitals and schools.

LOVE. Many kinds of love are represented in the Bible — the sensuous love between man and woman; affection; concern; the theological idea of love between man and God. The most common term used is *ahav*. Parents have a special compassionate love for their children; affection, esteem and loyalty formed the essential relationship between *David and Jonathan, or Naomi and *Ruth. Love between man and woman is almost always connected with marriage or the intention to marry. The Song of Songs, described by the rabbis as an allegory of God's love for Israel, has been classed among the world's great love poetry. Its lyric quality and range of imagery have pictured the generosity and understanding which love creates and sustains, and have made these the ideal in human relationships. Love of God is sometimes signified indirectly, such as loving justice, or loving His commandments. This is discussed in

Opposite: Painting by Maurycy Gottlieb depicting Jews at prayer on the Day of Atonement, the holiest day of the Jewish year, during which the love and fear of God are epitomized in the prayer *Avinu Malkeinu,* "Our Father, Our King."

*Love and Fear of God.

Love of one's fellow man is a biblical commandment: "Love your neighbor as yourself: I am the Lord" (Leviticus 19:18). This law is the basis for all the other laws which prohibit unfair dealings and the bearing of grudges, and stress concern for the defenseless. The great sages *Akiva and *Hillel regarded love of one's fellow as a basic precept of the Torah. From this commandment was drawn moral responsibility toward all men, including gentiles. In the last century, technology has brought the world and all its people closer together so that all mankind are essentially "neighbors." Recent Jewish philosophy has stressed this. Samson Raphael *Hirsch makes the love of all mankind a condition of being a Jew. Sympathy for one's neighbor is basic to Martin *Buber's I-Thou philosophy.

LOVE AND FEAR OF GOD. Just before he died, and on the eve of the Children of Israel's entry into the Promised Land, Moses made a farewell speech to the Jews. In it, he reviewed their history and gave direction for their future. In one sentence (Deuteronomy 10:12) he summed up what the Bible considers to be the entire purpose of human existence: "And now, O Israel, what does the Lord your God demand of you? Only this: to revere (fear) the Lord your God, to walk only in His paths, to love Him, and to serve the Lord your God with all your heart and soul."

The Hebrew word for "revere" is יִרְאָה *(yirah)* which is usually translated as "fear," and that for "love" is אַהֲבָה *(aha'vah).* These two concepts, although they may seem contradictory at first glance, are the essence of Judaism's view of man's attitude to God.

The "fear" referred to is not the fright or scaredness which a person feels when he is confronted, for example, with a hungry lion. It is rather a feeling of awe or reverence felt when witnessing greatness or grandeur. The view of a major natural wonder, for instance, is breathtaking and inspires the beholder with awe. It is this kind of feeling that is meant by the "fear of God"; that is, awe at the thought of the infinity and greatness of God.

Love of God implies a more intimate relationship, which is much closer to a personal relationship; a person does not love a natural phenomenon but something near to him.

The two terms, then, express the paradoxical

nature of man's relationship to God. On the one hand, God is infinite, great and far away (the philosophers use the word "transcendental") and on the other He is close and involved in every human being's affairs ("immanent"). This idea is expressed very frequently in the prayers by the way God is addressed. The phrase *Avinu malkeinu,* "Our Father, Our King," in particular is indicative: you are close to and love your father but you stand in awe of a king.

Another aspect of these two ideas is that awe or reverence implies obedience, while love means the willingness to sacrifice for one's beloved. This is very strongly expressed by the first sentence of the *Shema:* "You shall love the Lord your God with all your heart and with all your soul and with all your might" (Deuteronomy 6:5).

The idea of love and fear of God has played a central role in all Jewish thinking throughout the ages because believing in God demands an explanation of man's relationship to Him. The Jewish view is that He is both near and far; both Father and King.

LUBLIN, a city in east Poland. Anti-Jewish feeling here has been marked since the 14th century when Jews first came to the town. The Jewish community

Corner of a street in Lublin, photographed in the 1920s, showing some typical Jews of the period.

remained in Lublin, however, and expanded. Jews were brewers, bakers, furriers and brush-makers, and they traded at the fair for which Lublin was famous in the 16th and 17th centuries. The venue of one of the twice-yearly meetings of the Council of the Lands was the Lublin Fair. There was bitter rivalry between Jews and their Christian neighbors and *blood libels and attacks on Jews frequently took place.

In spite of these difficulties Jewish communal and cultural life flourished. Lublin's yeshivah was famous throughout Poland; the Jewish community also produced several well-known physicians in the 16th and 17th centuries. The town was the home of some of Judaism's great rabbis, among then Solomon ben Jehiel Luria (1534-72), Mordecai ben Abraham Jaffe (1535-1612) and Meir ben Gedaliah Lublin (1558-1616). Ḥasidism played a prominent role here and Lublin had its own dynasty of *zaddikim* (the Eigers); Jacob Isaac, the Seer of Lublin, was a renowned *zaddik.* During the 19th and 20th centuries Jews expanded their businesses, built factories, and founded cultural and political associations (such as Poalei Zion, Agudat Israel, Beth Jacob).

Anti-Semitism, always prevalent, increased during the 1930s. Lublin was occupied by the Nazis in 1939; in 1942 deportation to the death camps began. About 40,000 Jews from Lublin died in the camps. In 1944 the Red Army liberated the town. Anti-Semitism among the population remained rife and many of the surviving Jews left the town after 1946. By 1968 no Jews remained in Lublin.

LUDOMIR, MAID OF (1805-1892) is the popular name of a "woman-*zaddik,*" the leader of a ḥasidic sect. (For more on the role of such a person, see also *Zaddik; *Ḥasidism.) Her real name was Hannah Rachel, and she was the only child of Monesh Werbermacher of Ludomir in the Ukraine. She was an extremely pious person and prayed with ecstatic emotion; she also studied Midrash, *aggadah,* and *musar.* During a serious illness she experienced a vision in which, she claimed, she received "a new and sublime soul." Soon afterward she began to observe the religious duties of males, putting on *tallit* and *tefillin* when she prayed. She also recited *Kaddish* for her deceased father. A synagogue was built with an adjoining apartment for her. At the *se'udah shelishit* repast on the Sabbath, the door to her room was opened and she delivered a scholarly talk to her followers. Although she was betrothed at an early age, the engagement was later cancelled. Prominent rabbis tried to persuade her to marry, and at the age of 40 she finally did. Her popularity waned after her marriage, and she later emigrated to Erez Israel. She continued her mystical studies and engaged in rituals designed to hasten the coming of the Messiah.

LURIA, ISAAC (1534-1572). "Come, let us go up to Jerusalem!" said the Ari to his disciples one Friday just before sunset. "Oh, but first we must go and tell our wives," they answered. "You have lost the opportunity!" he cried in anguish. "We could have brought about the redemption and the coming of the Messiah just at that moment . . . Now we must wait." Luria, the great kabbalist, is referred to as *Ha-Ari Ha-Kadosh*, the sacred lion – "lion" derived from the initials הָאֱלוֹהִי רַבִּי יִצְחָק, *Ha-Elohi Rabbi Yizḥak*, the godly man, Rabbi Isaac. The yearning for the Messiah underlies the Ari's teaching that the mystical task of the Jewish people is to correct the imperfection in the world – the existence of evil and impurity. This can be done through devout prayer and strict observance of the precepts of the Torah. Only then will the Messiah come.

Traditions surrounding Isaac Luria's youth, his life in Egypt and his introduction to Kabbalah are shrouded in legend. It is known that his father emigrated from Poland or Germany to Jerusalem and married into a Sephardi family. Isaac Luria was a young child when his father died, and the widow took the boy to the home of her brother in Egypt. He was an outstanding student and collaborated with his teacher, Bezalel Ashkenazi, in the writing of halakhic works, particularly the *Shitah Mekeubezet*, a major compendium of talmudic commentaries. He married his cousin, and for some time engaged in business. For seven years he lived and studied in seclusion on an island near Cairo and there he wrote his only book, a commentary on a section of the *Zohar*. Luria settled in *Safed with his family about 1569 and studied Kabbalah with Moses *Cordovero. He began to develop his own kabbalistic system and drew many students, among them distinguished scholars. His most celebrated disciple was Ḥayyim Vital. Luria already had a reputation as a man of striking personality who possessed the holy spirit. He often took long walks with his disciples, pointing out the long-lost graves of saintly men which he had discovered through spiritual intuition and revelations. Luria himself wrote very little, but his teachings were assembled by Vital in a special book. It includes kabbalistic and non-mystical works and there are a number of handwritten copies in existence. Luria's system in Kabbalah was revolutionary and all subsequent systems were based on it. For more on this aspect, see *Kabbalah.

Another facet of Luria's fertile mind expressed itself in poetry, some of which appears in the liturgy. The best-known are three Sabbath hymns which have his name in acrostic. They describe the special relationship between man and the world of spirit on the Sabbath day. Luria occasionally preached in the Ashkenazi synagogue in Safed, but he preferred the Sephardi liturgy and based his mystical meditations on it. This is why Ashkenazi kabbalists and Ḥasidim pray according to the Ari's variation of the Sephardi rite. The Ari's activity in Safed, although it was very brief, had wide and prolonged impact on the entire Jewish world. In 1572 he died in an epidemic. The two synagogues and his grave have remained places of pilgrimage to this day.

LUTHER, MARTIN (1483-1546), German religious reformer. At the beginning of his activities Luther held the firm conviction that many Jews, after listening to his teachings, would accept Christianity as truth. He often condemned the persecution of Jews and recommended tolerance toward them, based on the spirit of Christian brotherhood. He condemned the "Passion preachers [who] do nothing else but exaggerate the Jews' misdeeds against Christ and thus

1. Detail of the ark of the Sephardi synagogue of the Ari, Isaac Luria, in Safed. The synagogue is a focal point for pilgrimages.
2. Martin Luther, as portrayed in the anti-Semitic Nazi journal *Der Stuermer*, May 1937, which describes him as the fighter against the serpent of Judaism in the Christian church, and as one of the greatest Jew haters in German history.

embitter the hearts of the faithful against them." He also disapproved of the confiscation of the Talmud and rabbinic literature.

In his pamphlet on the Jewish question, *Dass Jesus Christus ein geborener Jude sei* ("That Christ Was Born a Jew"), written in 1523, Luther argued that the Jews were right not to accept the "Papal paganism" (i.e. Catholicism) presented to them as Christianity — "If I had been a Jew and had seen such fools and blockheads teach the Christian faith, I should rather have turned into a pig than become a Christian." The Church authorities branded him a "half-Jew."

Luther's attack on the Roman Catholic church was at first welcomed by Jews as a break in the monolithic power of that institution, and they hoped that greater tolerance might be the result. *Marranos in particular were strongly sympathetic to the Reformation which Luther was attempting. But when the Jews refused to convert *en masse,* Luther became increasingly hostile toward them. He complained of their stubbornness and his attacks on usury began to assume an anti-Jewish bias. He condemned the Sabbatarian sect of Protestants for adopting Jewish practices. In two pamphlets of 1542 and 1543 he attacked the Jews in a torrent of vile abuse. He suggested imposing forced labor on them or outright banishment, and the Jews of Saxony were expelled on on his advice. A number of Reformation thinkers criticized Luther's change of attitude and the Jews were bitterly disappointed by it.

LUXEMBURG, ROSA (1871-1919), German economist and revolutionary, was born into a family of merchants in Russian Poland and while still at school joined the Polish revolutionary movement in Warsaw. As a student in Zurich she worked in the underground Socialist movement of Polish emigrés in Switzerland. In the early 1890s she helped found the Polish and Lithuanian Social Democratic Party, which for a time cooperated with the Marxist Russian Social Democrats. Migrating to Germany in 1898, she obtained German citizenship by marriage (purely formal) to a printer. She became a leading figure in the revolutionary left wing of the German Socialist movement. In 1905-06 she was imprisoned after taking part in a revolutionary uprising in Warsaw. She escaped and resumed her activities in Germany, and became prominent in the Socialist International, devoting much time to developing the general strike as a political weapon. As a consequence of her

Rosa Luxemburg, the socialist revolutionary, who was murdered on her way to prison.

opposition to World War I, which she felt was an imperialist enterprise, she spent a long period in prison. The "Spartakusband," which she helped found became the Communist Party of Germany in 1918. Rosa was on friendly terms with *Lenin, although she disagreed with him on a number of issues and was highly critical of the Bolshevik reign of terror in the Soviet Union. Arrested in Berlin on January 15, 1919, with Karl Liebknecht, both were murdered by army officers while on their way to the Moabit prison.

Rosa Luxemburg believed that international socialism and national independence were conflicting ideas. She was indifferent to frequent anti-Semitic attacks on her person, and had no interest in a specifically Jewish labor movement, her "nation" being the international working class, and its means of independence the socialist revolution.

LUXURY LAWS. The elaborate wedding or bar mitzvah which many Jews are accustomed to today could not have taken place in many communities several hundred years ago. The reason: there were strict laws issued by rabbis and communal leaders restricting the lavishness and cost of such celebrations.

These laws, known as sumptuary laws, placed limitations on dress, jewelry and the size of banquets. They were meant to eliminate the temptation of massive spending and to insure that each man lived according to his means. In many cases, they were designed to put an end to anti-Jewish agitation which stemmed from resentment of the Jews' ostentatious living.

In 1418, a conference in Forli, Italy, limited the number of guests who could be invited to a wedding to 20 men, ten women, five girls and all relatives up to second cousins. A 1432 law in Spain forbade Jews aged 15 and over to "wear any cloak of good thread, olive-colored material, or silk, or any cloak trimmed with these materials" except on festive occasions. In 1659 the number of guests at a circumcision depended on the wealth of the host: "a person who pays two zlotys in taxes can invite 15 persons, four zlotys 20 persons, six zlotys 25 persons, including the rabbi, the cantor and the beadle."

In the 16th and 17th centuries the communities of Salonika, Mantua and Rome issued periodic anti-luxury laws, and in Cracow, such laws became part of the community ordinances. In 1637, the Lithuanian Council gave local rabbis the authority to decide how many guests could be invited to festive meals.

A few years ago a group of rabbis in Jerusalem, seeking to revive this tradition, published a list of regulations aimed at sparing people from self-impoverishment through trying to keep up with the Cohens.

LUZZATTO, MOSES ḤAYYIM (1707-46), kabbalist, moralist, and Hebrew poet. Moses Luzzatto, known also by his Hebrew acronym RaMHaL, was the leader of a group of religious thinkers concerned with redemption and messianism. Born into one of the most eminent of Italian Jewish families, Luzzatto was regarded as a genius from childhood, and had an extensive knowledge of Bible, Talmud, Midrash, halakhic literature, classical languages and literature, and Italian culture. He also had a good scientific education.

In 1727 Luzzatto underwent a religious experience which changed his life. He thought he heard the voice of a *maggid* (a divine spirit inclined to reveal heavenly secrets to human beings). Thereafter the voice spoke to Luzzatto frequently. When it became known that Luzzatto's followers were taking part in mystical activities, he was accused of being a Shabbatean heretic (see *Shabbetai Ẓevi) and a vehement controversy followed, involving many of Italy's leading rabbis. As a result, Luzzatto ultimately agreed not to record the conversations of the *maggid* any longer, and to refrain from teaching *Kabbalah. But criticism continued, and so in 1735 he left Italy for Amsterdam. On his journey he contacted Jacob ha-Kohen who, instead of helping him, burned some of his writings and hid the rest. In 1743 Luzzatto went to Ereẓ Israel, probably in order to be free to teach Kabbalah. There he lived for a short time in Acre, but with his family, died of plague.

It is clear from his writings that Luzzatto saw himself as a reincarnation of Moses, the man who was to rescue his people from the *galut*. His chief writing was the *Mesillat Yesharim* which is still a standard text for the study of Jewish ethics. He also wrote kabbalistic works and was the author of one of the first plays to be written in Hebrew. Long after his death Luzzatto became a saint in the eyes of most East European Jewry. The three chief Jewish movements of the 19th century — the *Hasidim, the Mitnaggedim, and the *Haskalah writers — all found relevance in his thinking.

LVOV (German: Lemberg), a town in the Ukraine at a commercial crossroads between East and West. It has been under Polish, Russian and German rule and today is part of the U.S.S.R. The first Jews probably came to Lvov during the 14th century from Byzantium, Germany and Bohemia. A majority were

1. *Mesillat Yesharim,* a standard text on Jewish ethics by Moses Ḥayyim Luzzatto.
2. The fish market in the Jewish quarter of Lvov.

1. Part of the vaulted
ceiling and the ark of the
Taz synagogue in Lvov, built
in 1582 by Isaac ben
Naḥman after the plan of an
Italian architect.
2. The old section of Lydda
(present-day Lod), 1953.

shopkeepers, peddlers, and craftsmen; some became prominent and played an important role in trade, leased estates, operated brandy distilleries, and loaned money to the king and the nobility. The townsmen who were economic competitors of the Jews, hated them, but the nobles generally supported them, and their rights were guaranteed by the kings of Poland.

In spite of tension between Jews and Christians, relations between them remained stable. During *Chmielmicki's rebellion of 1648-49, Lvov's Jews were active in the defense of the town against him and contributed to the ransom for the lifting of the siege. Large numbers of Jews, however, especially those living outside the town walls, were massacred by the insurgents.

Possibly because of the deep shock of Chmielnicki's massacres, *Shabbetai Ẓevi was eagerly welcomed as the messiah by many of Lvov's Jews at the beginning of the 18th century. In the disillusionment that followed his apostasy, large numbers turned to *Hasidism, although no ẓaddikim settled in the town.

By the middle of the 19th century, the *Haskalah was attracting support, and one of Europe's first Reform temples was established in Lvov. During the First World War, the Jews suffered under the Russian occupation (1915) as they did during the Polish-Ukrainian battle for the city in 1918. In the interwar years (1918-1939), local anti-Semitism increased, and German troops were welcomed by the Ukrainians in 1941. A ghetto was established and most of Lvov's 150,000 Jews perished.

Today 40,000 Jews live in Lvov, and the Soviet Union conducts a strongly anti-Jewish policy against them.

LYDDA (Lod), a town in the coastal plain of Israel, 10 miles southeast of Tel Aviv-Jaffa, is first recorded in Thutmose III's list of towns of Canaan (1465 b.c.e.). According to the Bible it was founded by Shemed, a Benjaminite (I Chronicles 8:12). In the Hellenistic period Lydda was outside the boundaries of Judea. In 145 b.c.e. it was detached from Samaria and given by Demetrius II to Jonathan the Hasmonean. In Maccabean times it was a purely Jewish town, and later Julius Caesar is reported to have restored the privileges of its Jews, taken away by the Greeks. In 43 c.e. Cassius, the governor of Syria, sold its inhabitants into slavery. The Roman proconsul of Syria, Cestius Gallus, burned Lydda on his way to Jerusalem in 66 c.e. Captured by John the

Essene at the beginning of the first Jewish war (66-70), it was occupied by Vespasian in 68 c.e.

Between the First and Second Jewish Wars the town flourished. It had a large market, raised cattle and ran textile, dyeing and pottery industries. It was a seat of the *Sanhedrin, and its scholars included *Akiva and Eliezer ben Hyrcanus. It also had a Christian community at the time of Peter (Acts 9: 32-35). In the year 200 Septimus Severus, the Roman emperor, established a Roman city there. Still partly Jewish, it took part in the revolt against the emperor Gallus in 351 and was punished when this failed.

By the Byzantine era, the town was predominantly Christian. It was the legendary birthplace of St. George, patron saint of England, and was called Georgiopolis. Captured by the Muslims in 636, it served as the headquarters of the province of Filastīn. The Crusaders occupied the town in 1099; there was only one Jewish family there in 1170, according to *Benjamin of Tudela. But more Jews settled there again after the conquest by Saladin. During the early Ottoman period there seem to have been no Jews living there, though a small Jewish community was founded in the 19th century. The Jews were forced out by the 1921 Arab riots; by 1944 Lydda had a population of 17,000 Arabs, one-fifth of them Christian. During the War of Independence, Israel forces occupied Lydda in July 1949. The majority of Arabs abandoned the town. At the end of 1980 the population numbered 38,700 including 4,300 Muslim and Christian Arabs.

Israel's international airport, renamed in honor of David Ben-Gurion, was originally built on the outskirts of Lydda by the British Mandatory government in 1936. It is the home base for Israel's *El Al airlines. Almost three million passengers passed through it in 1980. Both the airport and Israel Aircraft Industries are important sources of employment for the local population. Other industries include papermaking, food preserves, electrical appliances, cigarettes and oil refining.

MACAULAY, THOMAS BABINGTON (Lord; 1800-59), the English historian and politician, was a member of a family which had been in the forefront of the movement against slavery. He was elected to Parliament in 1830 and in his maiden speech in the House of Commons introduced a bill for the removal of political discrimination against Jews. In an article in the Edinburgh Review of 1831 he wrote: "The points of difference between Christianity and Judaism have very much to do with a man's fitness to be a bishop or a rabbi. But they have no more to do with his fitness to be a magistrate, a legislator, or a minister of finance than with his fitness to be a cobbler." Rarely had the case for Jewish emancipation been presented with the literary force of Macaulay's essays and speeches; his support of this cause as a leading writer had a significant effect on public opinion.

MACCABI WORLD UNION is an international Jewish sports organization. It was founded in 1921 and was closely connected with the growing Zionist movement. Its aims were threefold: instilling a new self-confidence and self-respect into Europe's downtrodden Jews; fostering a sense of Jewish identity; and transforming the town-dwelling ghetto Jew into a strong and active pioneer, capable of building a national homeland in Palestine.

In 1898, in a speech at the Second Zionist Conference at Basle, the well-known Zionist leader, Max *Nordau, proclaimed the necessity for physical training, and the number of Jewish sports clubs increased after this time. In 1903 the existing sports clubs were associated as the Union of Jewish Gymnastics and club membership reached 1,500. The movement continued to grow, and the Maccabi World Union was formed in 1921 to integrate the many clubs. By the following year Maccabi had almost 100,000 members. Headquarters were at first in Vienna (1921-27), then from 1927-29 in Brno, Czechoslovakia, and in 1929 were moved again to Berlin, where the Union flourished under the presidency of Heinrich Lellever (1891-1947). In 1929 the first international sports competition was held in Prague and the next year in Antwerp, Belgium. These games were the forerunners of the Maccabiah Games, the Jewish Olympics, which were staged for the first time in 1932.

The idea of the Maccabiah was conceived by Joseph Yekutieli, a founder and veteran leader of Maccabi in Palestine. He succeeded in persuading the mayor of Tel Aviv, Meir Dizengoff, to build Palestine's first sports stadium. In 1929 Yekutieli's proposal for the Maccabiah Games was approved and in 1932 the first Maccabiah was held in Tel Aviv, with 500 athletes from 23 countries participating.

Many athletes remained in Palestine after the games, particularly following the Second Maccabiah in 1935 when rabid anti-Semitism was sweeping Europe. The Maccabiah thus became an important means of promoting *aliyah.* The third Maccabiah was delayed until 1950 because of World War II; the fourth was in 1953, and it has been held every four years since then. Participants in recent Maccabiahs have come from more than 30 countries. The main sports in the Maccabiah are track and field, gymnastics, swimming, water polo, wrestling, tennis, soccer, and basketball.

The membership of the Maccabi World Union, the sponsor of the games, had increased to about 200,000 by 1939. After the war, Jews in communist countries were forbidden to engage in sports activities as Jews, but new branches of Maccabi were developed in North and South America, South Africa and Australia. Since 1948 the activities of Maccabi have been centered in Israel, and the headquarters are in Tel Aviv.

MADABA MAP. In 1884, a huge mosaic map of the biblical Holy Land, measuring 72 feet by 23 feet, was discovered in the floor of a sixth-century church in Madaba, Jordan.

The Maccabi football team of Mazeikiai, Lithuania, photographed in the late 1930s.

1. Parchment amulet bearing the *magen David,* invoking God "in the name of the seal of Solomon."
2. The Madaba Map of the biblical Holy Land, with Jerusalem in the center and the Jordan River and the Dead Sea above.

This map is really more of a pictorial history of the area rather than an accurate geographical representation. Cities are allotted space, not according to their actual size, but according to their historical significance. Thus, Jerusalem is one of the largest portions of the map, located directly in the center. This reflects ancient belief that Jerusalem was the center of the world, and its most important spiritual point. Its area in the mosaic is filled with pictures of the major sites in the Holy City, including two colonnaded streets, the Tower of David, the Church of the Holy Sepulcher, a church on Mount Zion, baths, and perhaps even the Western Wall.

The place names, historical notes, and biblical quotes are all given in Greek. Important places and tribal areas are marked in red and natural features are indicated by pictures. For example, ships are seen sailing in the Dead Sea, animals wander in the deserts, and ferries cross the Jordan River.

The original mosaic, based on a Roman road map, represented the area from present-day Beirut, Lebanon, in the north, to Thebes, Egypt, in the south.

It was tilted toward the east so that the Mediterranean Sea was at the bottom. It was obviously a tremendous project to lay down each individual tile in this enormous area by hand. Unfortunately a large part of the mosaic was destroyed during the erection of a Greek Orthodox Church on the site, so that today, all that remains is the area from Nablus to Egypt, which was restored by a German archaeological expedition in 1965-66.

MAGEN DAVID ("Shield of David"), the six-pointed star, has become the generally accepted emblem of the Jewish people. Tradition tells us that King David wore a *magen David* on his shield, and that King Solomon had the symbol inscribed on his ring in place of the name of God to give him dominion over demons. In spite of its long history, it is however only recently that the *magen David* has become an exclusively Jewish symbol.

Through the ages it has been used as an ornamental and as a magical sign by Jews and non-Jews alike. There are examples from the Bronze and

Iron Ages from areas as far apart as India, Briton and Mesopotamia. At the beginning of the common era it was still being used in Jewish and non-Jewish decoration alongside the five-pointed star and the swastika (this latter was taken by the Nazis in the 20th century as their symbol).

During the early Middle Ages, Christians decorated their churches and cathedrals with the *magen David.* For Muslims it was a magical sign; in Arabic sources the *magen David* was also known as the "seal of Solomon" and this alternative name was taken over by Jewish groups as well.

In the 14th century the *magen David* was increasingly used in secular, non-magical connections. In 1354 the Jewish community in Prague was granted its own flag, and chose the *magen David* as the emblem – this was the first occasion on which it was given a specifically Jewish connotation. After 1492 it was used as a printers' symbol by printing houses in Prague, Italy and Holland. In 1655 the *magen David* appeared on the seal of Vienna's Jewish community, and the Jews of Amsterdam adopted it shortly afterwards.

In the 18th century the kabbalists appropriated the sign. To them it was a secret symbol of redemption, for they saw it as the Shield of the Son of David, that is the Messiah.

It was not until the 19th century, when Jews looked for a symbol of their own to parallel the cross of Christianity that the *magen David* was generally adopted. The use of the *magen David* became more and more widespread – it decorated Jewish ritual objects

and synagogues, and the seals and letterheads of private and charitable Jewish organizations. It was adopted by the fledgling Zionist movement, and the first issue of Herzl's Zionist journal, *Die Welt* (1897) bore a *magen David* as its emblem. (In modern Israel the counterpart of the Red Cross first-aid organization is known as *Magen David Adom, the Red Shield of David.)

As early as 1799 the six-pointed star was being used by anti-Semites to satirize Jews. The Nazis used it as a badge of shame to single out and degrade their Jewish victims, and the hope and suffering of the Jewish people came to be symbolized by the *magen David.* See also *Badge, Jewish.

The State of Israel has chosen the *menorah,* the Temple candelabrum, a much older Jewish symbol, as its emblem, but the *magen David* is retained on the national flag, and is widely used in Jewish life in both Israel and the Diaspora.

MAGEN DAVID ADOM, translated from Hebrew as "Red Shield of David," is the Israel first aid society, the Jewish Red Cross.

Magen David Adom was founded in Tel Aviv in 1930 as the medical wing of the *Haganah, the pre-State underground military organization. On July 12,

1. Seal of the Sephardi community of Jerusalem in the 19th century. Around the *magen David* is engraved a verse from Isaiah about the Redemption and the Return to Zion.
2. The yellow *magen David,* the badge which the Nazis forced the Jews to wear. This one is worn by a Dutch woman, 1942.

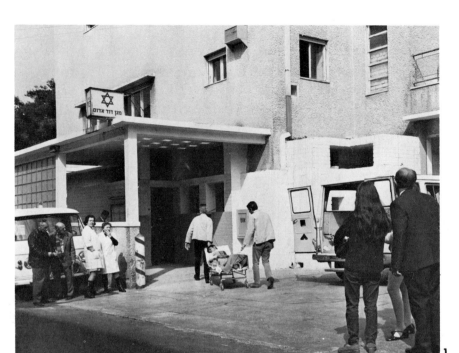

1. The victim of an accident being taken from the ambulance to the Magen David Adom emergency station in Tel Aviv, 1970.
2. Bowl placed in the foundations of a building as protection against devils and evildoers, Erez Israel, third-fourth century c.e. In the center is a man encircled by a snake and around the rim is a kabbalistic inscription in Hebrew and Aramaic.

1950, a law was passed by the Knesset recognizing Magen David Adom as the sole first aid organization in Israel. In 1980, Magen David Adom had over 60 branches, about 10,000 trained volunteers manning its stations, and 700 ambulances in use. During the *Six-Day War of June 1967, 180 ambulances were placed at the disposal of the Civil Defense Units and Army Medical Corps. Many more civilian-manned vehicles operated in battle areas, particularly in and around Jerusalem.

Magen David Adom operates the Volunteer Blood Donors' Association, founded in 1935 which assures a regular supply of fresh blood for transfusions, and it provides about 80% of all blood used in Israel's hospitals. Blood banks issue plasma on request both to hospitals and to first aid stations. The David Marcus Blood Fractionation and Plasma Drying Institute at Jaffa processes blood for longer storage.

Magen David Adom cooperates with the International Red Cross in taking care of prisoners of war as well as in the repatriation of wounded prisoners. In times of international need, Magen David David Adom sends emergency rescue teams, medical supplies, food and clothing to areas of distress throughout the world. The International Red Cross, however, has not accepted the Magen David Adom for full membership although it has accepted the Red Crescent (the Arab "Red Cross").

Funds for Magen David Adom are raised in Israel

through an annual lottery authorized by the government, as well as by Friends' organizations abroad. Branches of Friends of Magen David Adom function in Argentina and other Latin American countries, as well as in Australia, Belgium, Canada, France, Great Britain and the U.S. Donations to Magen David Adom from abroad consist largely of ambulances, medical supplies, and funds for first aid stations.

MAGIC, the attempt to change natural or human events by occult, ritualistic means, was never approved of in Jewish teaching, although the possibility of performing magic was never totally denied. The opposition stemmed from the fact that belief in the power of magic implies the recognition of supernatural powers independent of God. It thus challenges Jewish belief in God's omnipotence and providence. In addition, magic usually involved the adoption of idolatrous practices. In early Semitic cultures priests were magicians and priestesses practiced witchcraft. However, a magical approach to the world was common throughout the ancient Near East, and as a result, the Israelites were exposed to a great deal of magical lore, especially when they came in contact with the Canaanites and Babylonians, among whom occult practices were a part of daily life. Similarly, during the time of Persian and Greek domination, as well as throughout the period of the Diaspora, Jews were not infrequently exposed to magical practices and beliefs, and some penetrated in

strangely evolved forms into Jewish folk-culture and practice.

In The Bible. Several types of magicians are mentioned in the Bible, including the soothsayer, sorcerer, charmer, medium, wizard, necromancer and diviner. All are characterized as "abominations unto the Lord." The Bible, however, does not dismiss magic as foolishness or delusion, and records several episodes of what appear to be effective employment of magic. Thus, Pharaoh's magicians successfully imitated Moses when the latter transformed his rod into a snake, and the waters of the Nile into blood. Similarly, the witch of En-Dor succeeded in raising the spirit of the dead *Samuel at *Saul's request. Nevertheless, the biblical accounts stress the distinction between these occult practices and the *miracles which such men as Moses perform. The latter are the result solely of the command of God, who changes the laws of nature in accordance with His will, and not human designs.

In the Talmud. The rabbis of the Talmud maintained the biblical opposition to the practice of magic. However, there were occasions during the Mishnaic period when learned and pious men resorted to what might appear to be magic — for a good purpose. Ḥoni ha-Me'aggel (Ḥoni "the drawer of circles") several times drew a circle which he then entered, swearing that he would not budge until God caused rain to fall. Moreover, under Persian influence certain magical practices became popularly accepted and were necessarily tolerated by the rabbis. Included in these were magical procedures and incantations that proved effective in healing or were considered to be capable of combating the hold of "black" or harmful magic. Because of their supposedly protective nature, the use of *amulets was also countenanced.

Furthermore, even the rabbis themselves were influenced by the widespread belief in spirits and demons. Descriptions of the human and angelic qualities possessed by demons can be found in several places in the Talmud, as well as various suggestions as to how best to avoid their evil influence. The rabbis, however, repeatedly emphasized that all these strange powers are subordinate to divine government and that, moreover, they cannot hurt the pious. See also *Angels.

Middle Ages. During the Middle Ages, the reliance on magic increased among non-Jews, and this had a corresponding impact on certain Jewish groups. The *Ḥasidei Ashkenaz (12th and 13th centuries) were particularly susceptible to magical influences as can be seen reflected in their central text, the *Sefer Ḥasidim.* It tells, for example, of a Jewish baby born with teeth and a tail. The rabbi of the community cautiously advises that these be cut off lest the child grow up to be a werewolf. Among this group there also developed the idea of the creation of the *golem.

The belief in magic greatly influenced medieval anti-Semitism. Thus many Christians looked upon the Jews as evil magicians and as actual demonic figures, and this served as an excuse for persecution and harassment (see *Anti-Semitism).

With the rise of *Ḥasidism in the 18th century, the belief in magic became part of the common folk-culture. Many of the leaders of Ḥasidism, including its founder, the *Ba'al Shem Tov, were known as wonder-workers and as "possessors of the good name." Stories of possession by an evil spirit, a *dybbuk, became common, and corresponding ceremonies of exorcism were developed.

Modern Times. In our scientific and technological age, man tends to believe that he has overcome the need for magic to master the powers of the world. Yet, even today, people cling to superstitious beliefs and practices. For example, the belief in an "evil eye" is still prevalent, and many Jews, especially those of Eastern European origin, always add *"bli ayin ha-rah"* ("without an evil eye") whenever they make a favorable comment about someone else, lest it be construed as a jealous comment that might trigger off a detrimental effect.

MAHARAL OF PRAGUE is the name by which one of the greatest rabbis of his time, Judah Loew ben

1. A Yemenite amulet of unknown date, written on paper, expresses the owner's wish that his heart be opened to the Torah and wisdom.
2. Statue of Judah Loew ben Bezalel, the Maharal of Prague, executed by Ladislav Saloun, 1917.

1. Gustav Mahler, symphonic composer and brilliant operatic conductor. 2. Moses Maimonides, prolific writer of philosophical and halakhic works.

Bezalel (1525-1609) was known. The name is an acronym of his titles and name (Moreinu Harav Rabbi Loew — Our Teacher, the rabbi, Rabbi Loew) and that is how he is generally referred to. He was an outstanding talmudist and thinker and was revered for both his piety and scholarship. His great knowledge was not confined to religious subjects, but embraced secular matters as well. In particular, his mastery of mathematics and astronomy won him the esteem of Jews and non-Jews alike. Moreover, the Maharal advanced a significant view on the education of the young; he believed in teaching children concepts that were within their grasp, a view which only much later became accepted.

As a rabbi and talmudist, Rabbi Judah was an important community leader. He served as rabbi of Moravia, Posen and finally as chief rabbi of Prague, where he remained until his death. Among his accomplishments there, was the founding of the yeshivah, Die Klaus. An influential figure, the Maharal was granted an audience with Emperor Rudolph II, king of Bohemia in 1592, but the purpose of this interview is not known.

The Maharal is particularly well-known for his philosophy and writings. Since the time of *Judah Halevi, no one had stressed the unique nature of the people of Israel, its mission and destiny, as did Rabbi Judah Loew. His works discuss the Exile, and stress the belief that the Divine Presence will never forsake Israel. He was an expert on the *Kabbalah and integrated that discipline into general Jewish philosophy.

A prolific writer, the Maharal wrote many works on ethics and philosophy in addition to a commentary on the Bible, Targum and Midrash, known as the *Gur Aryeh.* His strong attachment to *aggadah* is evidenced by his life work which was a new interpretation of the *aggadah* based on traditional sources.

The Maharal's place in Hebrew literature is unique since he did not belong to any defined school and was not followed by disciples. He was a lone thinker who developed his own original philosophy. Strangely, this philosophy was less well-known to later generations who connected the Maharal with the unfounded legend that he was the creator of the famous Prague *Golem. However, his original and profound ideas were revived in the 20th century by several Jewish thinkers, notable among whom were Rabbi A.I. *Kook, and Elijah Eliezer Dessler. He was so well-thought of that in 1917 a statue of him was erected at the entrance to the Prague town hall.

MAHLER, GUSTAV (1860-1911), Austrian composer and conductor. He began his career conducting operettas. In 1897 he became director of the Vienna Court Opera, having first been baptized into the Catholic faith in order to secure the position. Although his tenure in Vienna brought the opera there to a level of achievement previously unknown, in 1907 he resigned because of hostile intrigues. His remaining winters were spent in New York, where he conducted the Metropolitan Opera and the New York Philharmonic. He died in Vienna.

Known today as a symphonic composer, his creative efforts were overshadowed in his lifetime by his success as a conductor. Although he wrote no operas, his sense of musical drama is evident in his brilliance as an operatic conductor, in his song cycles (including *Das Lied von der Erde, Lieder eines fahrenden Gesellen,* and *Kindertotenlieder*) and in his ten symphonies, the last uncompleted.

MAIMONIDES, MOSES (1135-1204), rabbi, scholar, physician, scientist, philosopher, known in rabbinic literature as Rambam, the acronym formed from the initial letters of Rabbi Moses ben Maimon.

Over 800 years ago the day, hour and even the minute of the birth of Maimonides was recorded, and the impact of the event remains strong to this day. "On the eve of Passover (the 14th of Nissan) which was a Sabbath, an hour and a third after midday, in the year 4895 of the Creation," Moses ben Maimon was born in Cordoba, Spain, the greatest figure in Judaism in the post-talmudic period, and one of the greatest of all time. His father, Maimon, was *dayyan* (religious magistrate) of Cordoba and member of a distinguished family of scholars. In 1148, as a result of religious persecution, Maimon and his family had to leave Cordoba to wander until they settled in Fez, Morocco, about 1160. Maimonides describes those years as a period "while my mind was troubled" but he was actually laying the foundation of his vast and varied learning and his masterful literary work. He was 23 when he began the draft of the *Siraj,* his important commentary on the Mishnah. In that same year he wrote a short essay on the Jewish *calendar, one on *logic and other works. In Fez Maimonides studied under Rabbi Judah ha-Kohen ibn Susan, whose reputation for learning and piety was widespread. He also continued his general studies, including astronomy and medicine. Here also he wrote his *Iggeret ha-Shemad* (Letter on Forced Conversion) in which he concluded that a Jew should not live in a country where he is faced with forced conversion. Following his own teachings, Maimonides and his family escaped when religious oppression increased in Fez, and they spent five months in Acre, in Ereẓ Israel. They visited Jerusalem and other holy sites before sailing for Egypt where they settled in Fostat, the old city of Cairo. Maimonides' failure to fulfill the *mitzvah* of living in the Holy Land caused him soul-searching anguish which he was never able to resolve, even though he knew how important his presence was to the threatened Jews in Egypt. In Fostat he lived a life free of financial care. For eight years he was supported by his brother David, who managed the family business. Maimonides devoted himself entirely to his writings and to his work as both religious and lay leader of the Cairo Jews. Then tragedy struck — David was drowned, leaving a wife and two children. Maimonides suffered a deep personal loss and now faced the need of earning a living. He abhorred the thought of using Torah learning as a means of support. This was a serious point of contention between him and the *geonim* of the religious establishment, and he turned to the profession of medicine. Jews and Muslims were

among his patients. His ideas on medicine were advanced and sympathetic: he rejected the use of magic and charms in healing, and added that the doctor must know the whole patient in order to diagnose properly. His medical treatises, almost all in Arabic, were translated by Samuel ibn *Tibbon into Hebrew and Latin, and brought him international recognition. Most of these writings have been preserved and some were published recently in English. When he was appointed physician to the sultan of Egypt in 1185 his fame spread. A legend arose that Richard the Lion-hearted wanted Maimonides as his physician. These were busy years and the most fruitful of his life. His first wife had died young, and in Egypt he remarried. His only child was a son, Abraham, to whose education Maimonides lovingly devoted himself. He was deeply involved in his medical practice and in the broad Jewish community. In a letter to his translator Samuel ibn *Tibbon, Maimonides wrote : "My duties to the sultan are very heavy. I am obliged to visit him every day, early in the morning; and when he or any of his children, or any of the inmates of his harem, are indisposed, I must stay during the greater part of the day in the palace. Even if nothing unusual happens I do not return until the afternoon. Then I am almost dying with hunger . . . I find the antechambers filled with people, both Jews and gentiles, nobles and common people, judges, friends and foes — a mixed multitude who await the time of my return. I dismount from my animal, wash my hands, go forth to my patients, and entreat them to bear with me while I partake of some slight refreshment, the only meal I take in the twenty-four hours. Then I write prescriptions. Patients go in and out until nightfall, and sometimes even until two hours or more in the night. I converse with and prescribe for them while lying down from sheer fatigue; and when night falls, I am so exhausted that I can scarcely speak.

In consequence of this, no Israelite can have any private interview with me, except on the Sabbath. On that day the whole congregation, or at least the majority, come to me after the morning service, when I instruct them as to their proceedings during the whole week; we study together a little until noon, when they depart. Some of them return, and read with me after the afternoon service until evening prayers. In this manner I spend that day."

It is hard to imagine that there would be time for anything else, yet the prodigious Maimonides

Title page of *Moreh Nevukhim, The Guide of the Perplexed,* Maimonides' important philosophical work.

מֹשֶׁה בֶּן מַיְמוֹן

Maimonides

Maimon," an extraordinary tribute. (For information about the *Kaddish,* see *Death and Mourning.) Maimonides wrote *Ma'amar Teḥiyyat ha-Metim* to refute accusations that he denied or ignored the doctrine of personal resurrection in his works (see *Life and Afterlife). In the essay he asserted and confirmed his belief in the doctrine. The thirteen principles of faith which he formulated, which include his affirmation of resurrection, have become part of the daily morning prayer.

As head of the community, Maimonides took vigorous steps to curb the influence of the Karaites. On the one hand he regarded them as Jews, entitled to benefit from community services such as circumcision, burial, etc. However, because of their divergent views, they were not to be included in a *minyan* (quorum) of Jews.

Although the impression which emerges from his great works is that of an aloof and austere intellectual, the correspondence of Maimonides reveals a sensitive and sympathetic human being, warm-hearted and open to the suffering of his people. When he died on December 13, 1204, public mourning was declared in all parts of the Jewish world. His remains were taken to Tiberias for burial, and his grave is a place of pilgrimage to this day. His son Abraham succeeded him as the leader of the Egyptian Jews. The Torah ark thought to be from the Rambam's community is in the Israel Museum, and some manuscripts in Maimonides' handwriting are in the British Museum and the Bodleian Library.

Mishneh Torah, also called *Yad ha-Ḥazakah* ("The Strong Hand"), is a complete statement of all Jewish law. It was written in simple, beautiful Hebrew and carefully organized so that its contents could be easily reached and understood, even by the ordinary Jew. In addition, Maimonides' brilliant arrangement of *halakhah* demonstrated his grasp of philosophy, science, medicine and astronomy. But the method of presentation raised strong objections among some rabbis. (For more on *Mishneh Torah* and its critics, see *Law, Jewish.)

Maimonides wrote the *Guide of the Perplexed,* a work directed to intellectuals, after the completion of the *Mishneh Torah.* It was originally in the form of letters to a beloved student, Joseph ibn Sham'un, and restates Maimonides' belief that philosophy and science are handmaidens to the study of religion; that firm faith and sound reason can be reconciled for the traditional Jew. In that period, many scholars regarded this view as heresy, but the Guide had

1. Stamp issued by the Spanish post office in 1967 depicting Moses Maimonides.
2. Statue of Maimonides erected in 1964 in Cordoba, the town where he was born.

conducted an extensive exchange of letters with every part of the Jewish world (see *Letters and Letter-writing). Because of his great learning, his dynamic approach and his warmth, Maimonides was approached for responsa to many questions of *halakhah* and to provide leadership in dealing strongly with the complex problems which beset the Jewish community. The most serious of these were the influence of the *Karaite Jews who were active and outspoken against rabbinic law; the threat, in many parts of the Arab world, of forced conversion to Islam; and the undermining of faith by the impact of secular philosophy. It was also during this period that Maimonides wrote his great classic works – *Mishneh Torah* and the *Guide of the Perplexed* – (discussed below) and two important essays *Iggeret Teiman* (Letter to Yemen) and *Ma-amar Teḥiyyat ha-Metim* (Essay on Resurrection). The Jews of Yemen had been given the choice of conversion to Islam, or death. In despair they turned to Maimonides, who wrote his letter, a historic message of guidance and inspiration, urging his brothers to remain firm in their belief. Strengthened and encouraged, the grateful Jews of Yemen introduced into the *Kaddish* prayer an invocation for "the life of our teacher Moses ben

important significance for medieval Jewish philosophy, and a formative effect on modern Jewish thought. Among the thinkers who were influenced by Maimonides are *Moses Mendelssohn, Samuel David Luzzatto and *Ahad Ha-Am. Maimonides also had an impact on Christian scholastic thought, for example on Thomas Aquinas. And his treatises on logic are among the classical works used in universities. Works by and about Maimonides would fill a library. They have appeared in many languages and in many new translations. The commentaries on his works number over one thousand. His impact on Jewish life and thought is immeasurable.

The Maimonidean Controversy. The criticisms which greeted the appearance of Maimonides' *Mishneh Torah* also brought into sharp focus related troublesome issues, some of which had been problems long before Maimonides. Some of these issues were reason and philosophy in their relation to belief and tradition; the proper understanding of anthropomorphism, that is, descriptions of God and His qualities in terms that apply to human beings; the question of the literal belief in resurrection of the body. The essential argument erupted over the form of the *Mishneh Torah,* and its attitude toward the Talmud. The author had stated in the introduction that one purpose was to supersede the Talmud for popular use as a source book of *halakhah.* It omitted sources and the flow of discussion; and it used a classification code which was attacked as a system adopted from the Greek philosophers. At the same time, Maimonides was challenging the traditions of the Babylonian academies whose leaders, the *geonim,*

sought financial support for scholars and sages engaged in full-time study of Torah. This was a double attack — against the core of life in the academies, that is, the continuing flow of discussion, and against its economic foundation. When the *Mishneh Torah* reached the rabbis and scholars of southern Europe, it evoked another attack. The intellectual and social climate of the Christian countries was sharply different from that of the Muslim. There was explosive opposition to *ḥokhmah yevanit* — the attempt to synthesize the Greek philosophy of reason with the revealed faith of Judaism. Leading the opposition was Abraham ben David of Posquieres. Bitter arguments followed. The disputes became harsher and more extreme in their views; and overflowed to include the rabbis of northern France. A *ḥerem* was placed on Maimonides' philosophic works. Great scholars including Maimonides' son Abraham, were bitterly involved on both sides, and the controversy was halted only by a shock from without — Maimonides' books were burned as heretical by the Dominicans in 1232! Many who were opposed to Maimonides reconsidered their extremist opinions. The conflict between rationalists and anti-rationalists flared again 150 years later, and the conflict between faith and reason persists to this day. The *Mishneh Torah* did not replace the Talmud as its opponents feared, but proved instead to be a useful guide. So strong was Maimonides' personal influence that even at the height of the controversy his opponents emphasized that it was the work and not the man they opposed. An oft-repeated saying is: From Moses (the law-giver) to Moses (ben Maimon) there has been none like Moses.

MAJORCA, largest of the Balearic islands in the Mediterranean, situated off the east coast of Spain. The earliest evidence of Jews of Majorca dates from 1135. When James I of Aragon captured Palma de Majorca (1229-32), several Jews were among his retinue, and were granted properties on the island. The fortress of Almudaina came to be known as "the fortress of the Jews" since a residential area for them had been set aside within its walls. With the consolidation of Christian rule, Jews arrived from southern France and North Africa and even from Alexandria in Egypt.

The Jews of Majorca owned Muslim, Turkish and Tatar slaves, whom they customarily converted to Judaism, although the local church authorities tried

A square in Cordoba's former Jewish quarter named after Moses Maimonides.

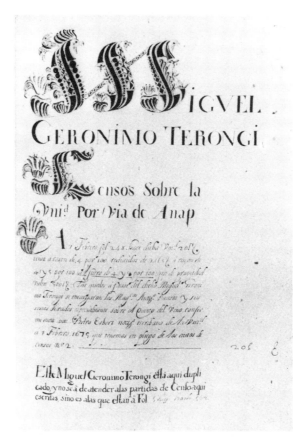

A page from the account books of the Inquisition, listing properties confiscated from the descendants of the Jews of Majorca. 1679.

to prevent this. The Jews became renowned for their skill as gold-and silversmiths, and as shoemakers; they also engaged in international maritime trade.

In 1285 Alfonso III seized the island. The Jews paid him a huge sum of money for the right to appeal to him against legal decisions taken by his officials; in 1290 he imposed a heavy fine on them for allegedly taking excessive interest. For the right of establishing a "Jewish street" he received a further large sum.

Anti-Jewish riots broke out in 1305 and in 1309 the island's first *blood libel occurred. In 1346 Pedro IV ordered the establishment of a separate Jewish quarter in Inca to prevent undue familiarity and disputes between Jews and Christians. The community suffered severely during the *Black Death and again during plagues of the 1370s and 1380s, and Christian mobs called for their expulsion from the island.

In 1391 anti-Jewish persecutions sweeping Spain spread to Majorca and many Jews were massacred; some communities were completely wiped out and many Jews fled to North Africa. In September 1391 the peasants demanded that the remaining Jews be

either baptized or put to death. Early the following year the authorities ordered the handing back of plundered Jewish property. Although the crown attempted to resettle Jews on the island and granted privileges as inducements to return, and a number of families arrived from Portugal in 1395, a blood libel was renewed in 1432 and by 1435 the community had ceased to exist — 200 persons having been converted and the rest having fled to North Africa.

In the late 15th century Majorca's Conversos (baptized Jews) fell under the shadow of the *Inquisition and by 1771, 594 had been burned at the stake. After the French conquest of the island, the Inquisition was abolished in 1808. But in 1856 further riots broke out against Conversos after several had sought to join an exclusive island club. By 1980 an estimated 300 Converso descendents were living on the island, mainly as silver-and goldsmiths. Some were successful businessmen, and a few had even settled in Spain. Majorca is today one of the Mediterranean's most popular holiday resorts, and one of its hotels caters especially for Jewish tourists.

MALAKH, ḤAYYIM BEN SOLOMON (1650?-1717?). Born in Kalish, Poland, Ḥayyim Malakh was a highly respected rabbinic scholar, kabbalist and preacher, who became a leader of the Shabbatean sect many years after *Shabbetai Ẓevi had converted to Islam.

Nothing is known of his early career, but in 1690 he went to Italy where, for several months he studied the Shabbatean writings, learning the secrets of the sect. From 1692-94 he acted as a Shabbatean missionary in rabbinic circles. Shabbateanism was a heretical movement and discredited in Poland, and so he moved on to Turkey where some of the outstanding followers of Shabbetai Ẓevi lived.

He became one of the founders of the "Association of the Ḥasidim" which advocated an immigration of ascetic scholars to Jerusalem to await the Messiah. Malakh, of course, secretly believed that this Messiah would be Shabbetai Ẓevi and predicted that the redemption would come in 1706. He went to Germany and Moravia on behalf of the association and in 1698 attended a council of Shabbatean leaders of the Ḥasidim of Nikolsburg, Moravia. In Vienna, he challenged kabbalists to a debate on Shabbatean beliefs, but the dispute, which lasted two weeks, ended inconclusively. Malakh then went to Erez Israel where, in October 1700, he was chosen as leader of a ḥasidic sect. He was given the surname of Malakh, which is the Hebrew for angel, either because of his outstanding abilities as a preacher or because of the very ascetic life he led. His popularity, however, was short-lived and his radical views led to his expulsion from Erez Israel and his persecution by rabbinical authorities. He was forced to wander from Constantinople to Salonika, Poland, Germany and Holland. He returned to Poland in about 1716 and died shortly thereafter.

MALBIM, MEIR LOEB (1809-79), rabbi, preacher, and biblical scholar. Born in Volochisk (Volhynia), Malbim studied in his native town until he was 13. He married at the age of 14 but divorced his wife soon after. After a period in Warsaw, he moved on to Leczyca, where he married the daughter of the local rabbi, Ḥayyim Auerbach, who supported him financially so that he could devote himself to literary work. In 1839 he was appointed rabbi of Wreschen, where he remained for seven years. In 1858 he became chief rabbi of Rumania.

Because of his uncompromising stand against *Reform Judaism, he was imprisoned in Kempen, and only released on the intervention of Sir Moses *Montefiore, and on condition that he leave Rumania. During his subsequent wanderings he suffered persecution and calumny. He served as rabbi in Leczyca, Kherson and Mogilev, and was persecuted by assimilationists, the *maskilim* and the Ḥasidim. He died in Kiev.

Malbim's fame and literary popularity rest on his commentary on the Bible, completed in 1876. His aim was to strengthen the position of Orthodox Judaism against what he regarded as a threat to its foundation in the Reform movement. He prophesied that the Redemption would occur between 1913 and 1928 "when the Temple will already have been established."

MAMLUKS. The word "Mamluk" in Arabic means "owned." The Mamluks were originally a group of white male slaves, mainly Turks and Circassians from southern Russia who, from the mid-13th century, were used by the caliphs of Baghdad to strengthen their armies, and who gradually took power into their own hands. Taken as children and brought up as

1. Meir Loeb Malbim, chief rabbi of Rumania and prominent Bible commentator.
2. The Mamluk tower at Ramleh, built between 1267 and 1318.

1. Facade of the 13th-century Ibrahim Tushtumur mausoleum, a typical example of Mamluk architecture.
2. The Mamluk fort and caravanserai of Antipatris, which was built on the remains of a Crusader fort.

pistols and scimitar, these amazing horsemen and brutal, treacherous murderers were yet keen admirers of beauty and built in their 500 year rule some of the most breathtaking mosques and minaretted tombs in Islam. Although theoretically bound to pay annual tribute to the Sultan in Constantinople, this practice lapsed among them.

*Saladin, himself a Kurd, employed Mamluks as the spearhead of Muslim resistance to the invading Crusaders in the Middle Ages. Mamluk sultans ruled over Egypt, Cyranaica, Syria, the Hejaz and northern Nubia, until they were overthrown by the Turkish sultan Selim I in 1516. The Ottomans retained Mamluks as local governors, and by the 18th century they had again displaced their masters and recovered much of their former power. There were 100,000 of them in 1798, mainly in Cairo. When Napoleon invaded Egypt that year neither Mamluk horsemanship nor reckless bravery could stop him. The setback to their prestige proved fatal and they were finally destroyed in a massacre in 1811.

Jews under the Mamluks did not fare well. Their original hostility to the Christians, especially the Copts of Egypt, soon spread to include the Jews too. The Jewish minority was subject to intermittent pogroms, the closure or seizure of synagogues, destruction of property, and heavy taxes. Like Christians and Samaritans, they were forced to wear distinctive dress, in their case a yellow turban. They were forbidden to ride horses or swift asses, and were at some periods, not allowed to drink wine. They were also subject to legal discrimination. The Mamluks did not, however, interfere with Jewish judicial autonomy in civil law, and did recognize the *nagid* as head of the Jewish community.

warriors, they avoided marriage, remained without dependants and devoted their lives to war and the acquisition of women, horses, jewels and slaves. It was their habit to import white Christian slave-children from southern Russia, whom they brought up as their heirs, after converting them to Islam. A striking sight to behold in their green caps wreathed with yellow turbans, their chainmail coats and red pantaloons, each man heavily armed with a brace of

MANASSEH was only 12 years old when his father, King Hezekiah of Judah, died leaving the boy to occupy the throne in 698 b.c.e. It was no easy task for a youth to rule a nation, and Manasseh's job was doubly difficult in those days because the Assyrians controled most of the area, imposing restrictions and forcing the Jewish leader to obey their laws.

There is evidence that Manasseh tried many times during his 55 year reign to overthrow Assyrian domination. He fortified Jerusalem and probably took part in various revolts. At one point the Assyrians dragged him off to Babylon in chains and kept him in prison before eventually allowing him to return to Jerusalem.

But despite these attempts at freeing his people,

Manasseh ben Israel

Manasseh is remembered as a wicked king who abolished the religious reforms of his father, introduced alien rites into the Temple, and treated the people cruelly. "And he made his son to pass through the fire, and practiced soothsaying and used enchantments . . . he wrought much evil in the sight of the Lord," says the Bible.

The aggadic literature is also filled with stories of Manasseh's wickedness — of how he built an idol so heavy that it required 1,000 men to carry it, and that new teams were employed daily because the king had each group executed at the end of the day's work. According to these tales, he ridiculed the Torah, committed incest, and condemned his own grandfather — according to tradition, the prophet Isaiah — to death. The prophets of his day attributed the ultimate destruction of Jerusalem to Manasseh's sinful behavior.

MANASSEH BEN ISRAEL (1604-57), Amsterdam rabbi, scholar and mystic. Manasseh was born to a *Marrano family on the Atlantic island of Madeira, but the family escaped when he was still a child and settled in Amsterdam.

A child prodigy, Manasseh began to study in yeshivot when aged only 14; he gave his first public oration at 15 and wrote his first book when he was 17. A year later he became preacher to the Neveh Shalom congregation in Amsterdam, and in 1626 he founded Amsterdam's first Hebrew printing press. He was a gifted linguist and wrote books in Hebrew, Spanish, Portuguese and Latin. His theological knowledge was extensive; many of his works were addressed to non-Jews, and among scholars he was regarded as the leading representative of Hebrew learning. His friends included *Rembrandt, who engraved his portrait, and the Dutch statesman, historian and theologian, Hugo Grotius.

Manasseh is also remembered for his role in the negotiations for the return of Jews to England. They had been formally banished from England in 1290, and the small communities of Marrano refugees that had lived there since had no legal guarantee of existence. Manasseh's interest in the return of the Jews to England was a mystical one: the medieval name for England was *Angle-Terre* ("the end of the earth"), and the Bible tells (Deuteronomy 28:64) that once the Jews are dispersed to *kezeh ha-arez* ("the end of the earth"), the Messiah will come. Thus Manasseh hoped to hasten the coming of the Messiah.

He traveled to England, dedicated a book, *The Hope of Israel,* to parliament, and petitioned the English Protector, Oliver *Cromwell. Cromwell demonstrated his personal sympathy to Manasseh by granting him a pension of 100 pounds sterling a year, but Manasseh was bitterly disappointed as all he had officially achieved was permission to establish a synagogue and a Jewish cemetery in England. He returned to Holland in 1657 and died soon afterwards. In fact his mission was a success, for although there was no formal recall of the Jews to England, their settlement there was never seriously questioned again.

MANCHESTER is a city in the north of England and the home of the second largest Jewish community in Britain.

In 1780 the first Jews came to Manchester from Liverpool, and in the next 20 years established a synagogue, cemetery and philanthropic society. This small Jewish community swelled after 1848 when political refugees fled the liberal risings in Europe. In 1869 Rumanian Jews escaping the persecutions arrived in Manchester, and in the 1870s young men avoiding military conscription came from Russia. Small groups emigrated from North Africa and the Levant in 1871 and set up a Sephardi community in the south of the city. Between 1881 and 1914 came the great Russo-Polish immigration, and the Ashkenazi community settled increasingly in the northern suburbs.

The earliest settlers had manufactured waterproof garments, but this industry was superseded by the technologically superior "rainproof" wear in which Jews were not involved. The mid-19th century European refugees were merchants, and the Russo-Polish immigrants worked as tailors and capmakers, jewellers and street traders. Today large numbers of Manchester Jews are involved in the garment and bag-making industries.

There are an abundance of Jewish communal institutions in the city, among them a Jewish hospital, 68 synagogues, several Jewish schools and a *bet din.* There are two boards of *sheḥitah,* the second set up by the ultra-Orthodox Jews of Manchester. Both the ultra-Orthodox and the Reform communities in the city have active and numerous members.

Manchester was the home of Chaim *Weizmann from 1904 to 1916, and many prominent British Zionists and personalities have lived there including Lord Simon Marks and Israel and Rebecca Sieff (of Marks and Spencer), Harry Sacher and Leon Simon. There have been a number of Jewish lord mayors of Manchester and Jewish Members of Parliament for the Labour Party. The Jewish population of Greater Manchester numbered 35,000 in 1981.

MANDATE FOR PALESTINE. The temporary administration of certain former overseas possessions of Germany and parts of the Turkish Empire granted

1.   Ark of the Law in the synagogue of the Congregation of Spanish and Portuguese Jews, Manchester.
2.   Stamp issued by the British mandatory government in Palestine, September 1, 1920.

הלכות יסודי התורה יש בכללן   היסורות ועתיר החכמות וירע   היו שבין אותם לטהים פרית
עשר מצות שש מצות עשה ו   שיש שם מצר ריושון והוד הלר   היו לסרב ינותרוןזיזין לשתיר יומרת
וארבע מצות לא תעשה וזה ה   הוורך עליר כל העוריו וכל העוריות   כוניתו והיי שהתורה ללורות יין
פרטן יד לידע טישטם אוד   מן שמריוביורן ומה בעתהבלי   ער מירבה כלומיון שם מצי ים
ב סלוי יעלה בניהטבה שיש   מריצו ולין מירומתתהמריצן ריא   יגתתמלתריון כמיות ג הריצי
שם טהה חלד יד ג ויחזד ד   יעלה על הדעת טיין שהויו יעי   זה היו לה העלב ירון כל היוד
לאהם ה לריהה מיחט לקש   מעיי ין דבר יוחד יכול להמריצו   והיו המהנא הלעל כמה שיין לב
שמי ז שלו להל את טגד ח   ריב יעלה על הדעת שיין לה המר   דץ ותכלית נכה טיזין לה הפסק שו
שלו לאכר דברים שנקדין שם   העריצים מלכדו מעייכ היון ל   שהגול סובב תניר יר יפשר ט
שהווע עליהם ט לשוווע מן הנבי   ובהו מעי ולי יכטו היו לבתוב   שיסוב כלין מיכבכ והוד כתד הזי
הנדבר נטוויה י שלו למות   שכלה העי לאוכ עריכין לו והיוד בר   הנוככ זיותח כליו יד וליוע רל
וכיוד כל המריצות יון נמקים   כתד היו יזע עריך להם ולו לא   ל
יולן   ליוחר מהב ב כיר יון יום   וידעתדבר זה מצות עשה שנ
פרק א יסדי   וולסתן ביוזת יוחר מהב הד   יוכב יי ווהך וכל היומעלה עלרעת
                                                                            טיש שם טלה יוחר חזק מזה עמד

Maimonides. Title page from *Sefer Madda,* a part of the *Mishneh Torah* by Maimonides. This edition is from southern Germany, 1310.

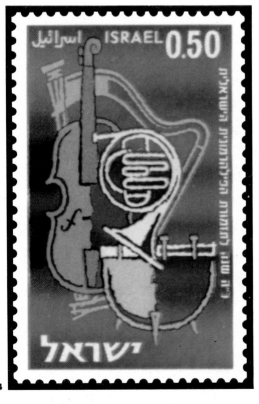

1. **Medicine.** Stamp issued on August 5, 1964, for the Sixth International Convention of the Israel Medical Association.
2, 3 and 4. **Music.** Stamps of Israel depicting musical instruments mentioned in the Bible.

1. Herbert Samuel taking the oath as high commissioner for Palestine at the beginning of the mandatory period, September 1922.
2. British mandatory forces dispersing an Arab riot near the "New Gate" of the Old City of Jerusalem, 1933.
3. Jews of Tiberias training in self-defense following the massacre of October 10, 1938.
4. Jewish supernumerary policemen on guard duty in Haderah, 1942.
5. British soldier guarding the Me'ah She'arim quarter of Jerusalem toward the end of the mandatory period, March 1947.

by the League of Nations under the Treaty of Versailles after World War I included the British Mandate for Palestine. These administrations were intended to lay the foundations for the ultimate independence of mandated territories. The British mandate over Iraq, and the French mandate over Syria ended in 1932 and 1936 respectively. The mandate over Palestine differed from the others in that its primary purpose was the establishment of a national home for the Jewish people. Palestine was not chosen arbitrarily; it was recognized as the historic land of the Jews, to which they had a closer connection and more justifiable claim than any other group. The national home was not to be established, but re-established after a 2,000 year exile.

A Jewish Agency was to be set up and Jewish immigration into Palestine facilitated; the Zionist Organization was recognized as the appropriate agency until establishment of the Jewish Agency in 1929. Hebrew was recognized as one of the three official languages of the territory. The mandate was also to safeguard "civil and religious rights of all the inhabitants of Palestine, irrespective of race and religion." Each community was allowed to maintain its schools in its own language. No modification of the mandate was permissible without consent of the League of Nations and the United States. Under

1. Jews celebrating the end of martial law in Jerusalem in March, 1947. After the British had despaired of solving the Palestinian conflict, they withdrew their forces and handed the problem over to the United Nations.
2. Tamarisk tree in the Sinai desert which some believe bears a fruit comparable to the biblical manna.

Article 25 of the mandate, Transjordan was severed from the territory destined to include the Jewish national home. The mandate ended with the establishment of the State of Israel on May 14, 1948. (See also *Balfour Declaration; *Israel.)

MANNA was the miraculous food which sustained the Israelites during the 40 years in which they wandered through the wilderness of Sinai.

Exodus 16:4 describes manna as white in color, and resembling a fine frost which covered the ground. It fell from heaven within the area of the Israelite camp every morning excepting the Sabbath, and it needed no cooking. One *omer* (measure) for each person was collected each day, and the amount gathered by every family was enough for all its members. Manna was to be eaten within 24 hours, for if left, it bred worms and rotted. The double portion which fell on Friday did not rot, however, but remained good for the Sabbath. This is commemorated today by the two loaves of bread on the Sabbath table.

Manna is called "bread from heaven" in the Book of Exodus, and "bread of the angels" in Psalms. The English name "manna" comes from the words, *man hoo?* ("What is this?" in classical Hebrew) which is what the Israelites exclaimed when they saw manna for the first time. In Hebrew it is called simply *man*.

The marvel of the heavenly supply of manna caused many legends to be told of it. According to the *aggadah*, it was one of the ten objects created in the evening of the Sabbath of the Creation. The *aggadah* also relates how the surface of the desert was swept clean by the wind and washed by the rain before manna fell. It fell directly in front of the

homes of the righteous, but the wicked had to go far afield to gather it. Legend also tells that to a child it tasted like milk, to the sick like barley steeped in honey, to the adolescent like bread and to the old like honey; to the heathens it tasted bitter and unpleasant. It had a fragrant odor and women used it as perfume.

Scholars have differing views as to the origin of manna. Some think it may have been a phenomenon of nature which sometimes occurs in the Sinai desert. Others believe it was an animal or plant parasite growing on the desert tamarisk trees.

MANNERS. Judaism has always encouraged social consciousness and emphasized the importance of man's relationship with his fellow man. The Jew, after all, functions within a society — he is not hidden away in a monastery or isolated in a hermit's cave. He is therefore instructed to show good manners (or *derekh erez,* as it is called in Hebrew) in all his activities, to be polite and considerate of the needs of others.

The Ten Commandments, the very first rules set down by God for the Jewish people, deal in part with the most basic behavioral standards — things which today we take for granted. The sages took this theme even further and wrote rules and regulations touching on almost every aspect of good behavior. In fact, one of the minor tractates of the Talmud (called, appropriately, *Derekh Erez)* is devoted solely to standards of behavior and etiquette.

Speech, for example, is the most common means of social contact and so the Talmud advises that man should speak pleasantly and refrain from interrupting and speaking abruptly. To this the great sage *Maimonides adds, "when speaking, a man should neither shout nor scream nor raise his voice excessively."

The rabbis realized that people are often judged by their outward appearances, and so advised the Jew to dress modestly, but always in a neat and orderly fashion.

Eating and drinking are also social functions and no one likes to sit at the same table with a slovenly dining companion. On this topic the rabbis wrote that a man should not eat in a standing position nor lick his fingers, both of which were considered examples of boorish behavior. And liquids should not be gulped down on one quick draught but should be sipped slowly and politely. It is not always pleasant to watch another person eat so the rabbis suggested

that people eat only at home and not in public places.

Scholars are to be particularly careful in their manners since they serve as an example to the people. Maimonides details how a scholar should act. He should not walk in a stiff and haughty manner with his neck outstretched, nor should he run in a public place.

The relationship between a man and his wife was also not forgotten by the sages as can be seen in the many exhortations to the husband to respect the honor and feelings of his wife and to consult her in all matters concerning the home. He should not be harsh toward his children but should be patient and understanding.

Although the rabbis often found references in the Scriptures to *derekh erez,* these references were not generally included as formal laws since they were considered to be recommendations rather than commandments, and would vary with the customs and lifestyles of the people involved.

MAPS OF EREZ ISRAEL. The oldest map of Erez Israel still in existence is in the form of a mosaic on the floor of a sixth century church in *Madaba, now

Map of the 40 years' wanderings of the Jews in the desert after the Exodus from Egypt. From a Hebrew-English *Haggadah*, London, 1813.

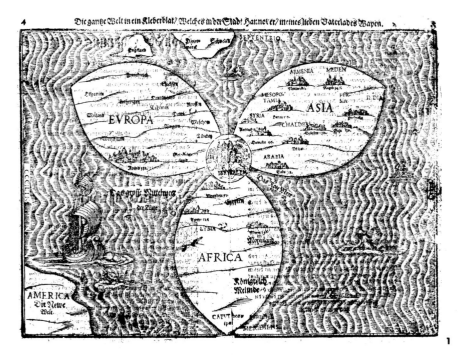

1. A 16th-century map printed from a woodcut, showing Jerusalem as the center of the world.
2. A French map of the Holy Land made from a copperplate engraving, 1713.

Before the 16th century almost all the maps that were drawn focused on Erez Israel and on Jerusalem in particular. This was because Erez Israel was thought to be at the center of the earth and because of its status as the Holy Land of Judaism, Christianity and Islam. For the Romans, Erez Israel formed the strategic center of the empire and thus many road maps were produced for the benefit of the army and the governors, which devote particular attention to Erez Israel. Early Christian maps which have survived depict in detail sights of Christian biblical interest and were drawn for the benefit of pilgrims.

By the late Middle Ages, maps were being drawn for use as sea charts to navigate ships, and many Jews are known to have participated in the production of such maps. These showed coastlines and ports in detail, with Erez Israel as the only country shown with inland information. They were meant as guides for armies as well as pilgrims.

Maps of Erez Israel were among the first to be produced in print and were popular throughout the Christian world. The French maps were the most accurate. In 1810, 47 maps of Egypt, Sinai and Erez Israel were drawn for Napoleon's military campaign. Precise details were taken by trigonometric surveys and place names were given in Arabic as well. Britain also made accurate maps of the country, the coastline and Jerusalem during the 19th century for

a city in Jordan. The map, like all ancient maps, is orientated toward the east, which means that East is on top, where we would expect North to be. It pictures Jerusalem in the center, with the Jordan River and the Dead Sea above it and the Mediterranean at the bottom.

archaeological digs and the admiralty.

In the 20th century aerial photography has enabled precise mapping to be made and the government of Israel has produced comprehensive maps of Erez Israel which are of great benefit to archaeologists and tourists alike.

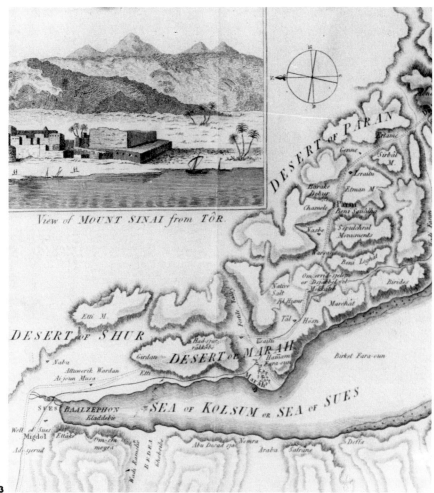

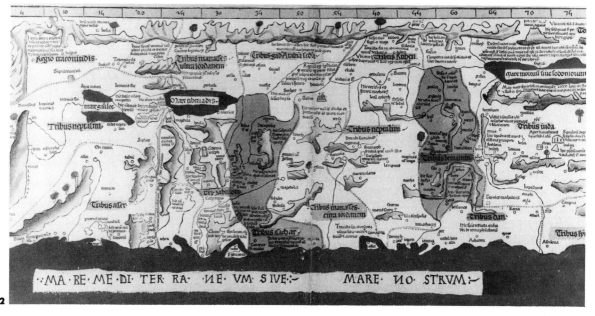

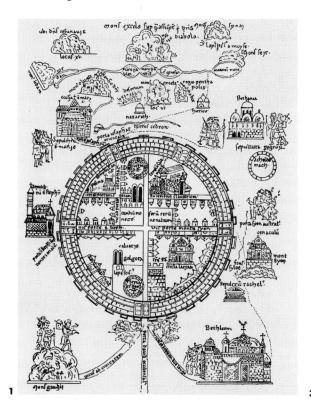

1. A pictorial map of Jerusalem and Palestine dating from the time of the Crusaders, from a 12th-century Latin manuscript.
2. A 14th-century map of Palestine.
3. Another view of Erez Israel "from Suez to Mount Sinai," this one made in the 18th century.

1. Colonel David "Mickey" Marcus, American officer accidentally killed while leading Israeli troops during the War of Independence.
2. Israel medal issued in 1964 in honor of the Tel Aviv International Trade Fair.
3. Marketplace in a Jewish quarter of London known as "Petticoat Lane," in the 19th century.

MARCUS, DAVID ("Mickey"; 1902-1948) was a soldier who fought with distinction for both the United States and Israel. He was born in New York on the Lower East Side, graduated in 1924 from the West Point Military Academy and also studied law. He left the United States army in 1927 in order to practice law, but rejoined after the outbreak of World War II. He attained the rank of colonel and received a number of major United States and British decorations. After the war he served in the military government in Germany and was appointed head of the War Crimes Branch.

In January 1948 he was invited by the Jewish Agency and the Haganah to serve in Palestine as David Ben-Gurion's military adviser, and adopted the name of Mickey Stone. In May 1948 he was appointed commander of the Jerusalem front in the Israel War of Independence, and was the first officer to receive the new rank of *aluf* (brigadier general). Before dawn on June 11, he went outside the perimeter fence of his headquarters near Jerusalem, and was accidentally killed by a sentry. His body was transferred with military honors to the United States and buried at West Point. A village in Israel, Mishmar David, is named after him and a monument stands at the site where he was killed.

MARKET DAYS AND FAIRS. Market days on Mondays and Thursdays was a central feature of Jewish life in Erez Israel in ancient times. Because large numbers of Jews who were ordinarily dispersed in the villages and the countryside would gather in the towns on these days, the rabbinical courts always met on them and they were designated for the public reading of the Torah. It is from this fact that the present Monday and Thursday Torah reading derives. For more information on this see *Torah.

In the Middle Ages market days and fairs performed an important function in Jewish life and it is to this period that this entry is devoted.

Jewish merchants were early and eager participants in the establishment and running of local market days and regional fairs — the central institutions of medieval European commerce and trade. The prominent role of Jews in these markets (held locally once a week) and fairs (held usually two or three times a year in selected cities located on strategic waterways) can be seen from the fact that as early as the first quarter of the ninth century, the market day in Lyons was changed from Saturday to Sunday in order to accommodate Jewish traders (a fact which aroused the ire of the local bishop Agobard), and from the fact that the cities of international trade which housed the fairs all had large Jewish populations. After the *Crusades, Jewish economic activity became restricted to northwestern Europe and Jewish merchants were no longer allowed to compete with Christians at the local markets or regional fairs. But in central and eastern Europe, Jewish participation in the fairs was welcomed, and the 16th century actually witnessed the creation of economic and social patterns which clearly reflect the attendance of large numbers of Jews at various fairs and markets. Thus, in Poland and Lithuania it was expressly forbidden to fix the dates of fairs and markets on the Sabbath or Jewish holy days, and the Jews' commercial rights were not legally subject to challenge by the competing Christian merchants.

Beside their purely commercial function, fairs played an important role in the development of Jewish social and legal institutions and customs. In the early Middle Ages, the fairs would serve as the meeting place of the rabbinic and lay leadership of the smaller communities which would gather together to discuss matters of mutual interest, and even occasionally to enact ordinances applicable to all the communities. Later, in the 16th century, the distinctive creation of Polish Jewish autonomy, the Council of the Four Lands, actually developed out of the practice of establishing a trans-communal *bet din* during the Lublin fairs. For other aspects of this, see *Self-Government, Jewish.

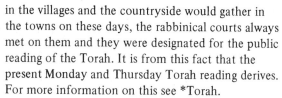

The social aspects of the fair were equally as important and were described somewhat fancifully by an eyewitness in the following terms: "At each fair there were hundreds of heads of yeshivot, thousands of pupils, and tens of thousands of youths and Jewish merchants. And whoever had an eligible son or daughter went to the fair and arranged a match, for everyone could find one to his liking. And at every fair, hundreds of matches were made, and sometimes thousands, and the children of Israel, men and women, wore kingly vestments at the fair."

In the *Pale of Settlement, the market square and the regular market days became the center of the *shtetl and the heart of its economy. The economic and social life in these townships was regulated by buying from peasants and selling to them on the fixed market day in the appointed place; quite naturally, taverns were erected around the market square and thus Jews became tavern-keepers as well. Jewish emigrants from eastern Europe carried over this type of market into the larger cities in western Europe — Petticoat Lane in London is a good example of such markets.

MARRANOS. Rarely during the 2000 years of Diaspora has there been a time in which Jews have been completely free from pressure to abandon their religion. Almost always, in some community or other, Jews were commanded to convert or die. *Anusim* — forced ones — is the name given to those who, fearing for their lives, left Judaism and adopted a new faith.

Various methods were used to force conversion upon Jews. In the 15th century King Manuel of Portugal's method was to take Jewish children away from their homes, baptize them, and hope that the parents would follow. For more on this see *Conversion, Forced.

Having converted against their will, many *anusim* secretly clung to and practiced Judaism. In Spain and Portugal such *anusim* were known as Marranos (a popular term of contempt meaning "pig"). Converted in the 14th and 15th centuries, prior to the expulsion of all of Spain's Jews in 1492, many of the Marranos tried to escape to countries where they could practice Judaism openly, using excuses such as "making a pilgrimage to the Pope" in order to obtain permission to leave the country. But many were not able to leave and, clinging to their Jewish heritage, developed a unique "underground" Jewish existence. They continued to practice in their homes some rituals whose observance would not expose them to the watchful eye of the *Inquisition, while maintaining, in public, a front of allegiance to Catholic doctrine and practice. They developed a theology of their own which saw their conversions both as a form of divine punishment and as a phenomenon already performed in the biblical story of Queen Esther (see *Purim). They maintained their social cohesion by marrying only amongst themselves, and most remarkably, they managed to transmit their consciousness of belonging to the Jewish people to their descendants so that Marranos actually could be found in Spain and Portugal until the 19th century. Even in the 20th century there are people, particularly on the island of *Majorca who identified themselves as descendants of Marranos.

World War II gave rise to a modern example of *anusim*. Fearing death in the gas chambers for being Jewish, many Jews lived outwardly as Christians. Only in utmost secrecy did they dare practice their Judaism. Countless children were handed over to the Church and baptized so that they at least would survive the *Holocaust.

Just how to evaluate *anusim* from the point of view of Jewish law remained a painfully difficult issue for the rabbinic leaders of the generations. On the one hand, living a Christian or Muslim life was an act of apostasy, tantamount to a complete abandonment of Judaism; on the other hand, the fact that many *anusim* persisted in performing *mitzvot* in secret, in constant danger of discovery and death, testified to their true allegiance and their steadfastness as Jews. The almost universal consensus of rabbinic opinion was to view such people as

Tartar merchants and traders gather in an old Russian marketplace in the 18th century.

"unwilling sinners" and to uphold their status as full Jews, so that those who managed to escape to freedom and resume normal Jewish lives were fully accepted back into the community without need for conversion or special rites of penitence. A particularly acute problem was the special case of the Spanish Marranos who remained practicing Christians for generations and who did not take advantage of any and every opportunity to flee to a country which would allow them to live openly as Jews. Many rabbis tended to view such *anusim* harshly and restricted their rights and privileges under Jewish law, while others continued to uphold their status as complete Jews.

MARRIAGE. In Jewish teaching, marriage is considered the ideal human state and a basic social institution established by God at the time of Creation. Both the Bible and the rabbis reject celibacy as unnatural and harmful to the human personality, and insist upon the need for marriage, not only for purposes of procreation, but also for companionship and human self-fulfillment: "It is not good that man be alone; I will make a helpmeet for him" (Genesis 2:15) and "He who has no wife is not a proper man; he lives without joy, blessing and goodness." The successful marriage in the eyes of the prophets and the rabbis was the most perfect symbol of a

1. *Kiddushin* — placing the wedding ring on the bride's finger.
2. "Mitzvah Tanz," the traditional wedding dance in which the couple grasp opposite ends of a handkerchief instead of holding hands. Painting by S. Alva.
3. "The Matchmaker," by Tully Filmus.

meaningful and purposeful relationship and was taken by them as the closest approximation to the idealized relationship between God and Israel, and between Israel and the Torah. The laws of marriage and the customs and practices of the marriage ceremony which developed over the generations are numerous and varied, but all take as their goal the glorification of marriage as a sanctified state and the desire to facilitate to the greatest possible extent the maintenance of a successful and harmonious marriage.

The biblical idea of marriage was essentially monogamous, although polygamy was common among the upper classes of society. Among the rabbis, polygamy was almost unknown, but it was not until the 11th century that multiple marriages were legally prohibited. Then an enactment associated with the name of Rabbenu *Gershom ben Judah was promulgated which established monogamy as the legal norm for all the Jews living in Europe.

A Jewish marriage consists, from the point of view of rabbinic law, of two separate acts, called *kiddushin* and *nissu'in*, which were originally performed at an interval of a year or more apart, but which from the 12th century onward became united in one ceremony.

Kiddushin is a legal act of acquisition of the bride by the groom: by handing over an object of value (usually a simple ring) to the bride in the presence of two witnesses and reciting the formula, "Behold

1. Wedding procession in 18th-century Germany. The bride is under the *ḥuppah* (bridal canopy), preceded by musicians.
2. Yemenite wedding, 1966.
3 and 4. Wedding rings from Austria (top) and North Africa.

you are consecrated unto me with this ring according to the law of Moses and Israel," the groom signifies his intent to reserve the bride exclusively to himself, and by accepting the ring the bride signifies her consent. (The *halakhah* also recognizes the validity of *kiddushin* performed through the writing of a contract or through actual cohabitation, but both these methods became obsolete at an early date and today *kiddushin* is uniquely performed through the transference of an object of value.)

Kiddushin is thus a legally binding form of betrothal, but it must be followed by *nissu'in*, the marriage proper, for the couple to be considered completely married. In the *nissu'in* ceremony, the bride is led under a canopy *(ḥuppah)* symbolic of the groom's house, and benedictions are recited, after which the couple may legally live together.

The separation of the two ceremonies in talmudic times allowed the arrangement of long betrothals, but the uncertainties of life in medieval Europe made such an arrangement impractical and perilous, and it was for this reason that it became customary to perform both ceremonies together. The actual wedding ceremony as performed today is an amalgam of customs and traditions which developed over the generations, but its basic features can be summarized as follows:

Before being led to the *ḥuppah* the groom, in the presence of witnesses, undertakes by an act of *kinyan* (see *Acquisition) the obligations of the *ketubbah* (marriage contract; see below). He is then escorted to the place where the bride is waiting and lets down the veil over her face, while the rabbi pronounces the blessing invoked on Rebekah, "O sister! May you grow into thousands of myriads" (Genesis 24-60). (This ceremony is known in Yiddish as *bedeken di kale* ("veiling the bride") and is not practiced by Sephardi Jews.) The groom is then led to the *ḥuppah* by his and the bride's father, while the bride is accompanied to the *ḥuppah* by her and the groom's mother. Among Ashkenazim, the bride customarily walks around

the groom seven times and then stands on his right.

The ceremony proper (customarily performed in the presence of at least a *minyan* of males — a precautionary measure eliminating the possibility of secret marriages) then begins with the recitation of the marriage blessing over a goblet of wine, from which both bride and groom drink. The groom then places the ring on the forefinger of the bride's right hand and in the presence of two witnesses repeats the marriage formula (see above). *Kiddushin* has now been performed, and in order to separate it from the *nissu'in* which is to follow, the *ketubbah* is read out loud. Seven marriage blessings are then recited over a second goblet of wine and the ceremony concludes with the groom crushing a glass under his right foot, as a sign of mourning over the destruction of the Temple. To the rejoicing of the invited guests, the couple are then led to a private room in which they spend some time together, while witnesses are stationed outside. After this *yihud* (being alone together) they are finally considered to be man and wife.

Both the week before the wedding and the week after are celebrated in special fashion. In the synagogue on the Sabbath preceding the marriage, the groom is called to the reading of the Torah and, in some communities, while standing at the *bimah* is showered with nuts and candies, in symbolic representation of everyone's wish for his fruitfulness and happiness. This custom is called in Yiddish *aufrufen.* During the days immediately preceding the wedding, bride and groom customarily do not see each other (the actual period varies in different communities from a week to the day of the marriage), and both fast on the day of their

1. Lithuanian matchmaker *(shadhan),* 1930s.
2. "Jewish Engagement Ceremony," mid-19th century painting by non-Jewish artist.
3. Moroccan Jewish bride as drawn by Eugene Delacroix, 1832.

wedding as an indication of the spiritual importance of marriage and the fact that they are about to start a new life together. Following the wedding ceremony a *festive meal is served, during which the guests entertain the newly-wed couple and following which the seven wedding blessings are again recited. The seven days following the wedding are known as the *Sheva Berakhot,* for festive meals in honor of the couple are arranged each day, and at the conclusion of each the seven wedding blessings are recited in the presence of a *minyan* of invited guests.

Ring. Although the act of marriage can be effected in different ways (see above) it has become the universal Jewish practice to use a ring (except in very few oriental communities where a coin is used). By law, the ring must belong to the bridegroom, and can be constructed of any material, as long as it is free of precious stones and its value is more than a *perutah,* the smallest denomination of currency in talmudic times.

Ketubbah is the marriage contract, the document which records the financial obligations which the husband undertakes toward his wife consequent to their marriage. In principle, the obligations recorded in the *ketubbah* are imposed upon the husband by law, independent of the writing of the contract, but the *halakhah* still dictates that a deed be written and that it is "forbidden for the groom to live with the bride until he has written and delivered the

ketubbah to her." According to the Talmud, the *ketubbah* was instituted in order to protect the woman, since it imposes a monetary punishment upon the husband in the case of a divorce, and it also assures the wife at least minimal compensation upon the death of her husband. In the *ketubbah* are spelled out the minimum compensation set by law, as well as all additional sums willingly offered by the husband.

The traditional *ketubbah* still in use today is written in Aramaic and in accordance with a standard wording and format which leaves room for filling in the specific details pertinent to each marriage. Conservative rabbis use a somewhat modified version of the traditional *ketubbah*, while Reform rabbis generally have abandoned the *ketubbah* in favor of a more modern, English-language marriage contract.

Throughout the Middle Ages and up to today, the *ketubbah* has been one of the favored texts chosen by artists for illumination. Brightly colored and intricately adorned *ketubbot* have survived which originate from most of the known Jewish settlements in the Middle Ages, including Persia,

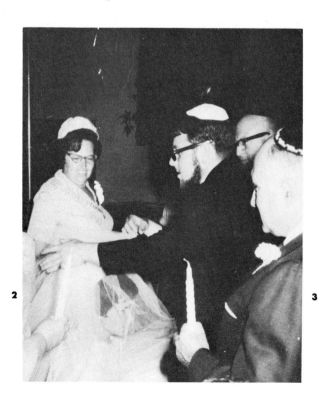

1. The custom in 19th-century Galicia, Poland, was to have the *badḥan* (entertainer) cause the wedding party to cry over the bride's imminent loss of the freedoms of maidenhood.
2. *Bedeken* — the groom lowers the veil over his bride's face before the wedding ceremony begins.
3. Groom cuts the special wedding *ḥallah* at a ḥasidic celebration.

1. Dutch woodcut, 1707, showing the bride and groom under the *huppah.*
2. A *get* (divorce paper) from Johannesburg, South Africa, 1958.
3. Signing the *ketubbah* (marriage contract).
4. Wedding in El Arish immediately after the Sinai Campaign, 1956.

Austria and Italy. Even today many young couples commission artists to design unique, decorative *ketubbot.*

Dowry is the property and goods given by a father to his betrothed daughter which she brings to her husband at the time of marriage. The giving of a dowry was a very ancient custom and is mentioned in several places in the Bible. By talmudic times the dowry had received legal status: the amount was usually stipulated in the *ketubbah* and was recoverable by the wife at the same time she recovered her *ketubbah,* i.e., upon divorce, or death of the husband. The custom of granting a dowry prevailed until modern times, especially among Jews of Eastern Europe. There the dowry often consisted of full board granted to the groom for several years so that he might continue his talmudic studies free from financial care. The custom was called in Yiddish *kest,* and the financial arrangements of the dowry were detailed in a document called *tena'im* ("conditions") signed at the betrothal ceremony.

Ḥuppah. Today, the term *ḥuppah* refers to the decorative canopy under which the wedding ceremony is performed. Originally, however, it referred to the actual bridal chamber, the tent or room of the groom to which the bride was brought in festive procession for the marital union. The custom of setting up a canopy for the wedding ceremony was apparently not widely practiced until late in the Middle Ages, for many medieval responsa deal with the question whether the act of entering the *ḥuppah* (canopy) was sufficient to constitute marriage or whether it was to be regarded only as a symbol which would still require the couple to retire in

privacy (as in today's practice of *yiḥud;* see above). The Talmud relates that there was an ancient custom to make staves of the *ḥuppah* from a cedar and a pine tree planted specifically for this purpose at the birth of a male and female child respectively. In medieval France, it was customary for the groom to cover the bride's head with his *tallit* as a symbol of sheltering her; and in modern-day Israel, for weddings of soldiers on active duty, it is not unusual to see a *ḥuppah* constructed of a *tallit* supported by four rifles held by friends of the bride and groom. Generally, the *ḥuppah* is erected inside the synagogue or the hall where the wedding is to take place, but among Orthodox Jews, the preferred custom is to erect the *ḥuppah* outside, or at least in a spot open to the sky, underneath the stars, because of God's assurance to Abraham that He would make his descendants "as numerous as the stars of the heavens" (Genesis 22:17).

Child Marriages. Minor children, i.e. males before the end of their 13th year and females before the end of their 12th, do not have the legal capacity to effect a marriage arrangement, and therefore no divorce is needed for dissolution of such a marriage, if attempted. In addition, a father does not have the power to contract a marriage on behalf of his minor son; however, he does have the right to contract a marriage for a minor daughter, with the provision that she understands the implications of marriage and gives her consent to it.

Forbidden Marriages. Incestuous marriages and marriages with a non-Jewish partner are not valid in

accordance with Jewish law; even if celebrated, such marriages are considered void, and no process of divorce is needed to terminate the marriage. In accordance with biblical law, a *kohen* (priest) cannot marry a divorcee, but if such a marriage is celebrated, a *get* must be given to terminate the marriage.

Divorce. A Jewish marriage can be terminated in one of two ways — either through the death of one of the partners or through the process of divorce. The regulations concerning divorce are very intricate and have undergone many changes in the course of the generations, but the basic act of a Jewish divorce is the giving of a *get,* a bill of separation, by the husband to the wife on the basis of mutual consent. Although the original biblical laws allowed the husband to divorce his wife at will, an enactment of Rabbenu Gershom ben Judah (11th century) which was accepted by all the communities of Europe — prohibits the husband from divorcing his wife against her will. For the *get* to be valid, it must both be given by the husband of his free will and received by the wife of her own free will and consent.

MARTINI, RAYMOND (1220-1285),
Spanish Dominican friar and missionary. Born in Catalonia, he lived for a long time in a monastery in Barcelona,

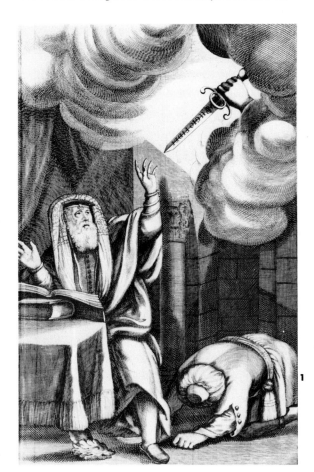

and for a period also in Tunis, where he engaged in missionary activities among Jews and Arabs. He studied Hebrew in order to be able to conduct religious *disputations with Jews, and was able to read rabbinic writings easily. He participated in the disputation with *Naḥmanides in Barcelona in 1263 and in 1264 became a member of the first censorship commission to examine Jewish books for passages allegedly offensive to Christianity.

Martini became a leading official in the anti-Jewish policy of the Church. His chief writing is the *Pugio Fidei* ("The Dagger of Faith") of 1280, most of which is devoted to anti-Jewish arguments. The book is an attempt to regain lost prestige after the Christian failure in the disputation at Barcelona. He is original in the use of talmudic sources in his attempt to affirm Jesus as the Messiah. *Pugio Fidei* became the most widely circulated anti-Jewish writing of the Middle Ages, and was used by friars, Christian scholars, and even Jewish apostates. Solomon ben Abraham *Adret wrote a refutation of Martini's main fictitious "proofs" from the *aggadah* for the validity of Christianity, and a defense against his charges of forgeries of the biblical text.

MARTYRDOM. The willingness to sacrifice life rather than faith, is one of the most significant concepts of Judaism, and has paradoxically been a factor in Jewish survival, where other oppressed groups have assimilated and disappeared. The laws of martyrdom were first formulated at the rabbinic council of Lydda in the second century c.e. when *kiddush ha-Shem* ("Sanctification of the Name [of God]") was declared obligatory with regard to three situations: idolatry, unchastity, and murder. Rather than worship idols, commit an unchaste act, or murder, the Jew is commanded to choose death. All other commandments may be violated rather than suffer death. But should a Jew be forced into breaking any commandment in the presence of ten Jews (or more) in order to demonstrate his apostasy (abandonment of faith) he is obliged to sanctify God's name by chosing death. If ten Jews are not present, he should transgress rather than be killed. These rules were to apply in "normal" times. In periods of persecution of the whole community, however, death was to be chosen even if no other Jews were present. The rabbis understood the first verse of the *Shema,* "And you shall love the Lord your God . . . with all your soul," as meaning even if He demands your soul from you,and, indeed, the

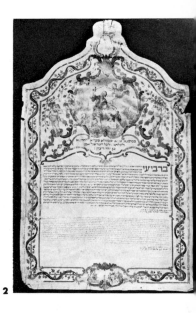

1. Frontispiece of a book written by Raymond Martini. The picture shows a Jew (seated) and a Muslim, surrendering to the Christian philosophy, symbolized by the victorious sword.
2. *Ketubbah* from 18th-century Italy.

A Jewish martyr being tortured during the Spanish Inquisition in the 15th century.

Book of Maccabees is almost entirely a sermon on the meaning and glory of self-sacrifice. Whereas in Christian and Muslim thought martyrdom is chiefly regarded as the act of individuals warranting canonization as saints, in Judaism it remains a task for each and every Jew to fulfill if the appropriate moment should come. In the war against Rome (66-73 c.e.), whole communities committed suicide rather than surrender to foreign domination. The idea of *kiddush ha-Shem* was strengthened during the Middle Ages as persecution under Christianity intensified. Such suicide became the only method by which the defenseless Jews of the time could express courage and opposition. In the 11th century, even before the *Crusades, the idea of a holy war became dominant in western Christian thought and cases are recorded of suicide to avoid forced conversion. During the Crusades both the crusading oppressors and their Jewish victims conceived their actions in terms of the glorification of God. Firmness of faith continued throughout the later centuries of tribulation, libels and massacres. (When the Nordhausen community was led to be burned on the pyre during the *Black Death massacres of 1349, it obtained permission to hire musicians and went singing and dancing to its death.) Medieval Jewish prayer books contain a benediction to be recited by the Jew about to kill himself and his children. *Kiddush ha-Shem* inevitably became part of the fate and suffering of Spanish Jewry under the tortures of the *Inquisition.

In modern times, the lessening of religious fanaticism, and growing secularization of Jewish life, accompanied by trends toward *assimilation and *emancipation, have led to the disintegration of Jewish values; as the necessity for self-sacrifice diminished, so the idea of *kiddush ha-Shem* appeared to lose its significance. However, renewed persecution under the Nazis revived the ancient tradition in the *ghettos and *concentration camps of Europe and very many cases of honorable death among the six million who perished must have gone unrecorded. The tradition has continued in defense of the revived State of Israel, with the qualification that the enemy, too, must *at last* be prepared for death. (See also *Akedah; *Akiva; *Masada; *Blood Libel; *Desecration of the Host; *Ḥasidei Ashkenaz; *Holocaust.)

proclamation of the *Shema,* "Hear, O Israel, the Lord is our God, the Lord is One," was the phrase with which martyrs went to their death.

Martydom when sacrifice was not obligatory became a matter of dispute. *Maimonides held that one who chose death when the law decided for life was guilty of an offense. Others, like the tosafists and most medieval Jews of *Germany, considered such voluntary death praiseworthy. The sages of the Talmud were divided as to whether gentiles are required to sanctify God's name by martyrdom. *Rava maintained that rather than break one of the Noachide laws, the gentile should choose death.

Jewish history is replete with examples of those willing to die for their faith from Shadrach, Meshach and Abednigo, who in the Book of Daniel refused to worship an idol and thus endangered their lives, up to the present generation of Soviet Jews who suffer indescribable hardships rather than give up their Jewishness. Under Antiochus Epiphanes, Hellenizers applied violent methods toward the Jews. The Fourth

MARX, KARL HEINRICH (1818-1883), German social philosopher whose writings have become the basis of the creed of hundreds of millions of socialists

throughout the world; in the Soviet Union and Communist China in particular they are revered as religious dogma.

Marx was born in Trier, West Prussia. His Jewish parents converted to Protestantism in 1817 in order that his father might continue to practice as a lawyer. Greatly influenced by the German philosopher Hegel, Marx joined the Young Hegelians and worked as a journalist after taking his doctorate in 1841. His writings convey a passionate longing for a new, free society in which individual man will truly benefit from the produce of his labor without the imposed restrictions of state-direction or capitalist profit. In 1848 Marx and his wealthy friend Friedrich Engels published the *Communist Manifesto,* the program of the League of the Communists. The *Manifesto* proclaimed: "The history of all hitherto existing society is the history of class struggles . . . oppressor and oppressed, stood in constant opposition to one another, carried on uninterrupted, now hidden, now open fight, a fight that each time ended either in a revolutionary reconstitution of society at large, or in the common ruin of the contending classes." It ended with the words: "The proletarians [industrial working class] have nothing to lose but their chains. They have a world to win. Working men of all countries, unite!" Exiled from several European countries thereafter, Marx lived his last years in London, where he died and was buried in Highgate cemetery.

His most famous work, *Das Kapital,* was based on years of research carried out at the British Museum library, but remained unfinished at his death. In *Das Kapital* Marx argued that the economic relations which bind society together are the true foundation on which legal, political, religious and moral institutions and ideas are superimposed. Workers are inevitably exploited by the owners of the means of production (land, factories, transport, housing, etc.) who use their surplus labor for their own profit ("surplus labor," is the value added to a commodity by the worker's sweat; this value is not received back by him as reward, but by the capitalist as profit).

Marx and the Jews. Marx's father Heinrich, whose original name was Hirschel ha-Levi, was the son of a rabbi and the **descendant** of many generations of talmudic scholars. His brother was chief rabbi of Trier. Marx described his attitude to Jews and Judaism as one of "self-hatred." At 15 he was confirmed a Protestant and became deeply attached to Christianity and to German culture. Marx associated Jews largely with greed, self-interest and love of money. He reveals a surprising ignorance of Jewish history and culture, and often refers to Jews as the symbol of financial power and capitalist mentality. This attitude did not protect Marx or his ideas from anti-Semitic attacks by his enemies. Ironically, the fascists and Nazis of the 1930s and 1940s used the term "Marxism" to denote a sinister worldwide "Jewish" plot against their national interests. Marx's Jewish origins, though hinted at in Soviet encyclopaedias up to the 1940s, were studiously concealed thereafter.

MARX BROTHERS. The U.S. comedy team known as the Marx Brothers consisted of Chico (Leonard, 1891-1961), Harpo (Adolph, 1893-1964), Gummo (Milton, 1894-1977), Groucho (Julius, 1895-1977), and Zeppo (Herbert, 1901-1979). Their irreverent, zany and impromptu humor had wide appeal and from the 1930s they became world-famous on film and television. Beginning as a vaudeville act, the team made its Broadway debut in a revue called *I'll Say She Is* in 1924. Chico was an accomplished pianist, and Harpo a harpist and both would break the comedy routine on film to show off their musical abilities. They also gave concerts. Groucho, the lead man, was master of

1. Karl Marx, father of modern Communism.
2. Harpo Marx takes aim (?) at the butler in the Marx Brothers film *Animal Crackers,* 1930.

the insult, and established a unique style, in swallowtail coat, large black moustache, chewing a long cigar and walking with a pronounced stoop which left his wrists sometimes trailing along the hotel carpet. Zeppo and Gummo left the act to become successful theatrical agents. Among the brothers' most successful films are *Animal Crackers* (1930), *Duck Soup* (1933), *A Night at the Opera* (1935), and *A Night in Casablanca* (1946). Harpo wrote *Harpo Speaks* (which, in the films, he never did) (1961), and Groucho,*Groucho and Me* (1959) and *Memoirs of a Mangy Lover* (1963).

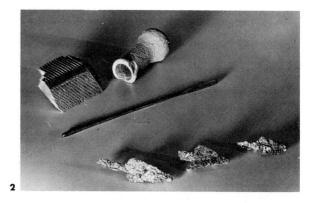

2

MASADA. The flat-topped rock that is called Masada soars majestically above the placid blue waters of the Dead Sea and the desolation of the Judean Desert. It is difficult to imagine that such a peaceful scene was once the site of fierce battles and a mass suicide by 960 Jews — men, women and children — unwilling to surrender to a hated enemy.

In 66 c.e., a band of Jewish resistance fighters led by Eleazar ben Yair fled the war with the Romans in Jerusalem and took refuge at the fortress on Masada, elaborately built nearly a century earlier by King *Herod, as a refuge from his Jewish subjects and from Queen *Cleopatra. For six years they lived a relatively quiet life. But in 72 c.e., two years after Jerusalem had fallen and the Temple was destroyed, the Roman governor Flavius Silva marched against them with the Tenth Legion; they were now beleagured in the last remaining *Zealot stronghold. The Jewish camp was pelted from below with catapulted rocks. A breach was made in the protecting wall; a huge ramp of light-colored earth, still there today, was erected on one side, but the Roman attempt to penetrate proved unsuccessful. Finally, after seven months of siege, the Romans set the wooden barriers alight, and the Jews were forced to make a fateful decision.

On the first day of Passover, Eleazar ben Yair addressed his comrades as follows: "We know in advance that tomorrow we shall fall into the enemy's hands; but we still have the free choice of dying a noble death together with our loved ones . . .Let our wives die undisgraced, and our children free from the shackles of slavery! And after they have preceded us in death, let us perform a service of love for one another, and then the glory of having sustained freedom will take the place of an honorable burial."

Accordingly, they chose ten men by lots to slay the others and one of the ten to kill those remaining and, finally, himself. The Romans had won, but it was an empty victory, for there were no men left to capture. The event became known through the historical writings of *Josephus Flavius, who spoke to two Jewish women and five children who escaped death by hiding away.

Masada was first identified in 1838 by the Americans E. Robinson and E. Smith, but it was not until the extensive archaeological digs between 1963 and 1965 by Professor Yigael *Yadin and thousands of volunteers that a great cache of information was discovered. One can now see Herod's unearthed and

1

1. Aerial view of Masada, last stronghold of the Zealots in their battle against Rome.
2. Some of the objects dating from the Zealot period, discovered at Masada.

1

1. **Marriage.** "Jewish Wedding" by Moritz Oppenheim, 1861. In
this painting of a German marriage ceremony, a *tallit* serves as a
canopy. The bridal couple have their belts symbolically tied
together.

2. **Marriage.** An 18th century Italian *ketubbah* (marriage contract).
The outer margin is decorated with signs of the zodiac and the
inner border is made up of exerpts from the Song of Songs
produced in very small print.

2

2

1

זה שלמה המלך העושה משפט משתי נשים"

3

1. **Morocco.** Headdress worn by young Moroccan Jewish girls
and women. Made of silver thread and ornamented with
enamel, filigree, semi-precious stones and colored glass, it is
interwoven at the base with horsehair, which is drawn in
bands across the forehead and falls over the ears.
2. **Lithuania.** Lithuanian family. The father wears a *kapote*
and his hat is called a *spodek*. The mother's head is
completely covered; the daughter being unmarried, is
allowed to have some hair showing. After L. Hollaenderski
Les Israelites de Pologne, Paris, 1846.
3. **Justice.** King Solomon passes judgement on the two
women who claimed the same child.

reconstructed Northern Palace, a villa rising from the highest point on the rock and adorned with intricate and colorful mosaics, among the earliest known in Israel. There are storerooms, pools, steamrooms, and a rainwater collection system that brought comfort to the king even through the scorching heat of desert summers. Many remnants of the Zealot period were also found, including skeletons, arrows, coins, pottery, a braid of hair, a synagogue, Hebrew scrolls and two *mikva'ot* (ritual baths).

Today Masada is not only a tourist attraction — with a cable-car to the top — but a source of inspiration and a symbol of courage to all Israelis. Every year, on that isolated rock, recruits to Israel's armored corps swear their oath of allegiance: "Masada shall not fall again!"

MASORAH, collective term embodying all the traditional information concerning the correct transcription and reading of the text of the Bible. Derived from the Hebrew root מסר, *masar*, "to transmit," the *masorah* was, for many hundreds of years, a purely oral body of knowledge which was transmitted from one generation to the next by an elite group of scholars, called *soferim*. It was their duty to ensure that the text of the Bible was maintained as received, i.e. that it was accurately transcribed in a particular form and style, and that it was read in accordance with rules of grammar and punctuation sanctified by tradition. In order to more fully understand the nature of his task, one has to look at the handwritten scroll used to this day for the public reading of the Torah in the synagogue. It is, in effect, merely a "skeleton" of letters, lacking all signs

of vocalization, accentuation, cantillation, and punctuation. Today anyone can learn to read the Torah scroll by first studying a printed copy of the Bible which is fully vocalized, punctuated, and divided into manageable verses and chapters, but for hundreds of years after the close of the canon (see *Bible), no such corresponding text was available, and it was the *soferim* who supplied the information which made reading possible.

Of particular importance in the work of the *soferim* was the preservation of certain oddities in the text of the Bible itself. At some very early stage in the transmission of the Bible, features such as letters with dots over them, letters suspended above their normal position on the line, letters smaller and larger than usual, made their appearance in the text, and they came to be viewed as sacred components which could not be tampered with even though their significance was not always understood. In addition, a fairly large number of words in the Bible are written in a form that does not correspond exactly to the pronunciation which tradition requires and in some cases words are read that in fact do not appear in the text; it was the duty of the *soferim* to ensure both that the text continued to be written with all these hallowed, though anomalous, features, and that it be read in accordance with the understanding that tradition dictated.

It is not known exactly when this large body of technical oral knowledge first began to be written,

1. A bar mitzvah service held on Masada.
2. Masoretic micrography (minute writing) used as outlines for the illustrations in an initial-word panel at the beginning of the Book of Leviticus.

The masoretic differences between Ben-Asher and Ben-Naphtali set in columns in the *Aberdeen Bible,* Italy, 1493. This column shows the differences for part of Proverbs, Ruth, and part of the Song of Songs.

but it is known that in the period between the seventh and ninth centuries c.e., the masoretes, the literary heirs of the *soferim,* reached the peak of their activity and set the basic mold for the literary recording of the *masorah.* The main center of masoretic activity seems to have been the city of *Tiberias, and although masoretes were at work in other parts of Erez Israel, as well as in Babylonia, the Tiberias school associated with the name of Aaron *Ben Asher predominated and it is their work which became accepted as standard.

In order to express in writing what was originally purely oral communication, the masoretes had to develop a new set of writing symbols which could convey in simple but exact fashion the required meaningful information. Thus, to enable the reader to correctly pronounce individual words, they devised a system of vowel signs which were placed under the consonental letters, and to enable him to read complete sentences in accordance with the traditional syntax, they devised a secondary system of accentuation or cantillation signs which were placed both above and below individual words and groups of words. The system of vowel signs chosen by the Tiberians was more or less arbitrary, and other signs could have been and were in fact designed (in Babylonia and elsewhere), but the system used by Ben Asher was a simple one and was accepted over all others. The system of cantillation signs on the other hand, seems to have been designed to serve as a type of visual mnemonic, for the shapes of the symbols approximate to the rise and fall of the voice which is demanded.

In addition to pioneering these two systems of notation, the masoretes set out to annotate in detail all the numerous orthographic and linguist anomalies of the Bible. Writing in the margins of the pages of codex editions of the Bible (i.e., texts not used for public reading) they would note, in abbreviated and epigrammatic fashion, all the words whose spelling did not correspond to the norm or words whose pronunciation did not correspond to the spelling. At the same time, they would point out all other places in the Bible where a given phenomenon appeared, or they would note its uniqueness, so that, in effect, these annotations add up to a veritable index of the linguistic features of the whole Bible. Today, when the term *masorah* is commonly used, it is to this latter aspect of the masoretes' activity which is most commonly referred.

Between the 10th century, when the last of the

formative masoretic work was completed, and the 16th, when the first Hebrew Bible was printed, numerous manuscript copies of the Bible were made containing the masoretic annotations. Many of the copyists, however, did not appreciate the technical exactitude of these comments, so that when Daniel *Bomberg set out to print the first complete Hebrew Bible and decided to include the *masorah,* it was found that there were enormous discrepancies among the various manuscripts. Bomberg hired a Jew from Tunis, Jacob ben Ḥayyim ibn Adonijah to correct this situation. He collected a large number of manuscripts and from them edited a new, clear version of the *masorah.* Bomberg then printed this version in his second edition of the Bible and it became the standard for all later printed Bibles. And today, when one refers to the "masoretic text" of the Bible, it is this version of Jacob ben Ḥayyim that is usually meant.

MATHEMATICS AND PHYSICS. The mathematical knowledge of the rabbis was derived from ancient Mesopotamian scientific traditions, and from the Romans and Greeks, though it was less exact than that of the Greeks. The rabbis did possess certain measuring instruments, but had rule of thumb methods for measuring heights relative to the lengths of the shadows of the object and the observer. They also had some knowledge of solid geometry. The Talmud is not clear about the methods used for fixing the *calendar. Rabbinic mathematics never progressed beyond what would now be considered the elementary stage, partly due to lack of interest in abstract mathematical reasoning. Another drawback was the lack of a metric system (based on 10) and an adequate symbol for zero. The use of the letters of the alphabet for numbers (i.e., *alef* = one, *bet* = two, etc.) was reinforced because of its connection with *gematria (see also *Hebrew Language).

The spread of Greek learning among Jews and Arabs during the Middle Ages included the dissemination of Greek mathematical theory. The earliest known medieval Jewish mathematician was the Egyptian astronomer Masha Allah (c. 770-820), known in Latin as Messahalla. Two centuries later, a Jewish convert to Christianity, Moses Sephardi (baptized Petrus Alfonsi), who became physician to Henry I, introduced Arabic mathematical-astronomical knowledge into England. One of the most outstanding figures of the 12th century was Abraham bar Ḥiyya, who wrote on mathematics, astronomy, optics, and music (see also *Astronomy). Abraham *Ibn Ezra was also the author of a number of mathematical works. He introduced the decimal system into Hebrew mathematics. Euclid's *Elements* was translated into Hebrew by Moses ben Samuel Ibn *Tibbon. The classic work on mathematical astronomy in Hebrew in the 14th century was *Yesod Olam,* written by Isaac ben Joseph Israeli, and the leading Jewish mathematician of the period was Levi ben Gershom. Notable Jewish mathematicians of the 15th to 18th centuries include Mordecai Comtino, Elijah Mizrahi, David *Gans, Joseph Solomon Delmedigo, and Elijah ben Solomon Zalman (the *Gaon of Vilna).

In the world of physics, medieval Jewish philosophers were confronted with two basic views of the nature of the material universe, those of Democritus (the atomic theory) and Aristotle (the matter and form theory). The Jews tended to favor the Aristotelian theory that matter and form exist eternally under unchanging natural law; although Aristotle's ideas imply the existence of God, they do not support creation of matter out of nothing, nor God's absolute power. *Maimonides accepted Aristotelian principles, but rejected Aristotle's views of the eternity of the universe. Levi ben Gershom was also an Aristotelian but considered the universe to be not eternal, but created from eternal matter. Both *Judah Halevi and Ḥasdai *Crescas opposed Aristotelian natural philosophy. The former attacked the idea that all matter consisted of four basic elements (fire, earth, air and water), arguing that it failed to fit in with the scriptural account of God's creation of natural objects as they are, rather than from more

basic constituents. Crescas considered the universe finite.

Following the emancipation of Jewry and the opening of universities to Jews, Jews have played a central role in the development of modern physics, no fewer than 15 having been awarded Nobel Prizes for work in this field. The most outstanding physicist since Newton, Albert *Einstein, developed a theory of relativity which has become the basis of modern physics. His theory of gravitation explains many facts inexplicable according to Newtonian mechanics. He also reformulated a corpuscular theory of light, invented the photon concept, stated the law of photoelectricity, the theory of random movement of small particles, and the quantum theory of specific heats.

Below is a list of other outstanding Jewish contributors to mathematics and physics:

Besicovitch, Abram Samoilovitch (1891-   ), descendant of a Karaite family, began his academic career in St. Petersburg (Leningrad). He left the U.S.S.R. in 1925 and settled in Cambridge, England. He was elected a Fellow of the Royal Society in 1934 and received its Sylvester Medal in 1952.

Bloch, Felix (1905-   ), U.S. physicist and Nobel laureate. Born in Switzerland, he worked in Copenhagen and Rome and settled in the U.S. in 1934. He took part in war work in Los Alamos (a secret atomic bomb center), and received the Nobel Prize for Physics in 1952.

Bohr, Niels Henrik David (1885-1962), Danish physicist and Nobel laureate. In 1911 he worked with the discoverer of the electron, J.J. Thomson, at Cambridge, and then in Manchester with Ernest Rutherford who discovered the atomic nucleus. Having produced a series of papers which revolutionized conceptions of the atomic structure, Bohr in 1916 became professor of chemical physics at the University of Copenhagen and in 1920 head of the Institute of Theoretical Physics. In 1922 he received the Nobel Prize (being the youngest laureate at that time). In September 1943 he and his family escaped the Nazis by going to Sweden in a fishing boat. From there he was taken to England in the bomb-rack of an unarmed Mosquito aircraft. There he became "consultant" to Tube Alloys, the code name for the atomic bomb project. He was chairman of the Danish Atomic Energy Commission, and took an active interest in the work of Israel's Weizmann Institute, which he visited several times. In the last 15 years of his life he worked tirelessly for peace.

1. Israeli physicists working with advanced electronic apparatus.
2. Medal struck in honor of Niels Bohr, Nobel Prize-winning physicist.
3. Felix Bloch, U.S. atomic physicist.

Bondi, Hermann (1919-   ), mathematician, born in Vienna, moved to England in 1937. His studies at Cambridge were disrupted by World War II, when he was interned and sent to Canada as an alien. He was allowed to return to England in 1941, and began secret research on radar. Appointed to the chair of Applied Mathematics at King's College, London in 1954, he became Director General of the European Space Research Organization in 1967, and in 1970 was made chief scientist to Britain's ministry of defense.

Courant, Richard (1888-   ), German mathematician, after fighting in World War I, became professor of mathematics at Goettingen. Driven from his post by the Nazis, he settled in the United States, where he became head of the department of mathematics at New York University. His work led to the invention of the electronic computer.

De-Shalit, Amos (1926-1969), Israel scientist and educator, born in Jerusalem. From 1954 until 1964 he headed the nuclear physics department of the Weizmann Institute, and was its scientific director (1961-63) and its director general (1966-68). He won the Israel Prize for natural sciences in 1965.

Fubini, Guido (1879-1943), Italian mathematician, professor of mathematics at Catania in 1901, Genoa,

1906 and Turin from 1908 until dismissed from his post in 1938 by the fascist anti-Jewish laws. He worked thereafter at Princeton and New York universities.

Ginsberg, Jekuthiel (1889-1957), mathematician and Hebrew writer. Born in Russia, he emigrated to the U.S. in 1912 and taught mathematics at Columbia University. In 1930 he was appointed head of the mathematics department of Yeshiva College. He founded and edited the *Scripta Mathematica Library*.

Glaser, Donald Arthur (1926-   ), U.S. physicist. For inventing the "bubble chamber" he won the Nobel Prize in 1960, and subsequently became professor of molecular biology at the University of California.

Michelson, Albert Abraham (1852-1931), physicist and the first American to be awarded a Nobel Prize for science. Born in Prussia, he was taken to the U.S. at the age of two. He was professor of physics at the University of Chicago (1892-1929), and received the Nobel Prize in 1907. Michelson developed a method to measure the volocity of light. In 1887, with Edward Morley, he preformed one of the most important experiments in the history of science. The experiment showed that light travels at constant velocity (186,000 miles per second) in any direction and under any circumstances. This law of light may be considered the one absolute natural law in the universe, and led directly to the work by Albert *Einstein on the relativity theory. Michelson aslo determined the diameter of Jupiter's satellites and was the first to measure the dimensions of a star (Alpha Orion).

***Oppenheimer, J. Robert** (1904-67), U.S. physicist.

Pekeris, Chaim Leib (1908-   ), mathematician, born in Lithuania, emigrated to the U.S. in his late teens and began research work at the Massachusetts Institute of Technology in 1936. After two years at the Institute for Advanced Studies at Princeton, he went to Israel in 1948, to establish the department of applied mathematics at the Weizmann Institute of Science. Under Pekeris an eight year mapping survey of Israel was undertaken, which laid the basis for the country's petroleum search.

Rabi, Isidor Isaac (1898-   ), U.S. physicist and Nobel Prize winner. He was appointed full professor at Columbia University in 1950. His work on molecular beams in determining the forces holding together the protons within the atomic nucleus, won him the Nobel Prize in 1944. He was a member of the board of governors of the Weizmann Institute of Science, Rehovot, Israel.

1. Isidor I. Rabi, U.S. nuclear physicist.
2. Otto Stern, physicist who worked with Einstein in Prague.
3. Advanced research at the Technion, Israel Institute of Technology, Haifa.

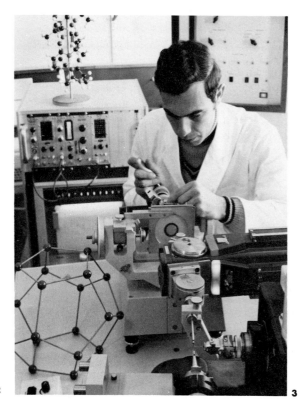

Segre, Beniamino (1903-1977). Italian mathematician, professor of mathematics at Bologna University until dismissed in 1938 under the fascist anti-Jewish laws. He was invited to England and taught until 1946 at the universities of London, Cambridge and Manchester. He went to Rome in 1950 and in 1968 was elected president of the Accademia Nazionale dei Lincei. He made important contributions to geometry.

Stern, Otto (1888-1969), physicist and Nobel Prize winner. He worked with Einstein in Prague and Zurich. He settled in the U.S. in 1933, receiving the Nobel Prize ten years later.

Szilard, Leo (1898-1964), Hungarian nuclear physicist. Regarded as one of the "fathers" of the work that led to production of the first atomic bomb, in 1934 he predicted the possibility of a nuclear chain reaction arising from nuclear fission. He tried to keep his own discoveries secret and to persuade other physicists to do the same, fearing that human ignorance in charge of such a powerful source of energy would doom mankind to destruction. However, alarmed at the possibility that the Nazis might develop a nuclear weapon he persuaded Einstein to write to President Franklin D. Roosevelt in August 1939. This letter led to the creation of the first atomic bomb, by the United States. However, four months before the bomb was used (on the Japanese cities of Hiroshima and Nagasaki) Szilard pleaded with the U.S. government not to use it and called for international control of atomic energy.

Teller, Edward (1908-   ), physicist. He left Germany after Hitler's rise to power in 1933. In 1935 he moved to the U.S. where he became involved in the production of the first atomic bomb. The key to the subsequent development of the hydrogen fusion bomb was his invention. He urged that hydrogen bomb development on a large scale be pursued in preference to the atom bomb both during and after the war. News of Soviet possession of a hydrogen bomb hardened Teller's conviction that such bombs were vital to the safety of western democracy.

Wiener, Norbert (1894-1964), U.S. mathematician, inventor of the science of cybernetics. He was a child prodigy, began reading science at four years of age and by seven was familiar with the theories of natural science. He entered Tufts University at 11, and received his Ph.D. at 18. His work during World War II led to developments in radar, high-speed electronic computation, the automated factory and cybernetics — the study of control (from the Greek for "steersman"). His book Cybernetics (1948) was a scientific best-seller. For the last 17 years of his life he refused to take part in military research. Another of Wiener's books, The Human Use of Human Beings (1950) sought to alert ordinary men to the dangerous social consequences of his theories.

MAZAR, BENJAMIN (1906-   ), Israel archaeologist and historian. Mazar was born in Ciechanowiec, Poland and studied at the universities of Berlin and Giessen. He settled in Palestine in 1929 and led archaeological digs at Ramat Rahel (1931), *Bet She'arim (1936-40) and En Gedi (1957-66). He conducted the historic excavation along the southern and western sections of the Temple enclosure in Jerusalem.

He was secretary of the Jewish Palestine Exploration Society from 1923 to 1943, and in 1959 became president of the Israel Exploration Society. Mazar has been on the staff of the Hebrew University since 1943, and in 1951 was appointed professor of the history of the Jewish people during the biblical period, and the archaeology of Palestine. In 1952 he became rector of the university and in 1953 was elected president. In 1968 he received the Israel Prize for Jewish studies. He has published several books and papers.

MEDALS, of both historic and artistic interest, commemorating Jewish events have been produced since ancient times. The Talmud mentions coins with the likeness of biblical figures, but the earliest extant Jewish medal dates from about 1500 c.e. and commemorates the physician Benjamin ben Elijah Be'er; its text is in Hebrew, Greek and Latin. Portrait medals of wealthy Jewish families were common during the Renaissance. Medals were also used for anti-Semitic propaganda: a typical example is the "Korn Jude." On one side was a picture of a bearded man wearing a Jew's hat, bearing a stick in his hand, and carrying a sack of grain on his back, on which sits the devil, ripping the sack open; on the reverse is an anti-Jewish inscription.

The events and persons commemorated by medals vary. Examples are the baptism of Jews in 1700, the fires in the Frankfort ghetto in 1721 and the 25th anniversary of the Jewish Loan Institute in Hamburg in 1841. Openings of synagogues, heroic deeds by Jews and the reduction of restrictions against them are commonly commemorated. Portrait medals were made of such eminent personalities as Moses *Mendelssohn, Nathan *Rothschild, and Chief Rabbi

1. Benjamin Mazar, Israel archaeologist and historian.
2. Cast bronze medal by Benjamin ben Elijah Be'er, the earliest known medal associated with a Jew, 1497-1503.

1. Medal honoring Israel's 25th anniversary, 1973.
2. Commemorative coin issued in Jerusalem, 1966, showing a stylized impression of Jerusalem.
3. "The Jewish Doctor" by Rembrandt.

Solomon Hirschel. The largest number of medals were produced in Germany, Holland, France, Italy and England. However, medals were also produced in America, Poland, Scandinavia and Russia. Not unexpectedly, Jewish sculptors often engaged in medal-making.

The first commemorative medals and coins in modern Israel were issued in 1958 on the tenth anniversary of the creation of the state. The Liberation medal showed the Roman "Judea Capta" coin issued at the fall of Jerusalem on the obverse and "Israel Liberata" on the reverse. Since that time medals commemorating Masada, the Warsaw Ghetto uprising, the Balfour Declaration, and the establishment of El Al Airlines are among the more than 200 medals minted by the Israel Government Coins and Medals Corporation. Commemorative coins appear every year on Israel Independence Day; half-shekels to be donated to charity at Purim, and shekels for pidyon ha-ben (see *Firstborn) are also struck for religious use.

MEDICINE. From the beginning of their history Jews have exerted enormous influence on the development of medical science. They have always cared greatly for the sick, and highly esteemed the medical profession. In ancient times the priest was also the custodian of public health. The physician came to be regarded as the instrument through which God effected cure, and so the practice of medicine was spiritually endowed. Great demands were made on the doctor, and his ethical standards have always been high. Many rabbis during the talmudic period were also physicians. As teaching and studying the word of God for payment was considered unethical. medicine was most often chosen as a means of livelihood; this was especially true in the Middle Ages, when almost all other professions were prohibited to Jews.

The medical knowledge of the East and much of ancient Greek medical lore was transmitted to the West by Jewish physician-translators. In the 20th century over 20% of all Nobel Prize winners for medicine were Jewish.

Medicine in the Bible. From the earliest times the Jewish faith sought to suppress magic customs and practices, including those related to health. The Hebrews were doubtless influenced by the highly developed medical knowledge of ancient Egypt. Nonetheless, like their neighbors, they did attribute health and disease to a divine cause. The uniqueness

of biblical medicine lies in its regulations for social hygiene, rules which are remarkable even by present-day standards, and which were transformed into religious dogma for the preservation of the nation. Of the 613 commandments, 213 have medical implications. Prevention of epidemics, suppression of prostitution and venereal diseases, frequent washing, care of the skin, strict dietary and sanitary laws, rules for sexual behavior, isolation and quarantine, the observance of a Sabbath day of rest, all these and other provisions, inhibited the spread of many of the diseases prevalent among neighboring peoples. Biblical treatment included quarantine, the use of oils, bandaging of wounds and bone fractures, bathing in therapeutic waters, especially in the case of skin diseases, sun rays and medicated drinks. Mouth-to-mouth resuscitation was known, but surgery is mentioned only with regard to *circumcision and castration. Embalming, though unusual, was not forbidden.

Medicine in Talmudic Times. Medicine, like much in Jewish life, was affected by ideas and practices with which the Jews came into contact as a result of invasion or exile. The influence of Persian and Babylonian magic medicine is clear from talmudic references to *amulets, demons, the *evil eye, etc. The medicine of the New Testament is almost entirely the miracle cure type. By contrast, the attitude of Jewish scholars of the time was generally rational and scientific. The Sabbath could be profaned for the treatment of the sick, since the sanctity of human life was paramount.

During talmudic times, patients visited the homes of physicians. *Hospitals apparently did not exist, although certain temple halls, parts of poorhouses and synagogues, were set aside for the sick. Reference is made to operating rooms, in which walls had to be made of marble for cleanliness. Free medical advice was not approved of since "a physician who takes nothing is worth nothing." At the same time, Jewish physicians had particular concern for the poor and frequently refused any payment from them. If a physician accidentally injured or caused death to a patient he was not held guilty.

Jewish doctors had the highest reputations throughout the Greco-Roman world, and mention is made of them by Celsus, Galen, Pliny and others. The personal physician of St. Basil was a Jew, as was that of Bishop Gelasius. At the same time, Christian bishops and emperors began promulgating numerous restrictions against Jewish doctors. The talmudic schools themselves taught medicine, and many talmudic scholars were physicians. The most distinguished of them was Samuel ben Abba ha-Kohen, who was personal physician to the Persian king, Sapur. During this time surgery was practiced, and included trepanning (boring a hole in the skull), amputations, removal of spleen, and cesarean sections.

Medicine in the Middle Ages. Knowledge of Hebrew was considered very important to the physician of the Middle Ages. Jewish physicians had this knowledge and often read Latin, Arabic, and in some cases Greek, too. They transmitted Greek medicine to the Arabs and later Arab medicine to Europe. International commercial links between Jews also helped them to obtain knowledge of drugs, plants and remedies from all parts of the globe. But from the fourth century onward there were innumerable restrictions forbidding Jewish doctors to practice among non-Jews, to hold official positions or enter the universities. The fact that Jews continued to hold key posts in the very courts which issued threats and restrictions against them testifies to the regard of others for their medical skill. Muslim countries were much more tolerant than Christian and consulting Jewish physicians was not forbidden to Muslims.

The oldest known medical book in Hebrew dates from the sixth century c.e. and was written by

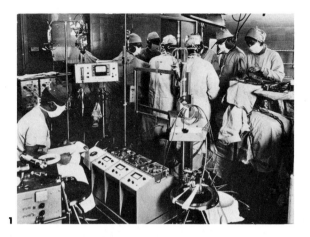

1

*Asaph Ha-Rofe (Asaph the doctor), founder of a medical school. His book encompasses all the then-known wisdom of Greek, Babylonian, Egyptian and Persian medicine as well as something of Indian medicine. It contains a "physician's oath" modeled on, but far surpassing that of Hippocrates in ethical content.

Following the Arab conquest of the Middle East and Spain, Jewish centers of learning began to flourish at Faiyum in Egypt, *Kairouan in Tunisia, and Cordova in Spain. A number of Jewish physicians or converts to Islam served as court physicians to the caliphs. In the 11th century Ephraim ben al-Zafran served as physician to the caliph of Egypt and left a library of over 20,000 books. Another famous Jewish physician of the time was Salama ibn Ramhamun who lived in Cairo. Judah Halevi, the Spanish poet-physician, exerted great influence on his contemporaries and later generations. Jonah ibn Bikhlarish was court physician to the Sultan of Saragossa, and Sheshet ben Isaac Benveniste served as court physician to the king of Barcelona. The most important scholar-philosopher-physician of the period was *Maimonides, who attained a world-wide reputation. In 1170 he became the personal physician to the family of the Sultan Saladin of Egypt. Maimonides stressed that the doctor must have not merely technical skill in curing physical disease but understanding of a patient's environment and intuition into his personality. Maimonides wrote his ten medical books in Arabic and they were translated into Hebrew and Latin. One of the most famous eye doctors of the Middle Ages was the Jew Benvenutus Grapheus of Jerusalem. Among a number of Jewish women physicians of the period was Sarah la Migresse, who lived and practiced in Paris in the 13th

2

1. An open-heart operation being performed at Hadassah Hospital, Jerusalem, 1970.
2. Law issued by Pope Gregory XIII forbidding Jewish doctors to care for Christian patients, 1581.

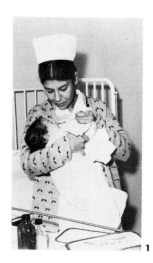

century. Rebekah Zerlin of Frankfort (c. 1430) became famous as an oculist.

During most of the 13th and 14th centuries Jewish physicians in Catholic Spain enjoyed the protection of reigning monarchs, although toward the end of the period the *Inquisition became more active. Even before 1492 and the expulsion from Spain, many Jewish physicians had emigrated to North Africa, Turkey, Greece, Italy, and Holland. One of the most famous was Amatus Lusitanus, whose life was a saga of adventurous flight from country to country, and who fought relentlessly against superstition and medical quackery. Other well-known practitioners of medicine during the period up to the 19th century include Abraham Zacuto and his grandson Zacutus Lusitanus, Antonio Sanchez (personal physician to Czarinas Elizabeth and Catherine II, until his Jewish identity was discovered and he was forced to flee to Paris), Joseph Hamon (court physician at Constantinople), Garcia de Orta (whose body was exhumed 12 years after burial and burned by the Inquisition), Cristoval d'Acosta, Isaac ben Mordecai (physician to Pope Nicholas IV), Kalonymus ben Kalonymus, Bonet de Lattes (physician to Popes Alexander VI and Leo X), and Philotheus Montalto (physician to Grand Duke Ferdinand of Florence and later to Queen Marie de Medici of France, by whose order he was allowed to be buried in a Jewish cemetery). Moses Cohen of Metz became physician to five successive sultans in Constantinople. In France Jean Baptiste Silva (1682-1742) became physician to the grand duke of Bavaria, Prince Luis Henry of Conde, and Voltaire.

The Modern Period. Following the French Revolution and the emancipation of Jews throughout Western Europe, the gates of universities and medical schools were at last thrown open to Jews. The subsequent contribution of Jewish doctors to medical science was enormous. Because of continuing restrictions in Russia, however, the youth of the world's largest Jewish community at the time went abroad to study. In Austria and Germany, though there was freedom to study and practice, Jews were unwelcome in "establishment" specialities such as surgery, and therefore were drawn to specialize in hitherto unpopular fields, and many became world renowned experts in these. Thus, for example, Jews dominated biochemistry, immunology, psychiatry, hematology, histology and microscopic pathology.

During the early 20th century there was an increased trend toward practical application of basic medical knowledge. During this period, August von Wasserman introduced the first diagnostic test (1906) and Paul Ehrlich the first effective drug for syphilis (1910). Casimir Funk revolutionized nutrition through the use of vitamin B (1911-14) in the treatment of beri-beri. He also coined the term "vitamin." Joseph Goldberger introduced nicotinic acid (1914) for pellagra, and Alfred Hess vitamin C for scurvy; Gustav Bucky invented the X-Ray diaphragm that bears his name.

The first Jewish doctors in the United States were of Sephardi origin, and were later joined by immigrant doctors from Germany and Russia. Following the Russian Revolution of 1917 many Russian Jews entered universities and the number of Russian Jewish doctors greatly increased, until unofficial quotas on entry reappeared in the later years of Stalin's rule. Emigration from Germany increased sharply in the 1930s after the rise of

1. The infant mortality rate in Israel has been greatly reduced due to modern medical methods implemented since the establishment of the State.
2. These student nurses will play an important role in Israel's hospitals, clinics and medical institutions.
3. A physiotherapist at Shaar Menashe Hospital in Israel treating a recent arrival from Algeria. The hospital is one of several maintained by United Jewish Appeal funds on behalf of aged, sick and handicapped immigrants.

Nazism. The majority of those who escaped and survived the Holocaust emigrated to the U.S. or Israel. Meanwhile in Britain, under the post-war Labor government, Baron Henry Cohen (Lord Cohen of Birkenhead) played a notable part in establishing the National Health Service. His own contributions to medicine, particularly in the field of diagnosis, gained him an international reputation.

The decades from 1930 to 1950 ushered in a golden age in scientific medicine, with the discoveries of antibiotics and cortisone, and great advances in molecular biology and medical technology. Jewish physicians in the U.S. greatly outnumbered those in any other country. There were approximately 27,000 Jewish doctors in private practice in the U.S., compared with 5,500 in Israel and 3,000 in France. *Jewish Physicians* by Nathan Koren lists around 7,000 Jewish doctors for whom there is documentary evidence from earliest times until the 19th century. There must, in fact, have been very many more for whose existence no evidence has survived. The Jewish contribution to medicine, however, cannot be assessed entirely in terms of numbers. Equally, if not far more, important has been the vast scope and extremely high quality of Jewish participation in the advance of medical science as reflected in research and education. (See also the articles *Haffkine, Mordecai; *Hospitals; *Hygiene; *Salk, Jonas E.)

MEGIDDO, an ancient Canaanite and Israelite city, lies on the southern side of the Jezreel Valley, and has been the site of many historic battles. The tell ("hill" – archaeological mound), near Haifa, was excavated in 1903-05 by G. Schumacher and by a Chicago team in 1925-39. Yigael *Yadin worked at Megiddo in 1960 and in later years. The excavations revealed the existence of over 20 levels of habitation each telling its own story.

The statue of an Egyptian official called Thuthotep, found in the excavations, shows that an Egyptian governor probably lived there during the 12th Egyptian dynasty (c. 1990-1780 b.c.e.). Megiddo, like all the Canaanite cities, fell to the Hyksos in the 18th to 16th centuries b.c.e. The conquerors strengthened the wall and built a gate. In a large palace near the gate were found jewels and ivories, which indicate the prosperity of the city at that time. In approximately 1469 b.c.e. Thutmosis III suddenly appeared before the walls of Megiddo and captured the city after a siege of several months. It remained under Egyptian rule for a long period thereafter, but was again destroyed in the second half of the 12th century b.c.e. The next settlement was poor and unfortified and the identity of its inhabitants is uncertain.

According to the Bible, Megiddo did not fall to Joshua, although its king was defeated. Most scholars date its capture by Israel only to the time of David. Solomon fortified the city; the Solomonic gate with three guardrooms is identical in plan with gates at Hazor and Gezer. A large palace built of well-hewn ashlar masonry was probably the residence of Solomon's governor. In the city were stables, which could hold 492 horses. Yadin, however, says these stables belong to the time of Ahab, who rallied 2,000 chariots against Shalmaneser III at Karkar. A water installation built sometime in the Israelite period consists of a pit 81 feet deep, with stairs leading to a horizontal tunnel and to a spring in the slope of the hill, which was thus connected with the city inside the walls. The Israelite city perished in 733-32 b.c.e. with the conquest of Tiglath Pileser III. The Assyrian king made Megiddo the capital of a province, which included Galilee and the Jezreel Valley. The third stratum was rebuilt on a uniform plan, with two large public buildings in the Assyrian style. Level II (630-609 b.c.e.) probably dates to the time of Josiah of Judah, who fell in the battle against Pharaoh Necoh near Megiddo (to which is related the statement about Armageddon in Revelations 16:16). The last settlement at Megiddo was a small city of the Persian period. Both Napoleon (in 1799) and Allenby (1918) defeated the Turks at Megiddo. The tell has been developed for visitors with a small museum illustrating the history of Megiddo. On his visit to Israel in 1964, Pope Paul VI was received by President Shazar at Tell Megiddo.

A kibbutz was founded in 1949 by settlers of Polish origin near the ancient mound.

1. Model of Tell Megiddo.
2. Bronze figurine of a Canaanite god, found in Megiddo.
3. Fragment of an Egyptian statue, also found at the Megiddo dig. It is more than 3,000 years old.

MEIR, was a second century scholar who played a decisive role in the development of the Mishnah. Born in Asia Minor, he studied in Erez Israel with the great sage, Rabbi *Akiva and while still a young man was ordained and promoted over Akiva's other disciples because of his great dialectical powers. Though forced to flee the country during the Roman persecutions following the failure of the *Bar Kokhba revolt, Meir soon returned to take a prominent part in the reestablishment of the Sanhedrin in the city of Usha. He was appointed *ḥakham*, deputy to the *Nasi of the Sanhedrin, and in this capacity brought about the adoption of an important grouping of laws known as the "Institutions of Usha." Toward the end of his life he became involved in a fierce power struggle with Simeon ben Gamaliel. Nasi of the Sanhedrin. Meir objected to what he considered to be unwarranted demands for prestige and authority on Simeon's part, and he attempted to have Simeon removed from office. Simeon, in turn, attempted to have Meir excommunicated. Neither succeeded, but as punishment for Meir's "rebellion," it was decreed — according to the view of some talmudic scholars — that all his subsequent legal contributions be recorded as anonymous statements, bearing the simple byline of *aherim* ("others").

The dialectical powers displayed by Meir in halakhic discussions became legendary. "He was able," says the Talmud, "to give 150 reasons to prove an object (ritually) clean, and as many more to prove it unclean." Because of this excess of dialectics, many of his *halakhot* did not receive the force of law: the pros and the cons offered by him were so nearly equal in strength that one never knew his real opinion on a subject.

Nevertheless, Meir's contribution to the development of *halakhah* was immense. He continued the labors of Rabbi Akiva in collecting and arranging much of the material of the *Oral Law, and it was his compilation, the Mishnah of Rabbi Meir, that Rabbi *Judah ha-Nasi used as his foundation when he set out to redact the final version of the Mishnah (for more information on this see *Talmud).

Meir also enjoyed great popularity as an aggadist (see *Aggadah). He is said to have composed more than 300 fables and many of his moral maxims are actually recorded in the Talmud.

Accorded the epithet "Holy" by his contemporaries, he was a man who demanded much of himself and of others. He observed the rules of ritual purity with a severity which went beyond that of his colleagues and he was the spiritual founder of a pietist community whose members devoted themselves to the three virtues of study, prayer and work. He was particularly noted for his hatred of ignorance, and this is reflected in one strongly-worded statement that "He who gives his daughter to an ignoramus is as if he put her before a lion." Yet he was also a remarkably tolerant man. This is seen in his relationship with his former teacher, *Elisha ben Avuyah. While all Elisha's former colleagues refused to associate with him after his apostasy, Meir alone continued to maintain close personal ties with Elisha, in the hope perhaps, that he could win him back to Judaism.

Meir died in Asia, but asked to be buried in Erez Israel. His exact place of burial is not known, but the tomb of Rabbi Meir Ba'al ha-Nes in Tiberias is generally assumed to be his.

Beruryah, wife of Rabbi Meir, was also an outstanding scholar and she became famous as the only woman in talmudic literature whose views were taken seriously and often quoted by her male contemporaries.

Many stories demonstrate Beruryah's piety and moral stature. For example, when certain evil men wronged her husband and he prayed for their death, Beruryah rebuked him, explaining that it was *sin* the Lord hated, not the sinners. You should be praying for the repentance of these evildoers, not their death, she said.

One tragic Sabbath, two of their sons died while Rabbi Meir was out. When he returned, she did not tell him at once what had happened, in order not to grieve him on the Sabbath. After *havdalah* she broached the subject saying, "Someone once gave me something to mind, and now he wants it back. Should I give it to him?"

"Of course!" the Rabbi answered.

Beruryah then led her husband to the room where the dead boys lay, and he began to weep. With her faith Beruryah comforted Meir. "The Lord giveth and the Lord taketh. Blessed be the name of the Lord," she said.

MEIR, GOLDA (née Mabovitch; 1898-1978), Israel prime minister and labor leader, was born in Kiev, Russia, where her father was a poor carpenter. She returned to Russia 50 years later as Israel's first minister to Moscow, and was received by thousands of Jews who came to the Moscow Great Synagogue to meet her.

Golda Meir in 1969.

גולדה מאיר

Golda Meir

Extreme poverty caused Golda's family to emigrate to the United States in 1906 and settle in Milwaukee, where she later studied in the Normal School for Teachers. Childhood memories of Russian pogroms influenced Golda in becoming a Zionist. Being a socialist as well, she settled in Palestine in 1921 with her husband Morris Myerson, joining kibbutz Merḥavyah. Although Golda Meir quickly adjusted to the hard conditions of kibbutz life, she soon became involved in political and social activities that took her away from the kibbutz. In 1928 she became the executive secretary of *Mo'ezet ha-Po'alot* (women's labor union) and was sent as an emissary to the Pioneer Women's Organization in the United States from 1932-1934. On her return to Palestine in 1934, she joined the executive committee of the Histadrut (Israel labor union) and later became head of the political department of the Histadrut, a job which helped train her for her eventual role as leading statesman of Israel.

In the 1940s, Golda Meir was a major figure during the struggle and difficult negotiations with the British mandatory government. She took Moshe Sharett's place in 1946 as head of the political department of the Jewish Agency in Jerusalem until the establishment of the State in 1948. After that she was appointed minister to Moscow, a post she held until April 1949.

After being elected in 1949 to the Knesset as a Mapai party member, Golda Meir was appointed minister of labor. She began large scale housing and road building programs, and supported a policy of unrestricted immigration. In 1956 she became foreign minister of Israel and held the post until 1965. As one of the few women to hold so high an office, Golda Meir became a famous international figure. Among her main achievements in foreign relations was extension of Israel aid to African nations. On her retirement from the foreign ministry, she became secretary-general of Mapai. After the death of Levi Eshkol on February 26, 1969, Golda Meir became the fourth prime minister of Israel. As prime minister she encouraged the emigration of thousands of Soviet Jews to Israel, and strengthened relations with the United States.

Disaster overtook her administration on Yom Kippur, 1973 when Egypt and Syria caught Israel's defenses off guard in a coordinated surprise attack. Following bitter recriminations, Mrs. Meir submitted her resignation and that of her government on April 11, 1974. She continued as head of the caretaker government which successfully negotiated a disengagement of forces agreement with Syria (following an earlier one with Egypt), until the appointment of a new government under Yiẓḥak Rabin on June 3. She then resigned her seat in the Knesset and retired into private life.

MEIR BEN BARUCH OF ROTHENBURG (c. 1215-1293), German rabbi, teacher, commentator and community leader. Meir was born in Worms into a family of scholars and community leaders. He studied under the finest teachers of his day in Germany and in France, and early gained a reputation as the greatest scholar of his generation. He held no elected nor appointed position as leader of German Jews as a whole, but his authority, in fact, was immense. He enjoyed this enormous prestige because of his powerful intellect and his knowledge of talmudic law. The Talmud was the "constitution" of Jewish community government and Meir, the greatest scholar of the land, was its best and most authoritative interpreter. For nearly half a century rabbis and judges from the German states and from the surrounding countries of Austria, Bohemia, Italy and France, and even from Spain, sent him their questions regarding law and ritual.

Sometimes Meir objected to the large number of responsa he was obliged to write, and was impatient of long-drawn-out questions. Sometimes he felt that his powers as an arbitrator were overestimated, and he was being asked to decide on matters over which he had no jurisdiction. His responsa were collected by his pupils, and were studied for generations. They

A representation of Meir b. Baruch of Rothenberg, from a 15th-century Italian manuscript.

are one of the sources on which the *Shulḥan Arukh* is based (see *Law, Jewish). He wrote profound commentaries on the Talmud. He also used to act as *ḥazzan* (cantor) and composed many *piyyutim,* religious poems, some of which are recited in the liturgy to this day.

In his interpretation of Jewish public law, he saw man as absolutely free, and the legitimacy of government as derived solely from the free consent of the governed. His support of democratic government influenced the European merchant classes who were in fairly close contact with the Jewish communities.

In 1286 Emperor Rudolph I attempted to impose taxes on the Jews of Germany, reducing them to the status of financial slaves. Outraged, Meir prepared to lead the Jews out of the country, but he was betrayed by an apostate Jew, arrested in Lombardy and imprisoned by the Emperor. Rudolph hoped to use the devotion of the Jews to Meir to force them to pay his taxes, but Meir would not allow them to pay a ransom and he died in prison. Fourteen years later, his body was redeemed by the Jews for a large sum of money and buried in Worms.

MELBOURNE, the capital of Victoria state, Australia, had a Jewish population of **34,000 in 1980** out of a total population of 2,400,000. Two Jews were among the 15 original founders of the city in 1835. The Jewish community was founded in 1841. The first synagogue was opened in 1847 and an influx of Jewish settlers in the mid-century led to the growth of working class districts in the city suburbs.

John Groton, former prime minister of Australia, visiting a Lubavitch Ladies College in Melbourne.

In 1872 a new St. Kilda synagogue was opened, and two years later the Melbourne Hebrew School was established. A United Jewish Education Board was set up to cover the Jewish communities of Melbourne, East Melbourne and St. Kilda in 1888. By 1900 the most popular occupations were textile manufacturing, general retailing, tailoring, cabinetmaking, and watchmaking. Fewer than 3% of Jews were in the professions.

The Judean League of Victoria was founded in 1921 as a roof organization for a number of secular Jewish societies which had evolved, including sports, literary, cultural, social and Zionist activities. A central public issue in the 1940s was the battle against anti-Zionist elements. A Mount Scopus College, the first Jewish day school in Australia, was founded in 1948 and gave a tremendous impetus to Jewish education in Australia. The first Liberal congregation was established in 1935, and relations with the Orthodox section of the population became strained. A conflict occurred between the Jewish Council to Combat Fascism and Anti-Semitism, many of whose members were Soviet supporters, and the Board of Deputies. The Board set up a public relations committee of its own, and eventually the Council modified its pro-Soviet stance.

By 1981 there were more than 180 Jewish organizations, including 21 synagogues, two homes for the aged, seven day schools, a number of foster homes and hostels, kindergartens, a library, art gallery and Yiddish newspaper. In the 1980s Melbourne Jewry was predominantly middle-class and suburban. The two most honored citizens of the city — Sir John *Monash and Sir Isaac *Isaacs — were both Jews. More than one million people lined the city's streets for Monash's funeral procession in 1931. Other prominent Jewish personalities have included Rabbi Jacob Danglow, whose ministry at St. Kilda's extended over 50 years, Rabbi Israel Brodie, who later became chief rabbi of the British Commonwealth, Professor Newman Rosenthal, and Samuel Wynn, a leading Zionist.

MENDELE MOKHER SEFORIM (Abramowitsch, Shalom Jacob; 1835-1917), Hebrew and Yiddish writer. Mendele wrote stories and plays all his life. He wrote about his own childhood, much of which was spent wandering through Lithuania after the death of his father in 1848; he wrote about social and literary problems, for he was deeply interested in the education and public life of Jews in Russia; he wrote

popular science, hoping to encourage the mass of Jews to study secular sciences as well as religious texts; and he wanted to translate the prayerbook and the Book of Psalms into Yiddish — but this project remained unfinished. He wrote novels and poems based on the history of the Jewish people, and he translated the regulations for compulsory service in the Russian army from Russian into Yiddish.

Mendele recorded the plight of Russian Jews suffering both exploitation from the Jewish upper classes within, and hatred and tyranny from Russian society without. His writings combine a satirical impatience with Russia's ghetto Jews and a sympathetic understanding of them and their problems.

He wrote both in Yiddish and in Hebrew and was acknowledged a classicist in both languages. He first wrote in Yiddish in order to reach a wider audience, but later came to believe that his Yiddish writing was of artistic value in its own right. He was one of the earliest popular Hebrew writers and did much to create a modern literary Hebrew style. He did this consciously, wanting Hebrew to be a "live creature, talking clearly and precisely," and he has influenced Hebrew fiction to this day.

MENDELSSOHN, MOSES (1729-1786). In early childhood Mendelssohn suffered from a disease which left him with a curvature of the spine and permanently affected his nervous system. Yet he grew up to be a great Jewish philosopher of the Jewish Enlightenment Movement, of *Haskalah as it is known in Hebrew, and a spiritual leader of German Jewry.

Born in Dessau, Mendelssohn received a traditional Jewish education and also broad general tuition. During the whole of his lifetime he worked as a merchant, while carrying on his literary activities in his spare time. In his conversation he was as outstanding as in his writing, and a circle of intellectuals gathered regularly at his home to discuss general and Jewish subjects. He was famous among both Jews and non-Jews for his wide-knowledge, his sharp intellect, and his moderate, patient and modest character.

Mendelssohn wrote several works on basic philosophical topics such as the existence of God, the immortality of the soul, and free will. His work *Jerusalem* secured him a place in the history of Jewish thought. He also published critical articles on German literature, and a commentary on his own translation of the Pentateuch, the *Biur,* which was condemned by certain leading rabbis.

Although it was against his nature and his intentions, Mendelssohn was forced to defend publicly, before the society of his time, his personal Judaism and the right of the independent existence of the Jewish religion. As a result of the furore raised by this debate with John Lavater, the Swiss clergyman who had challenged him to convert to Christianity, Mendelssohn considered himself obligated to bettering the status and condition of his fellow Jews. Nevertheless, when in 1770 a "person of high rank" submitted to him a project for the establishment of a Jewish state in Palestine, Mendelssohn rejected it. He held that after centuries of servitude the Jewish people were incapable of being moved by the spirit of freedom. In common with many Haskalah thinkers, he could not envisage any possible future for the Jewish people as a nation.

Mendelssohn's life thus became a testimony of the basic conflict of the *Emancipation — the conflict between *assimilation on the one hand and the safeguarding of the singularity of Jewish life on the other, the conflict of the modern Jew in the Diaspora who seeks integration, while at the same time desiring to preserve his Jewish identity.

Mendelssohn's grandson was Felix Mendelssohn, the acclaimed composer, who could not resolve the problem of his Jewish identity and who, like most of Mendelssohn's descendants, converted to Christianity.

1. Mendele Mokher Seforim.
2. Portrait of Moses Mendelssohn by one of his contemporaries.

Moses Mendelssohn

1. Cartoon ridiculing professional boxer Daniel Mendoza after his defeat, which is depicted as the defeat of the entire Twelve Tribes of Israel.
2. Pottery lamp decorated with a *menorah,* third to fourth century, Erez Israel.
3. The seven-branched *menorah* and various implements used in the Temple. From a Hebrew Bible, Spain, 14th century.

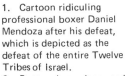

MENDOZA, DANIEL (1764-1836). An English middleweight boxing champion, Mendoza was born in Aldgate, London. He taught himself the art of boxing and won his first professional fight at the age of 16. He is known as the father of scientific boxing for he devised defensive moves which enabled him to defeat much heavier opponents.

His success in the ring brought him to the attention of the Prince of Wales, and he became the first boxer to receive royal patronage. Mendoza proudly billed himself as "Mendoza the Jew." His acceptance by royalty together with his boxing ability did much to help the position of the Jews in the English community. He opened his own boxing academy where he taught the "manly art"; he wrote two books on boxing and he toured the country giving boxing exhibitions. He finally lost his championship title to John Jackson in a ninth-round knockout on April 15, 1795.

In 1945 Mendoza was one of the inaugural group chosen for inclusion in the Boxing Hall of Fame in the U.S.A.

MENORAH, seven-branched candelabrum carried by the Israelites through the wilderness of Sinai. Today the *menorah* is the emblem of the modern State of Israel.

God showed Moses the prototype of the *menorah* when He handed down the Torah on Mount Sinai: from the central shaft of the *menorah* six branches,

1. Kabbalistic *menorah* in which each branch is given a symbolic meaning. Venice, 1548.
2. *Menorah* carved on a fourth century Italian stone coffin.
3. The *menorah* of the Second Temple being carried off by Roman soldiers. Detail from the Arch of Titus in Rome, built shortly after the destruction of the Temple in the first century c.e.
4. Marble pedestal from an Ereẓ Israel synagogue of the second to third centuries, decorated with a three-footed *menorah*.

1. The emblem of the State of Israel: the seven-branched *menorah* with the symbols of the Twelve Tribes of Israel along its base, flanked by olive branches.
2. Violinist Yehudi Menuhin.

three on either side, curved upwards, making seven branches in all; it was carved from one solid piece of gold. It was a sacred object to be used only in the *Tabernacle and later in the Temple, and no imitation was permitted. The special candleholder used on Ḥanukkah is a *ḥanukkiyyah* and not a *menorah* — it has eight branches.

The original *menorah* was 18 handbreadths high and burned in the Tabernacle as a perpetual light. When Solomon built the Temple in Jerusalem, he placed ten golden *menorot* inside it, probably in addition to the *menorah* of Moses. Both these and the original *menorah* were destroyed completely when the First Temple was desecrated in 586 b.c.e. The returning Babylonian exiles rebuilt the Temple in 516 b.c.e. and, following the custom of the Tabernacle, made a single *menorah* according to the descriptions of Exodus (25:31-40 and 37:17-24). In 169 b.c.e. it was removed by Antiochus Epiphanes (the king in the Ḥanukkah story); Judah Maccabee replaced it after the cleansing of the Temple. With the final destruction of the Temple by the Romans under Titus in 70 c.e., the *menorah* was seized and probably carried in the triumphal procession through Rome. There is no definite information as to the fate of the *menorah* after this time, but it is certain that it did not exist later than 1204.

After the victory of Titus, the symbol of the *menorah* was preserved by the Jewish people. During the Middle Ages it was used to illuminate manuscripts. Kabbalists (Jewish mystics) took it as a representation of the *sefirot* (emanations of God). Today the *menorah* remains a familiar symbol. One appears on Marc Chagall's stained glass windows in Jerusalem; the Ghetto memorial in Warsaw embodies two large *menorot;* and the large carved *menorah* of Benno Elkan stands outside the Knesset building.

MENUHIN, YEHUDI (1916-   ) was born in New York to parents who were educated in Palestine but had left to settle in the United States. As a child Yehudi spoke Hebrew. He started to learn the violin at the age of five, and appeared as soloist with the San Francisco Orchestra when he was only eight. He continued his studies in Europe, and in 1928 performed successfully in Paris, London and New York. By the time he was 17, he had performed in 63 different cities and had already acquired an international reputation.

During World War II he played for United States and Allied Forces and gave benefit concerts for wartime causes. In 1944 he was the first allied soloist to play in liberated Paris, and in 1945 he was invited to play in Moscow. In 1957 Menuhin began his own music festival in Switzerland, and in 1959 he started another one in England, where he also established a school for musically gifted children. He has visited Israel many times. In 1970 he was awarded the Jawaharlal Nehru Prize for International Understanding.

Menuhin's two sisters, Hephzibah (1920-1981) and Yalta (1921-   ), are both gifted pianists and have appeared with him frequently. His son Jeremy and his son-in-law Fu-Yong are also pianists and the whole family sometimes gives concerts and makes recordings.

MERCY. The exercise of mercy is an obligation for all Jews. By this it is meant that they must act with compassion and forgiveness towards all mankind, and perform deeds of charity and kindness. This quality is an essential characteristic of God who is known as *Raḥum* ("Merciful") and, in accordance with the tradition which sets as man's goal the imitation of God: "As He is merciful, so be you merciful." Just as God is bound by His covenant of mercy with His people, so is the Jew bound by specific commandments to act mercifully to the oppressed, the alien, the orphan, the widow, and indeed, every living creature.

The stress placed upon this quality is evident both in the many charitable institutions existing in Jewish communal life, and in the daily prayers which implore God to deal compassionately even with the undeserving man. Human beings are frail, imperfect creatures constantly open to error, and so they are totally dependent on God's mercy.

But God, as depicted by the rabbis, embodies a combination of justice and mercy, of strict judgment and lenient compassion. This combination of justice and mercy in God is represented by the two names of God — Elohim and YHWH. The former stands for justice and the latter for mercy. Though they may seem contradictory, one actually complements the other and, when there is a conflict between the two, God usually favors mercy. For a further discussion of this, see *God.

Judaism demands of its judges this same balance, and the principle of mercy thus assumes extreme importance in the administration of Jewish law.The prophet Zechariah (7:9) put it : " . . .execute the judgment and show mercy and compassion every man to his brother."

MERON, a settlement in the north of Israel. An ancient Canaanite city called Merom stood on the site of Meron from at least 1500 b.c.e. It lay on the "Way of Kings," an ancient route along which the warring armies of Egypt and of the north would march to do battle. Meron was conquered by two of the pharaohs of Egypt: Thutmosis III, whose dreams Joseph interpreted (Genesis 41: 14-57) according to some scholars, and Ramses II, probably the pharaoh against whom the Ten Plagues of Egypt (Exodus 7-15) were visited. Joshua defeated his enemies by the "waters of Merom" (Joshua 11: 5-7).

The Jewish historian, Josephus, who lived in the first century c.e. writes of Meroth, a city of 10,000 people, probably Meron, and in 1974 remains of the city described by Josephus were uncovered. Several talmudic sages are associated with the place (then referred to as Meiron) and *Simeon bar Yohai and his son Eliezer, according to tradition, are buried there. A popular festival is still held in Meron on *Lag ba-Omer, at what is believed traditionally to be the grave of the father and son (see *Lag ba-Omer and *Simeon bar Yohai).

Meron was settled after the Bar Kokhba war of the second century c.e., and the present-day village of Meron stands near the ruins of a synagogue from this period. A moshav, also called Meron, was founded near the village by Hungarian and Czechoslovakian immigrants in 1949. It belongs to the Ha-Po'el ha-Mizrachi Moshavim Association and specializes in hill farming, with deciduous fruit orchards, vineyards and poultry as major branches of production.

MERON, HANNA (1923-   ), Israeli actress, born Hanna Maierzuk in Berlin. She appeared in a film titled "M" and on the stage in Germany before emigrating to Palestine at the age of 10.

In Palestine she trained formally as an actress at the Habimah studios. During the Second World War she served in a British army entertainment unit, and in 1945 joined the new Cameri theater, of which she later became the star. She has been responsible for some of the company's greatest successes, and is also active in the management and policy-shaping of the theater.

In 1970 Hanna Meron was among the Israeli passengers attacked by Arab terrorists at Munich airport and as a result of the injuries she suffered, she lost a leg. After her recovery she resumed her acting career.

MESOPOTAMIA. "The land between the rivers" [Tigris and Euphrates] , Mesopotamia is the ancient name for the region today covered by Iraq, Iran and parts of Syria and Turkey. Western civilization (the establishment of written language, codified law, cities and trade) began in this region toward the end of the fourth millennium (i.e., four thousand years) b.c.e. when the Sumerians emerged as the dominant element in an intermingling of several migrant peoples. Sumer became the name of the land at the head of the Persian Gulf and Sumerian its language. To the Sumerians we owe the full development of

1. Grave of the second-century talmudic scholar, Simeon bar Yohai, in Meron.
2. Hanna Meron returning to Israel following the Munich attack.

1. Pyramid-like temple *(ziggurat)* in Mesopotamia, built about 2250-2233 b.c.e.
2. How one artist envisions the walled city of Babylon.

writing, possibly the invention of bronze metallurgy, the first accumulations of capital (wealth) and the beginnings of monumental architecture.

Mesopotamia for thousands of years contained numerous small city-states, the earliest of whose rulers were traditionally credited with incredibly long lives, but were eventually swept away in a catastrophic flood, followed by a confusion of tongues (possibly referred to in the biblical description of the Tower of *Babel). From the city of Kish derived the civilization of Akkad, to the north of Sumer. Akkad was the center of Semitic speech from which eventually developed Aramaic and Hebrew.

While the kings of ancient Egypt were regarded as gods, those of Mesopotamia's city-states were only considered mortal deputies appointed by the gods. Many of the city-states had their own gods, represented by statues, though in some cases the people of several cities might worship the same god under various names.

Rivalry between the city-states eventually led to the concentration of power in the hands of warrior princes, one of the most famous of whom was Gilgamesh of Uruk, whose wars are recorded in Sumerian epics. Uruk shared control over southern Sumeria with the city of Ur, from which came the patriarch *Abraham.

Around 2300 b.c.e. King Lugal-zaggi-si of Umma conquered all the other major cities of Sumer and laid the foundations for the first Mesopotamian empire. The first truly imperial ruler was Sargon of Kish, who ruled for more than 50 years, built a new city and palace at Akkad, and waged many far-off wars. He defeated Lugal in battle and united the entire country under his rule. His daughter Enheduanna became the first high priestess of the moon god at Ur, and is the first identifiable author in world literature (of poems celebrating the victories of the Sargonic kings).

By about 2150 b.c.e. Egypt and Mesopotamia

suffered collapse, possibly due to famine. Akkad fell into ruin so total that it was never reoccupied and it remains unlocated to this day. Ur asserted its independence. There is evidence that in the 21st century b.c.e. there was an invasion of Amorites from the west, and at the same time migrations into Syria-Palestine, which later formed the basis of the patriarchal narratives of the Hebrew Bible.

In 1793 b.c.e. one of the greatest rulers in history appeared in Babylon, Hammurapi, a successful military conqueror, zealous administrator and a lawgiver whose codification of the laws which had evolved in Mesopotamia was inscribed on a series of stelae (stone tablets) distributed throughout his kingdom. There are certain points of similarity between some of his laws and some of those of the Torah. Babylon was sacked by Hittites in an invasion around 1600 b.c.e. A hundred years later most of the Amorite city-states had been replaced by a few large non-Semitic ruling houses, and the native Semitic peoples reduced to peasant status. The one exception to the subjection of the Amorite peoples to foreign rule was a people known as the Habiru, who roved the Syrian and Palestinian hills in mercenary bands, and are thought by some to be the progenitors of the Jewish people.

Following the fall to the Greeks of Troy in Asia Minor in c. 1250 b.c.e., great migrations were set in motion by the movement of Greek peoples into the eastern Mediterranean and the subsequent displacement of others. At this time the Canaanite population of Canaan, displaced by the Philistines, first clashed with the Israelites moving into the land from south and east. The first direct contact between the rising force of Assyria and Israel occurred under Assyria's campaigning Shalmaneser III (858-824 b.c.e.). On five occasions a coalition of Israelites, Arameans, Cilicians, Egyptians, Arabians, Ammorites and Phoenicians faced Shalmaneser's armies. The Israelite house of *Omri fell in 841 and king *Jehu promptly surrendered to Shalmaneser. Around this time Babylonian scribes inaugurated a reform of the *calendar which was later taken over by the Jews and continues in use today. Under the usurper Tiglath-Pileser III (744-727 b.c.e.) the whole balance of power in the Near East was again upset. He destroyed Israel and many other states, and reduced the rest, including Judah, to vassalage. Sargon II of Assyria campaigned every single year of his rule reaching as far as Ashdod in the west and western Iran in the east, dying in battle on the northern frontier. *Sennacherib unsuccessfully besieged Jerusalem in 701 b.c.e. The final 40 years of Assyrian power were marked by constant warfare. The Assyrian capitals were annihilated around 615 b.c.e. by an alliance of Babylonians, Medes and *Josiah of Judah. The Chaldean empire inherited most of Assyria's conquests. *Nebuchadnezzar II (605-562 b.c.e.) conquered Jerusalem and Judah, and exiled the Judean aristorcracy to Babylonia. He also turned Babylon into one of the wonders of the ancient world, filling it with temples, palaces, a museum, ziggurat (kind of tower) and hanging garden. In a bloodless conquest in 539 b.c.e. Cyrus the Persian assumed control of all Babylonia (see also *Asia Minor, *Babylonia, *Iraq, *Syria, *Turkey).

MESSIAH. "I believe with perfect faith in the coming of the Messiah, and, though he tarry, I will wait daily for his coming." This is the 12th of Maimonides' 13 articles of faith and clearly expresses what has become a cardinal belief of traditional Judaism.

In the Bible there is no direct reference to the Messiah although certain passages are interpreted by later scholars to be referring to him. It seems that belief in the Messiah started to develop during the Babylonian exile after the destruction of the First

"Yearning for the Messiah," from Benno Elkan's bronze *Menorah* at Israel's Knesset building.

Temple, when the Jews came into contact with other religions, particularly oriental, mystical faiths. However, by Talmud times belief in the Messiah had become firmly a part of normative Judaism.

In traditional Judaism, the Messiah will be a human being — albeit it a perfect one — who will come and bring harmony to the world. He will not have a divine aspect other than having been chosen by God for his task. The Hebrew word for Messiah, *mashi'ah,* means "anointed" and indicates that the Messiah has been chosen by God. The coming of the Messiah therefore has come to mean the redemption of the Jewish people and an end to its suffering and tribulations.

Throughout history many men have presented themselves as the Messiah and because of the Jews' great longing for his coming, these "messiahs" have sometimes attracted large followings. Of course the most famous was *Jesus, although Christianity deviated from Judaism in ascribing to him divine characteristics. Of the purely "Jewish" messiahs, the best known is undoubtedly *Shabbetai Zevi who electrified the whole world, both Jewish and gentile. For more on this see *Messianic Movements.

According to the Talmud, the Messiah will be a descendant of the House of David and will be preceded by a secondary Messiah, from the House of Joseph. Folklore has it that he will arrive riding a donkey, although some sources have him arriving triumphantly riding the clouds. A widespread belief was that the Messiah will be born on the 9th of Av, the anniversary of the destruction of the First and Second Temples.

Throughout the ages there has been a great deal of speculation as to when the Messiah will come and many kabbalists and mystics worked out exact dates for his expected arrival. Most rabbinic authorities were against such speculation, probably because it always brought extreme disappointment to those who accepted the dates.

In modern Judaism, the idea of the Messiah has undergone great change. Reform Judaism has substituted a belief in a perfect world when mankind progresses sufficiently and many Orthodox thinkers describe the establishment of the State of Israel as "the beginning of the redemption," that is, the start of the messianic era.

MESSIANIC MOVEMENTS. Throughout Jewish history, Jews all over the world have yearned for the coming of the *Messiah. But at various times, especially in periods of trouble and suffering, the passive yearning turned into active preparation on the part of those who believed that the Messiah had indeed arrived and that the redemption was about to begin. The troubles afflicting them, such as the *Crusades or the *Chmielnicki massacres, were considered at the time to be the *hevlei mashiah* or "birth pains of the Messiah" which must be endured before his actual appearance.

Time and time again whole communities became convinced that their redemption was finally at hand. The excitement and jubilation would spread from town to town as the rumors and stories of signs and miracles were passed on. People sold their possessions, neglected their work and prepared themselves for their trip to Erez Israel. What terrible disappointment when in the end their Messiah proved to be merely a false hope!

An early example of messianic expectation took place during the period of the Second Temple in Judah. The turbulence accompanying the rule of King Herod and, later, that of the Romans led to the emergence of messianic leaders, each of whom claimed to be the "king of Israel," about to free the Jews from the hated foreign rulers. Many of these, like *Jesus of Nazareth, were crucified for their efforts.

In some cases, messianic movements took the form of revolts against the foreigners. It is said that the rise of Simeon *Bar Kokhba as one of the courageous leaders of the uprising of 132-35 c.e. against the Romans led the great sage *Akiva to consider him "the king messiah." The revolt, however, was quashed and Bar Kokhba was killed.

In the Middle Ages, the advent of the victorious Arabs and Muslims, and later of Crusader violence, brought about a general anticipation of the redemption. In the late seventh century in Persia, an illiterate tailor named Abu Isa led a reformist-like movement, attempting to introduce certain changes in the Jewish religion. He was later killed in battle.

One of the more remarkable messianic movements in the Muslim empire was that of David Alroy, in the first half of the 12th century. Born Menahem Alroy in Amadiya, Kurdistan, he took on the name of David, claiming to be king of the Jews. Menahem led a militaristic movement and attempted to take over the fortress of Amadiya by having masses of his followers enter the city with hidden weapons. The plan failed, however, and he was imprisoned by the sultan.

There are also indications that a rumor spread in Baghdad that Alroy would bring all the Jews of the city to Jerusalem. Apparently many were later ridiculed for selling all their worldly goods and waiting all night on the rooftops, expecting to be lifted off on the wings of angels.

In the 16th to 18th centuries, the messianic hopes often centered around stories of the *Ten Lost Tribes of Israel who were believed to be living far away, completely surrounded by the great river, the

Series of events linked with pseudo-messiah Shabbetai Zevi, whose activities caused a great upheaval in Jewish circles. An 18th-century German engraving.

Sabethai Sevi, der Falsche Messias.

Ware afbeeldinge van den genaemde propheet
Nathan Levi van Gaza:
Vray portraict du dit prophete
Nathan Levi de Gaza.

Sambatyon. When David Reuveni appeared in 1523, claiming to be a prince of those tribes, the Jews of Western Europe, recently having witnessed the tragic expulsion from Spain (1492), were eager to accept him as leader and redeemer. Reuveni did not actually claim to be the Messiah, but announced instead that he was in the service of his brother Joseph, king of the lost tribes of Reuben, Gad and half of Manasseh. As commander-in-chief of his brother's army, Reuveni's stated mission was to form an alliance between the Jews and Christians in order to launch a joint crusade against the infidel Muslims.

He made a grand entrance into Rome, riding a white horse, and was greeted warmly by Pope Clement VII. But his reception elsewhere was anything but cordial. The king of Portugal feared that, in the excitement stirred up by Reuveni's appearance, the Marranos would be tempted to revert to Judaism. When in fact one Marrano — Solomon *Molcho — actually did renew his Jewish faith,

Reuveni was forced to flee Portugal. After being harassed and hunted throughout Europe, both Reuveni and Molcho were said to have been burned at the stake.

By the 1660s the Jewish world was eagerly following the activities of *Shabbetai Zevi and later, Jacob *Frank (1726-1791); many convinced that the Messiah had at long last arrived. The Shabbatean movement was probably the most intense and widespread of all, involving almost all of the Jewish communities in high hopes and cruel disappointment.

In modern times, the Reform movement of Judaism and the Zionist experience have been viewed at one time or another as messianic activities. But, unfulfilled, messianism continues to be an important element in Judaism, providing a source of hope and inspiration.

METALS AND MINING. Six metals are mentioned in the Bible — gold, silver, copper, iron, tin, and lead. At various archaeological sites in Israel furnaces have been uncovered which were once used to smelt metals. The working of metals in biblical times was executed by special smiths and craftsmen, the first of whom was ". . . Tubal-Cain, who forged all implements of copper and iron" (Genesis 4:22). Metalcraft was especially important in the manufacture of spears, arrowheads and other weapons. Thus, *Nebuchadnezzar deported to Babylon not only Jehoiachin's army, but the craftsmen and smiths as well.

Gold. Specialized goldsmiths employed two methods in working gold. In some cases they beat the gold into very thin sheets, and in others they melted and cast it. Apparently there were seven recognized gradings of gold by quality. The gold entered Erez Israel via Egypt, Sudan, Saudia Arabia and India, where there

1. Nathan of Gaza, the prophet of Shabbetai Zevi.
2. Timna copper mines and processing plant near Eilat, Israel, where King Solomon had similar mines centuries before.

1 and 2. Workers at the Timna copper mines.

were mines. Filigree work was especially practiced by the Jews of Yemen.

Gold has always been a measure of wealth and status. It was rarely used as payment. Most graven images were made of gold as were the shields of King Solomon's guards, and gold leaf and gold casts were used in the building of the Tabernacle.

Silver. Silver mines in ancient times were located in Spain, Egypt and Anatolia. Like gold, siver was smelted with the use of bellows, and the slag extracted. Silver was used as a means of payment, in preference to gold, which was extremely soft. The Temple tax (the half shekel) was paid in silver.

Copper is referred to in the Bible, but it is not pure copper. It is in fact the alloy of copper and tin-bronze. From around 3000 b.c.e. until about 1200 b.c.e. it was the most useful and important of functional metals, being then gradually replaced by iron. Copper mines existed in Cyprus, Sinai and Egypt. It was the chief metal extracted in Erez Israel. It has been suggested that the protracted wars between Judah and Edom during the time of the kingdom of Judah were over control of the copper mines in the Aravah region.

The Timna copper mines are not considered to have been worked in Solomon's time, but were worked by Egyptians, Midianites, Kenites, and Amalekites. A copper snake dating to the time of the Exodus was discovered in an Egyptian temple excavated at Timna. The Philistine, Goliath, in the Bible is described in terms which show a highly developed military culture: "He had a helmet of bronze on his head, and he was armed with a coat of mail, and the weight of the coat was 5,000 shekels of bronze." A great many copper objects were taken to

Babylon by the conquerors after the destruction of the First Temple.

Iron. Isaiah describes the smith's technique of working iron with the help of charcoal to produce a metal suitable for making vessels. Iron was first exploited by the Hittites in Asia Minor, and it was brought to Syria and Erez Israel by Phoenician merchants. Iron was used primarily for weapons. Around 1200 b.c.e. the Philistines succeeded in gaining control of all the smiths ("Now there was to be found no smith throughout the land of Israel").

Tin and Lead. There was an extensive international trade in tin, which the Egyptians mined. It was also imported by the Phoenicians form Tarshish. The ancient sources of lead were Asia Minor and Syria. It was used in weights for fishermens' nets, as a cover of utensils, and may have been used in writing implements as well. Antimony, derived from lead, is mentioned in the Bible as an eye cosmetic.

The social standing of metalworkers in talmudic times was high, but there were distinctions between gold-and silversmiths and those who worked in base metals only. Rabbinic literature has many details of the processes of metalworking. According to the midrash, God created gold specifically for use in the Temple. In the famous basilica of the Sanhedrin in Alexandria, members sat on golden chairs. Also famous is the gold ornament *Akiva gave to his wife. On account of the idolatrous worship of the *Golden Calf, gold became a symbol of sin and was not to be used to sheath the *shofar* mouthpiece. On the Day of Atonement there was no gold on the vestments of the high priest; he officiated in robes of pure white linen. International treaties were inscribed on bronze tablets. Corinthian bronze, famous for its luster and quality, was used for the Nicanor Gates of the Herodian Temple in Jerusalem.

Despite many restrictions, Jews during the Christian era did participate in metal industries as lessees, managers, traders and even as miners. Their employment as minters of coins in Europe at a time when *Court Jews flourished, brought them into direct contact with gold and silver mining. In England Jews are recorded as having worked the Cornish tin mines in 1198 c.e. In Sicily there was a long tradition of Jewish mining dating from the time when the Emperor Tiberius sent 4,000 Jewish youths as slaves to the silver and iron mines. Two Jews organized the mining of lead in the Harz Mountains under Duke Frederick Ulrich of Brunswick in the 17th century.

Jews in modern times played a considerable part in

the mining and metal industries of industralized states. In Germany, from a small retail copper business, a huge international enterprise of Hirsch Kupfer-und Messingwerke A.G. developed. Another leading German metal firm owned by Jews was Metallgesellschaft. These enterprises were liquidated under Hilter. In Russia in 1807 there were 253 Jewish copper and tin workers in *Minsk, Kiev and Yekaterinoslav. By 1897 there were 15,669 Jewish smiths and 11,801 Jewish craftsmen in the various branches of the metal industry. Of the 96 large iron and tin plants in Odessa in 1910, 88 belonged to Jews. Jews were also represented on the boards of some of the largest gold and platinum mining companies. In the U.S. there were several prominent Jewish firms engaged in copper extraction, notably the Guggenheim family. In Poland and other European states Jews were also prominent in the coal industries, and in various parts of Czechoslovakia they were the first to extract coal. In South Africa Jews were among the pioneers in the extraction of coal, diamonds and gold and in base metal industries. Kimberley Jews played a major role in creation of the great mining groups which developed in the Witwatersrand. Notable were Barney Barnato, Lionel Philips, and Sir Ernest Oppenheimer, founder of the Anglo-African Corporation and chief of the De Beers diamond mining group. He also pioneered the copper industry in what was then Northern Rhodesia (now Zambia). Jewish industrialists were also first to engage in the commercial exploitation of petroleum products. (See also *Crafts, *Goldsmiths and Silversmiths, *Yemen.)

MEXICO is the largest country in Central America, with about 37,500 Jews out of a general population of 67,000,000. Jews have lived in Mexico since 1521, when the Spanish adventurer Cortes conquered the country. Those early Jews were Marranos, or secret Jews, and some forged documents proving four generations of Catholic ancestry to be allowed to enter the country. They suffered under the *Inquisition which came to Mexico in 1528, and which remained in operation there until the early 19th century — although the last mass burning of Marranos was in 1649.

In spite of persecution, Jews remained in Mexico and did much to develop trade and commerce there. They engaged in all occupations and many held official positions for the Spanish crown and even for the Church.

Mexico gained its independence from Spain in 1821, after which time the number of Jews in the country diminished. In 1862 Maximillian became emperor of Mexico, and Belgian, Austrian, French and Alsatian Jews came to the country with him. His personal physician, Samuel Basch, was an avowed Jew. Maximillian was overthrown by Benito Juarez, who believed in tolerance and religious freedom, and under him the Jewish population continued to grow. The rate of assimilation and intermarriage was high, but in 1885 the first organized congregation was formed.

Until the end of the century there was sporadic immigration from Russia and Galicia, followed by Jews from Aleppo, Syria, who brought a *shohet* (ritual slaughterer), Hebrew teachers and a *mohel* (circumcisor) to Mexico. They also built a *mikveh* (ritual bath house) and acquired a cemetery. Following the first World War, Jewish immigration from Eastern Europe increased. Many of the immigrants used Mexico as a stopping point *en route* to the U.S. When entry into America was restricted by the new immigration legislation introduced in 1924, however, Eastern European immigrants settled in Mexico instead and prospered. They introduced the system of selling on credit, which did much to raise the standard of living of the Mexican peasant.

From the economic depression of 1929-30 until Mexico entered World War II on the side of the Allies in 1942, there was growing anti-Semitism in the country. A quota was placed on immigration which effectively prevented many of Europe's Jewish refugees from entering Mexico. Anti-Semitism forced

1. Document appointing Pedro de Soto Lopez as an official of the Inquisition in Mexico, 1648.
2. Kosher restaurant in Mexico City, 1973.

Jewish stall operators to leave the public market and open private stores which, in fact, ultimately raised their economic status.

Following the war Mexico enjoyed an economic boom, and the Jewish population benefited from the situation. Today the majority of Jews are concentrated in Mexico City. There are separate Ashkenazi, Sephardi, Aleppo, German, Hungarian and American congregations. In 1967 there were ten Jewish educational institutions, 14 synagogues, and an active Jewish press. Mexican Jews sponsor many cultural activities: they hold an annual music month, and published a ten-volume Jewish encyclopaedia, *Enciclopedia Judaica Castellana* (1948-51).

Mexico's policy towards the Middle East conflict is one of neutrality. A trade agreement was signed between Israel and Mexico in 1952 and a cultural pact in 1969.

MEZUZAH (Hebrew: מְזוּזָה) is the name of the parchment scroll attached to the doorposts of a Jewish home. The word itself actually means "doorpost" but has come to refer to the scroll. On it are written verses from Deuteronomy (6:4-9 and 11:13-21) in square Assyrian letters, traditionally arranged in 22 lines. The Torah commands of these verses that "you shall write them on the doorposts *(mezuzot)* of your house and in your gates." The 12th century rabbinic authority, Maimonides, stresses that this commandment is to be observed purely from love of God, and that the *mezuzah* is not a good luck charm with power to ward off evil spirits. Many people, however, are accustomed to kiss the *mezuzah* or to touch it and then kiss the fingers when entering or leaving.

The parchment, made from the skin of a clean (permitted) animal, is rolled up inside a case with a small opening in such a way that the word *Shaddai* (Almighty), written on the back of the parchment, is visible through the opening. The three Hebrew letters which spell the word *Shaddai* are also the initials for the Hebrew words *shomer daltot Yisrael* (Guardian of the doors of Israel). The text of the *mezuzah* must be inspected twice in seven years to ensure that the writing remains legible.

The *mezuzah* is nailed to the right hand doorpost as you enter the room, in the top third of that doorpost, slanting inwards. The blessing, "Blessed are You . . . Who has commanded us to fix the *mezuzah*" is recited while affixing it. There should be a **1** *mezuzah* at the entrance to every home and on the

Mezuzot from around the world: 1) Italian, 15th century, in ivory case; 2) Eastern Europe, 19th century, wood carving; 3) Central Europe, 19th century, silver.

2   **3**

doorpost of every living room within the home – this of course excludes lavatories, bathrooms, storerooms and stables. It is also customary to place *mezuzot* at the entrances to synagogues and public buildings, including all government offices in Israel. In Israel a *mezuzah* must be put up immediately when a house is occupied by a Jew – outside Israel after the householder has lived in the house for 30 days. If the house is later sold to Jews, the *mezuzot* must be left on the doorposts. Today the *mezuzah* represents one of Judaism's most widely observed ceremonial commandments.

MICHELANGELO BUONARROTI (1475-1564), greatest of Renaissance painters and most admired of sculptors since the Greeks. He shared the common interest of his time in classic antiquity and expressed his passionate vigor and intense concentration in many subjects taken from

Jewish sources. His marble "David," a nude statue of the Goliath-slayer calmly awaiting his people's enemy, sling in hand, stands more than 13 feet high. It was carved from a huge, already partially-worked block that had been abandoned as unusable by an earlier sculptor. On September 8, 1504, the "David" was installed in place of Donatello's "Judith" at the entrance to the Palazzo Vecchio in Florence. Among the eminent group who had come together to choose the best site for the statue were Leonardo da Vinci, Botticelli, Pierro di Cosimo, and Filippino Lippi. A bronze "David," commissioned in 1502 and finished six years later, was sent to France and is now lost. Michelangelo's perfect knowledge of the human body exemplified in the "David" and in the *Cartoon of the Battle of Cascina* made him, at the age of 30, Italy's most renowned artist.

Among Michelangelo's most sublime works is the painting of the Sistine Chapel ceiling in the Vatican in Rome, commissioned by Pope Julius II in 1508. It depicts nine stories from the Bible and includes in all 300 human figures. The nine central pictures show the story of Genesis, from the Creation to the Flood, depicting the moral history of mankind — creation by God, the fall from grace, life in sin, and the wait for redemption. The painting took four years to complete and had a profound impression on Michelangelo's contemporaries, as it does on all who

have seen it since.

Between 1513 and 1516 Michelangelo completed a figure of "Moses," which was later augmented by others of "Rachel" and "Leah" as part of the Julius monument. Vasari in 1568 wrote of this statue: "When Michelangelo had finished the 'Moses' there was no other work to be seen, antique or modern, which could rival it." In its severe majesty it remains the most famous statue in all Rome.

MIDIAN. The Midianites were a group of nomadic peoples mentioned in the Bible as being among the sons of Abraham and Keturah who were sent to "the land of the East." Midianite traders are mentioned in connection with the sale of *Joseph, and Moses' father-in-law, *Jethro, was a Midianite priest. The elders of Midian displayed hostility toward the Israelites on the plains of Moab and the Israelites fought and slew many of them. After a war in which they were defeated by *Gideon, they ceased to be of political or military importance.

The range of the Midianites' wanderings was very broad: from Moab in the border region of Transjordan, along the border of the Arabian desert west of Edom, to the Sinai desert and the trade route between Erez Israel and Egypt. There was a Midianite settlement in northern Arabia during the Hellenistic-Roman period, which may have been a survival from

"The Creation of Adam," by Michelangelo, from the ceiling of the Sistine Chapel in Rome. God (right) is about to touch the outstretched hand of Adam to give him life. The figure of the Lord is carried on the wind and surrounded by cherubs. Eve, still uncreated, waits at His side.

a biblical settlement. In the Bible the Midianites are also referred to as "Ishmaelites." Some scholars connect these people with the Kushu tribes mentioned in an Egyptian text of the 18th century b.c.e., who wandered in the southern desert of Erez Israel. The Bible mentions a "Cushite woman" whom Moses married.

The Midianites were known as shepherds and traders. From time to time they would ally with other nomadic groups and attack permanent settlements around them. The Bible describes them as robbers.

According to the *aggadah* Midian allied with Moab against Israel. By making the Israelites drunk they succeeded in luring them to idolatry and forbidden relations with the daughters of Midian; for this reason the drinking of gentile wine was forbidden by Phinehas. It was he whom Moses commanded to lead the war against the Midianites, since Moses himself had previously found refuge in Midian when a fugitive from Egypt and felt that it would be an act of ingratitude to attack them even justifiably. Phinehas had already taken action against them by slaying the Midianite Princess Cozbi.

MIDRASH. The term *midrash* derives from the Hebrew root דרש, *drsh*, which means " to examine carefully," and is the name given to the process of intense examination of the Bible undertaken by the rabbis of the Mishnah, Talmud and later generations. The rabbis believed that the Bible, as the unique document containing the revelation of God to man, could not be understood merely in terms of a simple, surface reading of the verses. They recognized that the Bible was rich in information even on an elementary level, but since it was to serve as the legal and spiritual guide for all generations, it necessarily contained within it a wealth of hidden knowledge which could only be discovered by subjecting the text to a very careful process of literary analysis. Thus, the rabbis combed through the Bible in search of these concealed truths, guided, in the process, by established rules of interpretation, called *hermeneutics. The overall technique of analysis came to be called *midrash*. When it was applied to the strictly legal portions of the Bible, what emerged was called *midrash halakhah;* when it was applied to the narrative and historical material, *midrash aggadah*.

Midrashim of *halakhah* and *aggadah* can be found scattered throughout the Talmud, but most have been

Title page of *Midrash Rabba* to the Five Scrolls, among the best-known collections of aggadic midrashim.

preserved in separate anthologies which were collected and edited over a period of several hundred years. The earliest date from the time of the *tana'im* (sages of the Mishnah) and are midrashim of *halakhah*. They cover the main legal portions of the last four books of the Pentateuch (Genesis is purely narrative), and are known respectively as *Mekhilta de Rabbi Ishmael* (Exodus), *Sifra* (Leviticus), *Sifrei* (Numbers), and *Sifrei* (Deuteronomy). Their goal was to expand the limited legal information contained in the verse itself. Through the application of the hermeneutical rules, the full implications of a given law were spelled out. As a consequence, general principles could be established which allowed the adoption of legislation to cover new situations not elaborated in the verse itself. (For a fuller description of this process, see *Law, Jewish.) In later legal discussions, all four books are considered to be supplementary (but equivalent in status) to the halakhic material found in the Mishnah, and numerous segments can actually be found quoted by the *amora'im* in the Talmud.

Midrashim of *aggadah* are more numerous and more varied in quality. Some (like the midrashim of *halakhah*) consist of verse by verse commentaries on the biblical stories, but most take the form of extended essays or sermons. A large proportion of these actually originated as sermons delivered orally in the synagogue on the Sabbath or festivals, and only later were they written down in the form in which they have been preserved. In general, the goal of these sermons was ethical-spiritual. They sought to draw out moral lessons from the biblical stories, by employing all sorts of literary and rhetorical devices to expand upon the basic information supplied by the text. Biographical features of biblical heroes and villains would be filled in, and their behavior contrasted and compared in the attempt to bring the stories to life and thus instill in the listeners (readers) a particular moral appreciation of the events. Today's sermon is very much a continuation of this ancient form of preaching, and in fact the modern word for sermon, *derashah,* derives from the same root as *midrash.* Among the best-known collections of aggadic midrashim are those called *Rabba* (covering most of the Pentateuch and the Five Scrolls), *Tanḥuma,* and one of the last anthologies to be edited, the *Yalkut Shimoni* (see also *Aggadah).

MIGRATION, wandering from place to place, has been one of the major components of Jewish history, for since the time of the Patriarchs the "wandering Jew" has suffered from a lack of territory, government, and defense. Major Jewish migrations in search of favorable living conditions and in flight from harassment, persecution and expulsion, include the Exodus from Egypt, the Babylonian exile, Jewish settlement outside Ereẓ Israel during the Second

2

Temple period, the dispersion under the Roman and Near Eastern empires after the destruction of the Second Temple. The scattering of Jews throughout the Christian and Islamic states, culminating in the expulsion from the Iberian peninsula in 1492 and their settlement in the New World since the early stages of the European colonization, a process that greatly accelerated in the latter half of the 19th century. Throughout the period of the Diaspora, small numbers of Jews made their way back to Ereẓ Israel, the land promised them in covenant with their God.

Since economic motivation was far less dominant in Jewish migrations than in those of gentiles, Jews have tended not to re-emigrate to their countries of origin. The relative volume of Jewish migration in recent times has far surpassed that of any other people. There were an estimated 7.5 million Jews in the world in the 1880s. Since then six million Jews have taken part in international migrations. There have been three main periods of intensive recent migration.

1881-1914. Vast numbers of Jewish refugees (about 2.4 million) in this period left the Czarist empire, eastern Austria-Hungary and Rumania for the United States, which then allowed free entry, Canada, Argentina, Ereẓ Israel, and South Africa. The waves of pogroms in 1881 and 1905 in Russia increased the overseas movement of Jews, but the outbreak of World War I put an abrupt stop to the gathering momentum of emigration. The Jews often brought their wives and entire families with them and so had a higher proportion of women and children in their number than other immigrant groups. During this period about 70,000 Jews migrated to Ereẓ Israel, though a considerable number then left again, mainly

1

1. Jewish immigrants to the United States passing through the depot of Ellis Island in New York.
2. Jewish migrants from Eastern to Central Europe in the *Beriḥah,* the organized underground operation moving survivors of World War II out of Europe and on to "illegal" immigration to Palestine.

because of economic difficulties. Very many of the migrants were attracted to the U.S.

Within Europe some 360,000 Jews migrated from east to west before 1914. There was also considerable movement southward within Russia, toward Odessa. In addition, many Jews participated in the general movement of rural populations to urban centers.

1915-May 1948. During this intermediate period between migration to the U.S. and that to Israel, there occurred an event which entirely changed the demographic distribution of the Jewish people – the *Holocaust. During World War I, Jewish intercontinental migration dwindled, but there were large movements of Jewish refugees in Europe seeking to escape from the areas of hostilities. Thereafter overseas migration increased once more, comprising more than 400,000 Jews during 1921-25 (280,000 of them going to the U.S.). Between 1919 and 1926 almost 100,000 Jews immigrated to Erez Israel

following the *Balfour Declaration. Within Europe the drift from east to west continued.

Then, in 1921 and 1924 immigration restriction laws were enforced in the U.S. which drastically reduced the numbers of Jews allowed in from Eastern Europe. Between 1925 and 1930 only about 10,000 Jews per annum entered the country. Other countries which had previously been havens for Jewish refugees also introduced curbs. After the first few years of the communist regime, the Soviet government began to frown on emigration, and soon brought it to a virtual standstill. After World War I there was some stabilization within Europe, but by contrast, considerable unemployment in Palestine caused emigration from the area during the 1920s. Many Jews turned from the U.S. or Palestine toward Latin America.

In the 1930s, motives for migration from Europe tragically increased with the rise to power of Adolf

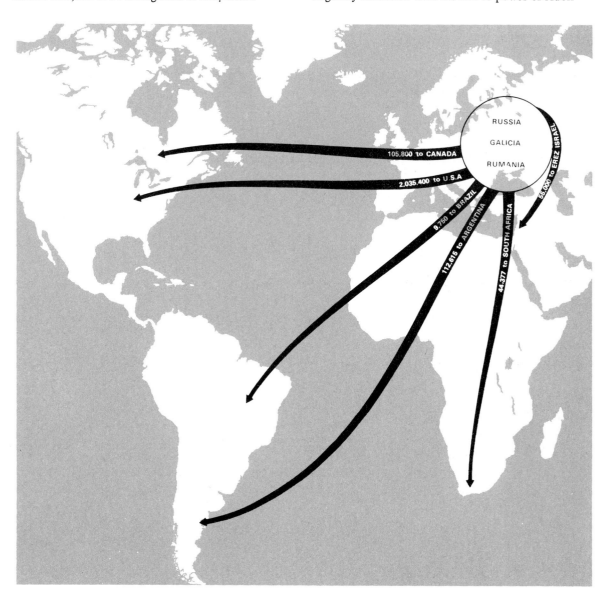

Intercontinental migrations, 1881-1914.

*Hitler and his Nazi party, the economic depression, and overt anti-Jewish policies in many European states. However, the more desperate the Jews became, the tighter did prospective countries of refuge close their doors against them. In the 1930s Jews made attempts to escape from the horrors of Nazism, from anti-Jewish hostility in Communist Eastern Europe, and from growing anti-Jewish fanaticism and intolerance in the Arab states, particularly since 1948.

Before the outbreak of World War II some 350,000 Jews left Germany, Austria and Czechoslovakia. They have continued leaving Eastern Europe, barring the Soviet Union, which greatly restricted their freedom of movement. Increasingly, the destiny of these refugees has been the reborn State of Israel. Between 1932 and 1939 almost 50% of intercontinental Jewish migrants turned to Palestine. The British Mandate White Paper of 1939, however, severely restricted Jewish immigration into Palestine, and was countered by organized *illegal immigration. Between 1938 and 1942 Jews again turned to the U.S.

As the Nazi armies swept across Europe, there were tragically few opportunities for Jews to escape, the most notable exception being in the east where many Soviet and Polish Jews managed to retreat eastward, some joining the armed struggle against the common enemy. Sweden gave refuge to the Jews of occupied Denmark. On the whole, however, the world, engrossed in war, was indifferent to the fate of these people and between 1940 and 1945, only 45,000 were allowed to reach Palestine. The rest, numbering seven to eight millions, were left to "migrate" within the area of the warring armies until most met their fate in the mass graves of the *concentration camps. The few who survived the war in Europe drifted back to their places of origin, though in some areas, like Poland, further pogroms occurred as late as 1946. Many therefore moved on to *displaced persons camps in Germany, Austria and Italy. The British allowed only 70,000 to go to Palestine between 1945 and May 1948, interning many others in Cyprus, and even sending some back to Germany. A small number of these refugees went to the U.S. The proportion of young adults, many with agricultural training, who entered Palestine between 1919 and 1948 was high, in contrast to the older generation which made its way to the U.S.

Within the Soviet Union after the 1917 revolution, hundreds of thousands of Jews took advantage of the ending of their former "ghettoization" in the Pale of Settlement to move into the central and southern parts of the country. Others were moved to Siberia to participate in the ill-starred experiment of a Jewish autonomous region — *Birobidzhan. In most cases, migrant Jews moved immediately to the large urban centers of their new countries.

From May 1948. This period is dominated by large-scale migration to the State of Israel. Unfortunately the U.S.S.R. and most Islamic countries of the Middle East placed obstacles in the way of would-be Jewish emigrants. In the early years of Israel, Eastern Europe and and the Islamic states were drained of most of their Jews. Within the short span of one or two years the vast majority of Jews from Iraq (123,000), Yemen and Aden (48,000), Libya (31,000), and Bulgaria (37,000), were transferred to Israel. Within Israel the *Jewish Agency and the new government organized massive settlement programs. Between 1948 and 1951 almost 700,000 Jews migrated to Israel, and a further 100,000 elsewhere. From 1955 to 1957 two-thirds of the almost 250,000 migrant Jews went to Israel (from Morocco, Tunisia, Egypt, Poland and Hungary). Half of a further 450,000 migrant Jews went to Israel between 1961 and 1964. (Virtually all Jews left Algeria for France during 1961-62.)

An undoubted change has occurred in the motive for migration since the 1880s. From that time on the main motive had been distress. By the mid-1960s, however, most of those Jews forced to migrate from their places of origin by such circumstances as war and intolerance had left. Thus, future migrations would depend on two main sources: the Soviet Union (where restrictions on emigration of its almost three million Jews continued in the 1980s) and the affluent west (nearly six million of whose Jews lived in the United States). For other aspects of migrations, see *Beriḥah.

MIKHOELS, SOLOMON (1890-1948). The Yiddish actor Solomon Mikhoels (stage name Solomon Vovsi) was head of the Moscow State Jewish Theater and chairman of the Jewish anti-Fascist League, which attempted to gain Western Jewish support against Nazi Germany after that country had attacked the Soviet Union in 1941. Born in Dvinsk, he studied law at St. Petersburg (Leningrad), but then joined Alexander Granovsky's Jewish drama studio. This moved to Moscow and became the State Jewish Theater in 1919. Mikhoels' distinction as an actor lay in his command of both tragic and tragicomic roles.

Solomon Mikhoels, Yiddish actor who was assassinated by Soviet secret police.

He played such famous roles as Shimele Soroker in *Two Hundred Thousand* and Benjamin in *The Travels of Benjamin the Third*. One of his most memorable performances was as King Lear in 1935.

On January 13, 1948, while on an official mission in Minsk on behalf of the State Committee for Theater Prizes, Mikhoels was brutally murdered, ostensibly by hooligans, or in a car accident. In fact, as was later admitted, he was assassinated by the Soviet Secret Police on the orders of Joseph Stalin, head of the Soviet Communist Party. Many thousands of Jews took part in his state funeral in Moscow.

Mikhoels' murder was the first step in the liquidation of all Jewish cultural institutions and of most outstanding Yiddish writers, artists and actors which occurred in Stalin's final years.

In Tel Aviv a square was named in his honor in 1962, the tenth anniversary of the execution of a large number of Russian Jewish writers by the Soviet government on false charges in connection with a so-called "doctors' plot" to murder Stalin.

MIKVEH (Hebrew: מִקְוֶה — "a collection [of water]"), a special pool of water constructed according to rigid legal specifications, immersion in which renders ritually clean a person who has become ritually unclean. (For details concerning the nature and laws of ritual impurity, see *Purity and Impurity, Ritual.) Like the synagogue and the cemetery, the *mikveh* is a basic element of Jewish family and communal life, and thus the erection of a *mikveh* was among the first projects undertaken by Jewish communities throughout the world from earliest times. In the ruins of many of the ancient settlements in Erez Israel, *mikva'ot* have been discovered intact, with perhaps the most famous of them being in the fortress of *Masada.

Just how to construct a *mikveh* in accordance with the numerous legal specifications involved constantly posed a technological problem of great seriousness, and over the generations rabbinic thinkers were repeatedly challenged to come up with novel solutions to this unusual problem which demanded a rare combination of technologic and halakhic ingenuity.

Briefly the basic legal requirements are these:
1) A *mikveh* must not be filled with water that has been drawn (i.e., has been in a vessel or a receptacle), but with water from a naturally flowing source; spring water or rainwater are the ideal sources, but melted snow and ice are also permitted.

1. Solomon Mikhoels in the role of King Lear in the production by the Jewish State Theater, April, 1935.
2. *Mikveh* in the basement of the 18th-century synagogue of Carpentras, France.

2) The water must be able to flow into the *mikveh* freely and unimpeded (any blockage renders the water "drawn water") and must reach the *mikveh* in vessels that are not susceptible to ritual uncleanness.
3) The minimum size of the *mikveh* is of a vessel which has a volume of "40 *seah*," variously estimated at between 250 and 1,000 liters (quarts).
4) The *mikveh* must be watertight and must be constructed of natural materials on the spot, for otherwise it is deemed itself to be a "vessel" and renders the water in it "drawn water."

Where large amounts of rainwater or spring water are available, the problem of establishing an adequate feed to replenish the *mikveh* is not great, but since most *mikva'ot* are built in urban centers where such supplies are not available, the technological and legal solution of a valid *mikveh* depends upon a fifth principle which stipulates that once a properly constructed *mikveh* is filled with the minimum amount of non-drawn water, drawn water can then be added to it indefinitely and not render it invalid. Several ingenious designs have been developed over the generations which take advantage of this principle, but no one design was ever universally accepted, and thus many of the *mikva'ot* differ in many of their details, in accordance with the rabbinic authority whose solution was adopted.

In modern times, many improvements have been

made in the physical and hygienic aspects of the *mikveh*. Now it is almost a universal custom to build baths and showers as an adjunct to the *mikva'ot* and in the United States in particular, many *mikva'ot* are even provided with such added amenities as steam rooms and beauty parlors.

MIKVEH ISRAEL is an agricultural school situated east of Tel Aviv. It was established in 1870 by Charles Netter of the *Alliance Israelite Universelle. He leased land from the Turkish government, gained financial support from such bodies as the Anglo-Jewish Association and individuals like Baron Edmund de *Rothschild, and opened his school. He took its name from Jeremiah (14:8 and 17:13) — "Hope of Israel," as he saw the agricultural development of Erez Israel as the future hope of the Jewish people.

Among Mikveh Israel's first pupils was a group of Russian immigrants (Bilu pioneers) who went on to found *Rishon le-Zion after their training at Mikveh Israel. When the German Kaiser, Wilhelm II, visited Palestine in 1898, Theodor *Herzl chose to greet him at the entrance to the school. Eliyahu Krause (1876-1962), the Russian-born agronomist, was director of Mikveh Israel between 1914 and 1955. Under him, both language and agriculture were developed: Hebrew became the official language of instruction, and numerous species of fruit and forest trees were pioneered and the improvement of farm branches studied. By the 1930s Mikveh Israel had become an important education center for *Youth Aliyah.

During the *War of Independence of 1948, the school was attacked several times, but survived. Today it is a state-run institution consisting of

schools for both religious and non-religious pupils. It has a cultural center, library, botanical gardens and a collection of 130 citrus species. Mikveh Israel has developed new techniques in citrus growing and introduced avocado cultivation and the acclimatization of many livestock strains. Its wine cellars produce select wines and liqueurs. The school is the home of over 1,000 persons: pupils, teachers and instructors.

MILITARY SERVICE. Jews have served in the armies of most of the countries in which they settled, although in many countries before the 20th century, they were denied the right to bear arms, just as they were denied civil rights, being considered second-class citizens. In the 20th century Jews played a full part in both World Wars, and more than one million served in each of them. In recent times the military achievements of the Israel Defense Forces in defense of the state have focused attention on the fighting qualities of the Jewish soldier.

In the United States Jews first served as militia during the colonial period, and stood guard against Indian attack. In the 1750s they took part in the

1. Entrance to the Mikveh Israel Agricultural School. 2. Members of the elite Jewish Municipal Guard in Warsaw, one of the limited forms of military service permitted to Jews during the uprising against Russian rule in 1830-31.

conquest of Canada, several being commanders in campaigns. A considerable number of Jews also served in the colonial armies in the American War of Independence (1775-83). Captain John Ordraonaux seized nine British prize vessels and later captured a British frigate, and Uriah P. *Levy, who joined the U.S. navy in 1812 rose through the ranks to become commodore; his ship sank 21 British vessels during the the second war between the U.S. and Britain. In the American Civil War (1861-65) about 6,000 Jews fought on the Union side and fewer in the Confederate forces, though these included the secretary of war, Judah P. Benjamin, the first surgeon general, David de Leon, and 23 staff officers. A number of Jews on both sides became generals during the war.

In World War I, 250,000 Jews fought in the army of the U.S. (representing 5% of the Jewish population of the U.S., whereas only 3% of gentiles served). Over 15,000 Jews were killed or wounded in the 18-month campaign. There were 10,000 Jewish officers, three of them generals, a number of high rank in the navy, and six winners of the Congressional Medal of Honor. Over 200 received the Distinguished Service Cross. During World War II, over 500,000 U.S. Jews served in the Allied forces. More than 50,000 were killed or wounded. In addition, 150,000 Jews served in the Korean war and 30,000 in Vietnam.

Until the repeal of the 1673 Test Act in 1828, British Jews were debarred from service as officers in the British army. Despite this, Wellington reported that 15 men of Jewish origin served under him at Waterloo in 1815. After 1828 a number of professing Jews became officers, especially in India. In the South African War (1899-1902), 127 Jews were killed under

2

arms. In World War I, 50,000 British Jews served, five winning Victoria crosses, the highest British military award. They formed their own unit, the Zion Mule Corps, and three Jewish units, the 38th, 39th and 40th battalions of the Royal Fusiliers, took part in Allenby's conquest of Palestine in 1918. The outstanding army commander of World War I was a Jew, Sir John *Monash. Over 60,000 Jews served in the British Army during World War II, two of them winning Victoria crosses. The Deputy Director of Military Intelligence at the War Office was a Jew, Brigadier Sir Edward Beddington. Abraham Briscoe was the first Jew to reach the rank of air commodore in the Royal Air Force.

In 1827 Jews living in Czarist Russia, under Nicholas I, began to be conscripted into the army for periods of up to 25 years. Ten in every thousand Jews were taken, most being between 12 and 25 years of age. Excluded from the officer ranks, they were continually pressured to convert to Christianity, and under the terrible conditions of service Jews tried as best they could to avoid conscription. For more on this, see *Cantonists. Under Alexander II the seizure of Jewish children for military service was abolished, and the maximum period of service reduced to 15 years. During World War I half a million Jews served

1.   The Zion Mule Corps on parade in Egypt in 1915, the year in which this body of Jewish volunteers, as part of the British Army, fought the Turks on the Gallipoli peninsula.
2.   Jewish soldiers in the Turkish army.

1

ימים שמונעין הכמי האומות להקז

מרצו	הוד ניסן	יום ל		בכניסתו		ייס	ג	ביציאתו
אפרילי	הוד אייר	ייס י		בכניסתו		ייס	יא	ביציאתו
מיי	הוד סיון	ייס ג		בכניסתו		ייס	ז	ביציאתו
זוניו	הוד תמוז	יס ז		בכניסתו		ייס	טו	ביציאתו
לוליו	הוד אב	יס יב		בכניסתו		ייס	י	ביציאתו
אגשטו	הוד אלול	ייס א		בכניסתו		ייס	ב	ביציאתו
סיטיברי	הוד תשרי	יום ג		בכניסתו		ייס	י	ביציאתו
אוטוברי	הוד מרחשון	ייס א		בכניסתו		ייס	ג	ביציאתו
נוביברי	הוד כסלו	ייס ה		בכניסתו		ייס	ז	ביציאתו
דיצימרי	הוד טבת	ייס ז		בכניסתו		ייס	ז	ביציאתו
יינרו	הוד שבט	יום א		בכניסתו		ייס	ג	ביציאתו
פירברי	הוד אדר	יוד ד		בכניסתו		ייס	ג	ביציאנו

Medicine. Doctor bleeding a patient — a primitive form of medical treatment. 17th-century illustration of a listing of "days when bleeding is prohibited."

1. **Marriage.** China platter depicting wedding ceremony.
England, 1769.
2. **Moon.** ''New Moon Prayers,'' painting by A. Bender,
late 19th century.

2

1

in the Russian army and several thousand won awards for bravery. Following the revolution of 1917, Jews were allowed to become officers. Four divisional commanders of the Red Army were Jews and a Jew became deputy commander of the air force. However, most of those Jewish officers who reached high rank were murdered during Stalin's purges. Grigori Stern, a full general, was an exception. He routed the Japanese army and later commanded Soviet Far Eastern Forces. Almost 500,000 Soviet Jews fought in World War II, at least 140 of them being awarded the title Hero of the Soviet Union. Jews constituted a disproportionately large number of senior officers — there were more than 70 Jewish generals. They held key positions in the Battle of Stalingrad and during the final assault on Berlin. Following the end of the war, Soviet policy toward the Jewish soldier changed for the worse. Most of the Jewish generals were retired by 1953.

Although free to bear arms in Gemany as early as the 12th century, this right was gradually withdrawn from Jews, especially following the Crusades of the 13th century. Jews were prominent in the following centuries as military contractors, however. Because of growing anti-Semitism in the 19th century, virtually no Jews became officers, though they had been allowed to commission in the Prussian reserve forces since 1845 and had shown exemplary conduct in

both the Austro-Prussian (1866) and Franco-Prussian (1870-71) wars. About 2,000 officers were commissioned during World War I and 12,000 Jewish soldiers were killed in battle on the German side. All Jews were removed from the army of the Weimar republic in 1933, when Hitler came to power.

In France during the Middle Ages Jews were generally forbidden to bear arms, except in emergencies. Their position did not change until the French Revolution of 1789, after which they became liable for service along with all other Frenchmen. The outstanding Jewish soldier of Napoleon's army was Henri Rottenberg, who was made a major general in 1814. Nevertheless, many gentile officers refused to allow Jews into their ranks, and restricted the right of promotion.

Under the Third Republic (1870-1940) there were 23 Jewish generals, though Jews were still subject to anti-Semitism, as the *Dreyfus case exemplified. Of the 39 French Jewish airmen of World War I, all but four were killed in action, as were more than 8,000 other French Jews. Following the French defeat in 1940, many French and East European Jews joined the Free French forces under Gen. Charles de Gaulle. Jews were also prominent in the French resistance movement.

In most countries of Europe and in the United States provision has been made for the appointment of Jewish chaplains to serve the spiritual needs of servicemen and servicewomen, and not a few of these were conspicuous for their gallantry under fire, some paying with their lives.

(For a description of military service in Israel see the section Israel Defense Forces in the article *Israel, and *War of Independence, Israel, *Sinai Campaign, *Six-Day War, *Yom Kippur War.)

MINORITY RIGHTS. The Jews have an extremely long history of having been a minority. In Egypt, in Babylonia, and all during the extended period from the dispersion by the Romans in 70 c.e., until the founding of the State of Israel in 1948, Jews have found themselves living in situations in which they had little or no power over the governments that ruled their lives. Unstable situations led some Jews to strive for security through assimilation into the majority group, in the hope of being treated as equals; or through autonomy, that is living apart and maintaining their own communal responsibility for internal matters. The security gained by either of these methods, however, often proved an illusion

Tombstones in the Israel military cemetery on Mt. Herzl, Jerusalem.

since it rested upon the goodwill of the majority around them.

At the Versailles Peace Conference after World War I, an attempt was made, partly at the urging of a strong Jewish group, to bridge the gap between equal rights for all and special treatment for minorities. In addition to calling for respect for the political rights of the individual, the treaty required certain states to acknowledge the right of minorities to their own language as well as to separate religious and educational institutions. This was necessary because the diplomats at the conference had prepared a new map of Europe, altering the shape of old countries and creating several new ones. The boundaries they drew on their maps often ignored the actual distribution of ethnic groups and created a number of minority situations which had not previously existed. With these other minorities the Jews were supposed to have their rights protected. But the machinery set up by the treaty for implementing its provisions did not function satisfactorily, and like the League of Nations itself, gradually ceased to operate.

Today in Israel Jews find themselves a majority and are facing the problem of putting into practice their traditional concern for minorities. Israel must

not only protect herself from attack by neighboring Arab countries, she must also fight the natural human inclination to be provoked by acts of war and terrorism into taking revenge upon the large Arab minority living within her borders.

MINSK, capital of the Belorussian Soviet Socialist Republic. Jews were first granted permission to live there in 1579, and by the 17th century were a firmly established factor in the town's commercial life. In 1685 a yeshivah was established by a local rabbi. During the 19th century Minsk's Jewish community was one of the largest and most important in the country. By 1897 its population had reached 47,562, making it the fourth largest community in the *Pale of Settlement. *Mitnaggedim* were influential and *Ḥasidism relatively weak. At the turn of the century Judah Leib Perelmann, (known as the *gadol* — i.e. great man — of Minsk) officiated as rabbi.

Minsk was one of the places where the Jewish labor movement originated and developed. Jewish Socialists were very active there during the 1880s and 1890s, and the Jewish Bund for a time had its headquarters there. Jews dominated the revolutionary meetings in the town in 1905 and were also the principal victims of the riots which, in the October of that year, were directed at liberal elements in general. Later Zionism became very influential, and the Second Convention of Russian Zionists was held in Minsk.

Following the establishment of the Soviet regime, Jewish traditional life was suppressed and replaced by Jewish-Communist cultural activities. At the outbreak of World War II in 1939 there were approximately 90,000 Jews in Minsk. By 1959 there were between 40,000 and 60,000. Many thousands perished during the war, when the German army seized the city and

1. A petition to Oliver Cromwell signed by seven London Jews headed by Manasseh ben Israel, March 24, 1655. It asks the Lord Protector of the Commonwealth for the right to conduct services in their own homes.
2. The synagogue in Minsk, 1973.

set up a Jewish slave labor camp and ghetto, and perpetrated a series of cold-blooded massacres and live burials. The resistance record of the Jews of the Minsk ghetto is unique. Many Jews escaped to join the partisans fighting in the surrounding forests, and Isaac Pavlovich Kozinets, later discovered to be a Jew, became leader of the whole underground resistance movement in the Minsk area. A memorial to the Jewish victims of the Holocaust was erected in the city immediately after the war — the only such monument in the Soviet Union bearing a Yiddish inscription. The Great Synagogue of Minsk was closed down in 1959 and *mazzah* baking was banned for several years. Periodic arrests and harassments of Zionists frequently occur.

MIRACLES. Extraordinary phenomena that seem to fall outside the pattern of normal, explainable occurrences are frequently referred to in English as miracles. In the Bible, such events are termed *otot* or *moftim* ("wondrous signs"), and in the talmudic literature as *nisim* ("heralds"). The terms point to the fact that both for the Bible and for the rabbis, miraculous events were caused by God and served as clear indicators of His controlling power in the universe. When the Red Sea parted to enable the Israelites to flee from the Egyptian armies that were pursuing them, and when the "sun stood still" at Gibeon to enable Joshua to be victorious in his battle with the Canaanites, miracles occurred; at a critical moment in human history, God altered the normal workings of physical phenomena (the sea, the sun), and by doing so, revealed His providential relationship to the people of Israel. Later thinkers, for whom "the natural order" had an existence independent of God, were troubled by the question whether biblical miracles were "natural" or "supernatural," but the Bible makes no such distinction and never questions God's ability to do anything, by any means.

The rabbis of the Talmud unquestionably accepted the biblical miracles as related, but they were troubled by the fact that they seemed to imply a lack of perfection in the very act of *Creation. They solved this theological problem by postulating that miracles were, so to speak, provided for already at the time of creation. Thus, although they were "extraordinary" they were still manifestations of the natural order. Many rabbis reversed this perspective and emphasized that the very regularity and harmony of

The miracle of "The Ascension of Elijah," depicted in a painting by Francesco Polazzo, c. 1730.

The miracle of the crossing of the Red Sea; woodcut by Jacob Steinhardt, 1921.

the natural world were in fact "miraculous." It is this thought which is vocalized in the thanksgiving prayer which is part of the daily *Amidah: "We thank You for Your miracles which are daily with us, and for Your wonders and benefits, which are wrought at all times, evening, morning and night."

The rabbis rejected, however, the belief in "miracle performers" as bearers of religious truth. Once the Torah had been revealed to man, it was no longer "in heaven." It could not be altered by extraordinary means, but only by a natural process of development which was purely in the hands of ordinary human beings. And although the rabbis emphasized the miraculous aspect of the story of *Hanukkah, they generally believed that by their time the age of miracles had ceased, since only in biblical times were people "willing to sacrifice themselves for the sanctification of the Name of God."

In the Middle Ages, the biblical miracles posed a great problem for Jewish philosophers. They could not be explained in terms of contemporary science and they flew in the face of the philosophers' strong belief in the existence of an unchanging order to the universe. As a solution, many of the medieval philosophers adopted the talmudic position outlined

above which attempted to "naturalize" the miracles by seeing them as having been woven into the order of nature from the very beginning; their miraculous nature stemmed from the fact that they were expressed at the key moment in history when they were most needed.

In modern times, some people have attempted to offer scientific explanations for several of the biblical miracles, such as the parting of the Red Sea. Others have "relativized" them by viewing them as natural occurrences which were recorded as if extraordinary and supernatural, because of the crucial role they played at the particular time.

MIXED SPECIES. According to Judaism, the world was created by God for man's use and benefit, yet God also placed certain restrictions on this use, among them those relating to mixed species.

From two verses in the Bible: Leviticus 19:19 and Deuteronomy 22:9-11, the rabbis learned that six types of mixed species called *kilayim* are forbidden: 1) sowing of different species mixed together or too close to each other; 2) grafting different species of trees and/or vegetables; 3) mixing of seeds in a vineyard; 4) cross-breeding of animals; 5) plowing with animals of different species yoked together; 6) mixing of wool and linen in the fabric of a garment. The prohibition against sowing mixed seeds is restricted to Erez Israel. The other limitations apply everywhere.

The reasons given for these restrictions vary. *Naḥmanides asserted that it is forbidden to change the order of creation. Mixing different things was also a practice of idolators and considered unnatural. *Maimonides explained that to breed animals of different species defies the laws of nature and of ethics. According to *Philo, restrictions in the vineyard were necessary because mixing produced "too great a burden upon the earth." On the other hand, *Rashi wrote that these statutes are "a royal (i.e. divine) decree, for which there is no reason." Whichever opinion is held, the fact is that the fields of the Jews were well cultivated and productive and the purity of plant species was preserved.

The details of the six restrictions are presented in the Mishnah tractate *Kilayim.* Possibly the most interesting relate to *sha'atnez,* garments made of cloth woven or sewn of wool and linen. The clothing of priests was exempted. Samson Raphael Hirsch, a German rabbi of the 19th century, understood this commandment to be a reminder to man that his assigned place and purpose in the world, and that of all other species, must be preserved.

In many cities with a large Jewish population, laboratories have been established to test clothing for *sha'atnez.*

MIZRACHI. "The Land of Israel for the people of Israel according to the Torah of Israel." This was the motto of the religious Zionist movement known as Mizrachi, which has played an active role in the World Zionist Organization since 1902.

The name Mizrachi which can mean eastward, was actually coined from some of the letters of the Hebrew words *merkaz ruhani,* "spiritual center" and reflects their aim of making Israel the spiritual and religious center of world Jewry.

Mizrachi was founded by Rabbi Isaac Reines who became its first president in the early days of the Zionist movement. Combining *Orthodoxy and *Zionism, it was a revolutionary idea and met with strong opposition on the part of Orthodox European rabbis, who considered Zionism to be a heretical movement. Even among Reines' followers, there were those who feared that the irreligious majority in the Zionist movement would denigrate the status of religion in the new Jewish state and replace it with secular "cultural" motifs. Nevertheless, during their first convention in March 1902, Mizrachi voted to set aside their fears and devote themselves wholeheartedly to the Zionist cause.

During its first year, Mizrachi succeeded in building 210 branches in Russia alone and soon spread throughout Europe. In 1905 the first branches opened in Erez Israel.

One of the most famous Mizrachi leaders to emerge at the early stages of the movement was Rabbi Meir *Bar-Ilan who coined the slogan mentioned above. Bar-Ilan served in a number of positions within the movement and under his leadership the first Mizrachi Conference to be held in the United States was convened in 1914 in Cincinnati, Ohio.

In 1920 the world center of the Mizrachi movement moved to Jerusalem, thus becoming the first Zionist party to establish its center in Erez Israel. They were soon joined by religious pioneer laborers who established Ha-Poel Ha-Mizrachi, the labor wing of the Mizrachi movement.

Under the impetus of Rabbi Abraham Isaac *Kook, Mizrachi helped establish the office of Chief Rabbinate in Israel and designed an entire educational

network in Israel, running from kindergarten through high school, yeshivot, vocational schools and teachers' seminaries. In 1954, these were incorporated into the government-run educational system.

The yeshivot have been the most outstanding achievement of Mizrachi education, being unique in that students receive both a yeshivah and a general education. Bar-Ilan University, established by Mizrachi of the United States, carries this tradition to the highest academic levels. Mizrachi also sponsors various youth groups such as *Benei Akiva (see section on youth movements in *Israel).

Ha-Poel Ha-Mizrachi has been responsible for establishing religious settlements in Israel, starting with moshavim in the 1920s and kibbutzim in the 1930s. A branch of Ha-Poel Ha-Mizrachi called *Ha-Kibbutz ha-Dati* (The Religious Kibbutz) formed blocs of religious kibbutzim in border areas, many of which (such as the Ezyon bloc in the Hebron area) were wiped out during the *War of Independence. Today there are about 80 such religious settlements in Israel.

Mizrachi has been an active partner in Israel's government since 1948, fighting for the preservation of the Jewish religious character of the state, and has consistently polled about 10 percent of the vote. In 1956, Mizrachi and Ha-Poel Ha-Mizrachi founded a united National Religious Party *(Miflagah Datit Leummit* — MafDal) which has often been the center of political controversy. Most of its members oppose the withdrawal from the territory on the west bank of the Jordan which was occupied in the *Six-Day War and its stand on the "Who is a Jew?" issue delayed its joining the 1974 Rabin Coalition government.

1. Mizrachi conference in Lida, Poland, 1903. Among the participants was Isaac Reines (no. 14) and Judah Leib (Fishman) Maimon, prominent religious Zionist leader (no. 10).
2. Hayyim Moshe Shapira, Mizrachi leader, member of the first Israel cabinet, 1949.

1. Papercut *mizrah* plaque, American or English, 1810.
2. Mnemonic form for remembering the order of the benedictions: *yayin, kiddush, ner, havdalah, zeman.* From a 15th-century German *Haggadah.*

MIZRAH. The Hebrew word *mizrah* means "east" and for most Jews it designates the direction to be faced when reciting the **Amidah* prayer. This tradition results from the fact that Jerusalem is east of most Jewish congregations in the Diaspora, and by facing *mizrah* they direct their prayers towards the sacred Temple Mount.

In the western hemisphere, most synagogues are built with the holy ark on the eastern wall. Of course, east of Jerusalem prayers are recited facing westward rather than *mizrah;* in the south, northward; and in the north southward. According to the rabbis, if a person is unable to determine the exact location of the holy city, he should direct his *heart* towards Jerusalem.

Mizrah is also the name given to a decorative plaque often placed on the eastern wall of traditional Jewish homes. This plaque is usually inscribed with scriptural passages incorporating the word *mizrah.*

MNEMONICS. Since it is impossible for anyone to remember everything, most people use devices of some sort to help them recall information. For 1,500 years the body of Jewish *law was passed on orally. There was no written text and the need for such devices was great. Even though students were rigidly trained to sharpen their memories, mnemonics, recalling an idea by relating it to something which suggests the idea, was the commonly used device to help, one which the rabbis deemed very important.

The fact that the scholars of Judah retained their learning while those in Galilee forgot it was attributed to the Judean students using mnemonics and Galileans not doing so. Popular mnemonics were: phrases from the text of the Bible which, of course, everyone knew by heart; popular proverbs; catchwords and well-known phrases from the Talmud. One example is a verse from Isaiah (33:6) which recalled the six orders, or division, of the Mishnah: "There shall be faith in thy times, strength, salvation, wisdom and knowledge." *Abbreviations and *acrostics were also popular mnemonics, such as: *DeZaKH ADaSH BeAHaB* for the Ten Plagues. The difference of opinion as to the order of the festival blessings for wine *(yayin)*, Kiddush, the festival *(zeman)*, the candle *(ner)*, and Havdalah is indicated by whether the reminder read *"YaKZaNaH"* or *"YaKNeHaZ."*

MOAB, an ancient land east of the Jordan and the Dead Sea, and one of Israel's neighbors in biblical times. Its highland extended south to the Zered river, east to the desert and west to the Dead Sea. The northern boundary was much disputed. Moabite tribes settled in the area around the mid-14th century b.c.e., not long before the exodus of the Hebrews from Egypt. The Moabites were of Semitic stock, closely akin to the Israelites.

According to Deuteronomy, Moab was inhabited by the Emim, "a people, great and many and tall," before the Moabites drove them out. "Moab" means "from my father," and according to the Book of

Genesis (19:30-38), Moab (the originator of the tribe) was born to Lot by his elder daughter near the town of Zoar at the southeast tip of the Dead Sea. The capital of Moab was Kir-Hareseth (present-day al-Kerak). Great importance attached to the "king's highway," a trade route passing through Moab and connecting Arabia and Egypt with Syria and Mesopotamia. The economy was based on trade conducted along this route, and on agriculture and cattle raising. The king of Moab, Mesha, was called a sheep-master. The national god of Moab was Chemosh. The Moabites practiced circumcision, and animal, and even human, sacrifice.

The land of Moab is mentioned in a geographical list of the Egyptian ruler, Ramses II (13th century b.c.e.) who undertook an expedition into Transjordan and captured Moabite cities. Northern Moab was occupied by Amorites before falling into Israelite hands after the king had refused the Israelites passage through his country when they were on their way to Canaan from Egypt. Because of this the Israelites were commanded in the Torah not to intermarry with Moabites even if they had converted to Judaism. Jewish tradition, however, understood the prohibition as applying to male Moabites only and the Book of Ruth in the Bible tells how Ruth the Moabitess converted and became an ancestor of King David. Throughout biblical history there was a great deal of animosity between the Israelites and the Moabites which often broke out into open war. King David subdued Moab and after Solomon's death, Moab came under the domination of the northern kingdom of Israel (see *Jeroboam). Later on in history, Moab became a vassal of the Assyrian empire,

its inhabitants lost their national identity and, as a separate people, it ceased to exist.

MODENA, LEONE (1571-1648), also called da Modena; Italian rabbi, scholar and writer. The vivid, fascinating, puzzling personality of Modena began to assert itself very early in his life. He was born in Venice and brought up in Ferrara where he became known as an infant prodigy. At the age of two and a half he was able to read the *haftarah*, the weekly prophetical portion; at three he translated biblical passages into Italian. His formal education was the usual one for a boy of good family and included rabbinic studies as well as Italian and Latin literature. At 12 and 13 he was writing and translating poetry in Hebrew and Italian. When his father suffered financial difficulty, Modena undertook to teach and preach in Venice, not a position of great dignity at that time. Yet his sermons attracted large and distinguished audiences, among them many gentiles. His Jewish learning was extensive and he was often consulted by learned contemporaries. He continued to write in Italian, particularly poetry. Most of the epitaphs on the tombstones in Venice at that time were of his composition. He wrote voluminously in a clear and beautiful handwriting so that much is known about him from his letters and responsa. These sources reveal a curiously contradictory type — a man of great learning whose piety was undermined by serious faults. He kept bad company, could not control his children and gambled away most of his money at cards. He vowed repentance many times. He undertook, by his own count, 26 different occupations in order to earn a livelihood, among them arranging marriages and writing amulets. He even acted in an amateur theatrical group.

Modena suffered much anguish because he could not keep his vows and break his habit of gambling. He enjoyed an enviable reputation among Jews and Christians as a wise and learned Jew, but he was not consistent; his condemnations and defenses were erratic. But in spite of his unstable character, he made a significant contribution to Jewish scholarship. In one of his most important works he used traditional Jewish as well as secular critical methods to show the limitations of the Christian interpretation of the Bible. Nevertheless, he himself considered his life a failure because he could not overcome his faults.

MODIGLIANI, AMADEO (1884-1920), Italian Jewish painter. Born in Leghorn, Amadeo studied art

1. Initial-word panel of the Book of Ruth, illustrating scenes from the story. On the right, Ruth the Moabitess, gleans after the reapers; on the left, Naomi is approaching Boaz who is sifting the grain. It is from the *Tripartite Maḥzor,* Germany, c. 1320, in which all the women are depicted with animal heads.

2. "Woman with a Blue Scarf," early work by Amadeo Modigliani.

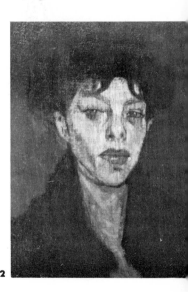

1

2

Modigliani's "Portrait of Jean Cocteau," oil on canvas, 1916-19.

Solomon Molcho

wife Jeanne Hébuterne. Modigliani was a superb draughtsman and a fascinating colorist: he achieved sparkling effect in his painting by the use of many layers of varnish. His portraits are characterized by long necks and noses, simplified features, and long oval faces. They convey an intimate and mute sympathy between painter and sitter.

Modligiani died at the age of 36. His wife threw herself from a window a few days later, killing herself and her unborn child. Soon after Modigliani's death, the value of his art began to be appreciated and his works were acquired by leading museums, galleries and collectors throughout the world.

in Florence and Venice and in 1906 went to Paris. While there, though he led a dissipated life, he learnt much from Cezanne, Gauguin, Toulouse-Lautrec, and from African sculpture, which he greatly admired, reproducing its simplified abstract forms in his own sculptures. Despite numerous love affairs, bouts of drunkenness, drug addiction, illness and poverty, Modigliani managed to produce a substantial body of work. More than 20 of his sculptures, 500 paintings and thousands of watercolors and sketches are in existence. The portraits include those of fellow artists and the two women who played leading roles in his life — the English poetess Beatrice Hastings, and his

MOLCHO, SOLOMON (c. 1500-1532). Dressed as a beggar and seated by the Pope's palace among the sick and poor of medieval Rome, Solomon Molcho spent 30 days without meat or wine, trying to prove that he fit the talmudic description of the suffering Messiah.

How did this young *Marrano, born in Lisbon, come to believe that he was the redeemer of Israel? It would seem that the turning point in his life was his meeting with pseudo-messiah David Reuveni (see article on *Messianic Movements). It was then that he decided to be circumcised and to change his name from Diogo Pires to the Hebrew Molcho (perhaps from the word *melekh* — "king").

As it was a crime for Marranos to openly embrace Judaism, Molcho was forced to flee from country to country, studying *Kabbalah in Salonika and preaching of the redemption throughout Europe. A collection of his sermons, entitled *Derashot* and later called *Sefer ha-Mefoar* ("The Wonderful Book") was printed in 1529.

These sermons attracted many followers, including Christians. He won the confidence of Pope Clement VII when his prophecies of a flood in Rome (1530) and an earthquake in Portugal (January 1531) came true.

Molcho was instrumental in preventing the spread of the *Inquisition in Portugal, mainly through his preaching. After being condemned to death because of his Judaizing, and saved through the personal intervention of the Pope, he was finally tried and burned at the stake by Emperor Charles V.

MONASH, SIR JOHN (1865-1931), Australian engineer and soldier, commanded Australian forces during World War I and gained a reputation as the most outstanding leader in the British army. He was

Sir John Monash

born into an immigrant family in Melbourne who had been printers of Hebrew books in Vienna. Besides his doctorate in engineering, Monash graduated in arts and law, and also studied medicine. He was never a professional soldier. Volunteering for the Victoria militia in 1884, he was commissioned three years later. In 1900 he won a gold medal for a number of articles on military subjects in the *Commonwealth Journal.* He was already a colonel in the militia when World War I broke out.

In April 1915, Monash commanded the Fourth Infantry Brigade at Gallipoli. Australian and New Zealand troops distinguished themselves in the action, and the valley there was named after Monash. In April 1917 he took part with Canadian forces in the capture of Vimy Ridge in France. In May the following year as lieutenant general, he was appointed to lead the entire Australian and New Zealand Army Corps (ANZACs) on the western front, and his troops played a decisive part in breaking the German lines on the Amiens front in the summer of 1918. The British prime minister, Lloyd George, described Monash as the only soldier of World War I with the qualities of leadership. Besides numerous military decorations, he received honorary doctorates from Oxford, Cambridge and London universities.

After the war he returned to civil engineering in Australia. In 1930, shortly before his death, he was made a full general, becoming the first Jew to attain this rank in any army. He took an active part in Jewish affairs in Australia and was president of the Zionist Federation in 1928. He wrote of his campaigns in *Australian Victories in France in 1918* (1920). A village in Israel is named Kefar Monash in his honor.

MONEYLENDING AND USURY. In Jewish tradition, the lending of money to the needy is a moral obligation of extreme importance. It is an essential component of the *mitzvah* of *zedakah* (charity). Lending money is, of course, also a basic component of any business economy, but both in biblical and talmudic law, no distinction is made between the two situations: no matter what the occasion, money lent by one Jew to another must not earn interest. Usury of even the most minimal amount is flatly prohibited by the Torah: "You shall not lend upon interest to your brother, interest of money, interest of victuals, interest of anything that is lent upon interest . . . ."

This prohibition proved to be one of the most universally violated obligations of biblical law. The prophets repeatedly denounce "evil-doers" who oppress the poor by taking interest on loans, and this would seem to indicate that even in biblical times there were many who did not live up to this moral requirement imposed by the Torah.

In talmudic times, a paradoxical development took place: on one hand, the laws pertaining to the prohibition of usury were broadened to encompass many situations not explicitly dealt with in the Bible. On the other hand, technical and legal devices were evolved to circumvent the prohibition in order to maintain business relationships which, in fact, included money earning interest for a lender or investor. Thus, the concept of interest was extended by the sages of the Talmud to include all benefits which might involve interest or appear to do so; these were called *avak ribbit* ("dust of interest") and included such things as not allowing a lender to live on the borrower's property without full payment of rent, or even something as minor as offering the lender information which might prove valuable to him. Changes in the economic conditions of Babylonia and Palestine eventually made such stringent restrictions almost impossible to enforce.

As in other conflicts between "law" and "life," the rabbis sought to preserve the law while submitting to the demands of life by seeking legal loopholes

Bust of General Sir John Monash, Australian soldier, engineer and Zionist.

which would make lending money at interest technically possible. Many such subterfuges were in fact invented. For example, a farmer who had received a loan was allowed to make a formal conveyance of his lands to his creditor and still remain on the lands as his creditor's tenant; the creditor would be entitled to the produce of the land, not as interest on the loan but as income from his property. Another form of evasion was to lend money at interest to a non-Jew, in order that the non-Jew might re-lend the money to the intended Jewish debtor; individually each lending transaction was perfectly valid. (For parallel solutions to the

economic hardships of the sabbatical laws, see *Sabbatical Year and Jubilee.)

Sanctions. Originally, courts appear to have been empowered to fine the creditor for taking interest. This was done by not enforcing even his claim for repayment of the capital. Although this particular sanction later lapsed, moneylenders who took interest continued to be regarded as having been morally tainted. As such, they were disqualified as witnesses and were not administered oaths. Even the borrower who paid interest was disqualified.

Post-Talmudic Law. The talmudic evasions of the prohibition against interest served as precedents for the later legalization of transactions involving interest. In time, a standard form of legalization was established known as a *hetter iskah,* meaning the permission to form a partnership. A deed, known as a *shetar iskah,* was drawn up and attested to by two witnesses, stipulating that the lender would supply a certain sum of money to the borrower for a joint venture; the borrower alone would manage the business and he would guarantee the lender's investment against all loss. He would also guarantee to the lender a fixed amount of minimum profit. In return, the borrower would be paid a nominal sum as a salary. The amount of the capital loan plus the guaranteed minimum profit would be recoverable at the stipulated time of maturity of the deed.

In the course of the centuries, this form of legalizing interest has become so well-established that nowadays all interest transactions are freely carried out, even in compliance with Jewish law, by simply adding to the rote or contract the words *al-pi hetter iskah.* (This is the basis of all interest-bearing bank accounts in the State of Israel.) Thus, today, the prohibition on interest has lost all practical significance in business transactions, and is now

relegated purely to the realm of friendly and charitable loans.

Transactions with Non-Jews. The Torah itself made a definite, although unexplained, distinction between money lent to Jews and to non-Jews. "You may charge interest to a foreigner, but not to your brother." The rabbis of the Talmud did try to modify this view, on the grounds that Jews should, in any event, keep their contacts with gentiles to a minimum. Nevertheless, in medieval Europe, moneylending to Christians became a widespread Jewish occupation. One reason for this was the 1179 Papal decree threatening all Christian usurers with excommunication, which rendered the Jews one of the few remaining sources of ready cash to the general public. The other was the increasing number of severe economic restrictions against the Jews, which virtually forced them out of any other trade or profession. One effect of this process was to give many Christians a pretext for their hatred of the stereotyped Jewish usurer. Hence, many of the late medieval persecutions acquired an economic as well as a religious character.

The Jewish moneylender, in his medieval role, declined in importance with the rise of modern banking procedures. For more on this see *Banking and Bankers.

MONTEFIORE, SIR MOSES (1784-1885). Under the shade of a stone windmill once propelled by Jerusalem's mountain breezes, stands a favorite tourist attraction – Montefiore's quaint carriage. Painted on its side is the celebrated family's coat of arms, adorned with the motto: "Think and thank." The man who, though childless, learned to be grateful for a useful life spanning 101 years, started off his business career as a humble apprentice to a firm of wholesale grocers and tea merchants. He later left to become one of the 12 "Jew brokers" in the City of London. After initial setbacks, he went into partnership with his brother Abraham and the firm acquired a high reputation. His marriage in 1812 to Judith Cohen made him brother-in-law of Nathan Mayer Rothschild, for whom his firm acted as stockbrokers. It was in his wife's memory that he later founded the Judith Lady Montefiore College. After his retirement from regular business in 1824, he had the time and the fortune to undertake communal and civic responsibilities.

Contrary to accepted opinion, Montefiore was somewhat lax in religious observance in earlier life;

but from 1827, after his first visit to Erez Israel, he was a strictly observant Jew, and was in the habit of traveling with his own *shohet*. His determined opposition checked the growth of the Reform Movement in England. He paid seven visits to Erez Israel and, anticipating the messianic restoration of a Jewish state, he attempted to acquire land to enable Jews there to become self-supporting through agriculture, but his scheme failed. He later tried to bring industry to the country, building the above-mentioned windmill and introducing a printing press and a textile factory, and inspired the founding of several agricultural colonies. The Yemin Moshe quarter overlooking the walls of the Old City of Jerusalem was established because of his efforts and named after him.

Montefiore enjoyed enormous prestige. His personal appearance (he was 6 ft. 3 in. tall), his commanding personality, his philanthropy, and his complete disinterestedness, made him highly respected and admired both in England and abroad. The support of the British government for his activities and the personal regard shown him by Queen Victoria added to his reputation. She was "desirous of giving an especial mark of our royal favor . . . in commemoration of these his unceasing exertions on behalf of his injured and persecuted bretheren." Thus, Moses Montefiore was both knighted by the Queen and given a baronetcy. He utilized his personal standing to further the cause of oppressed Jews elsewhere, as the *Court Jews had

2

Moses Montefiore

1. A landmark of Jerusalem, the windmill constructed at the end of the 19th century by Sir Moses Montefiore, as part of the new quarter, Yemin Moshe, he had built outside the walls of the Old City. Today, it houses the chariot used by Sir Moses during his many trips through Erez Israel.
2. Sir Moses Montefiore, latter-day Court Jew.

done in earlier years. For example, he intervened to help save the victims of the *Damascus blood libel in 1840; in 1846 he visited Russia to persuade the authorities to relax their persecution of the Jewish population; and the same purpose took him to Morocco in 1863 and to Rumania in 1867. Quite understandably, the 100th birthday of the former grocer's apprentice was celebrated by Jewish communities the world over as a public holiday.

MONTREAL is the largest city in Canada and contains its oldest established Jewish community, estimated at 100,000 in 1981. The flourishing Jewish community of Montreal dates back to 1760, when the first Jewish settlers were merchants and fur traders. In 1768, these settlers founded Canada's first synagogue, the Shearith Israel of Montreal, and modeled it after the Spanish and Portuguese synagogue of New York. Much later, in 1858, the first Ashkenazi synagogue was established; the German and Polish synagogue, later renamed Shaar Hashomayim. In the years which followed, Jewish immigration to Canada increased, and as Montreal's Jewish population grew, so did the number of congregations. Thus by 1980, there were over 30 synagogues in the city, most of which were Orthodox.

The enlarged Jewish community grew more self-sufficient and influential and organized numerous Jewish social welfare and health agencies, Jewish hospitals, old-age homes, vocational services and summer camps included.

Another significant accomplishment of the Jewish community was in the educational system; after many years of negotiation, community leaders succeeded in convincing the provincial government to give official recognition to Montreal's Jewish day schools, but continued grants depend upon a very significant increase in teaching in the French language as required by the new language law.

In politics as well, Montreal's Jews have

distinguished themselves, and have held various government posts. In 1970, the first Jewish cabinet minister, Victor Goldbloom, was appointed to the Quebec provincial government.

MOON. The months, the festivals, indeed the whole of the Jewish year, are based on the periodic reappearance of the moon. The *Kabbalah relates this to the rise and fall of the Jewish destiny. The Bible records the creation of the moon on the fourth day (Genesis 1:16). An *aggadah* (legend) relates that the sun and moon were originally the same size; they quarreled and were envious of each other, and the moon was punished and made smaller because it had "intruded" into the sphere of the sun (the moon can sometimes be seen during the day). The Hebrew word for moon is *yare'ah;* in poetic and rabbinic literature it is *levanah.*

New Moon. *Rosh hodesh,* the new moon, can be one day or two. For more on this see *Calendar. It is observed as a minor holiday symbolizing renewal and hope. Determining the New Moon is a biblical commandment based on a verse in Exodus (12:2).

1. Pavilion of Judaism at the EXPO '67 World's Fair, Montreal, Canada.
2. Facade added to the old synagogue of Congregation Sha'ar Hashamayim in Montreal, 1967.
3. The blessing of the new moon recited outside the "old synagogue" in Frankfort. It was subsequently destroyed.

The celebration begins the Sabbath before *(Shabbat mevarekhim)* when the New Moon is announced in the synagogue in a special prayer following the Torah reading. Originally the New Moon was proclaimed by the Sanhedrin, the High Court assembled in Jerusalem, after testimony by reliable witnesses that they had actually seen the new crescent; they then "sanctified" the moon. Bonfires were lit on the Mount of Olives to inform the whole nation. As soon as these beacons were seen, others were lit on hilltops by waiting scouts, and so the word was spread over the entire land and in parts of the Diaspora. Later the *Samaritans began to light misleading beacons and word had to be sent by messenger. In the fourth century c.e. the sages established a uniform permanent calendar, based on astronomical calculation, in force to this day. In Temple times, an additional sacrifice was offered on the New Moon. In our day, a *musaf* prayer is added, a special portion is read from the Torah, and half-*Hallel* is recited (see *Prayer). Since it is a joyous day, one may not fast and funeral eulogies may not be made. Everyday work is permitted. However, some women observe the custom of abstaining from certain tasks. This half-holiday was a reward to the women for not having given their jewelry for the creation of the Golden Calf. The very pious fast on the day before the New Moon, called *Yom Kippur Katan.*

Blessing the Moon. A prayer of thanksgiving is pronounced at the reappearance of the moon. In Hebrew this is called *kiddush levanah* or *birkat ha-levanah.* It can be said, preferably with a *minyan* (quorum of ten) from the third evening after the appearance of the new crescent until the 15th of that month. It should be recited outdoors, when the moon is clearly seen. The time recommended is immediately after the departure of the Sabbath when one is wearing one's best clothes and in a festive mood. The prayer includes psalms and a benediction praising God as creator and master of nature. The phrase, "David, king of Israel lives on!" is repeated three times and the greeting *"Shalom aleikhem"* (Peace be with you) is also repeated three times to others in the group who respond *"Aleikhem shalom."* This part of the service recalls Roman occupation of Ereẓ Israel in the time of *Judah ha-Nasi (second-third centuries c.e.). The Romans forbade the public consecration of the New Moon which therefore had to be done in secret. "David, king of Israel, lives on!" was the password that it had been accomplished. It also voiced the hope for Israel's redemption by the *Messiah, of the dynasty of David, whose kingdom would be as eternal as the moon. The ritual regards the moon as the symbol of the renewal in nature, as well as of Israel's hope for renewal and redemption.

MOROCCO. According to legend, Jews first settled in Morocco, the westernmost country of North Africa, before the destruction of the Second Temple in 70 c.e. According to one legend, they even came in the days of Solomon to purchase large quantities of gold from the Carthaginian gold market near present-day Rabat; according to another, Joab in King David's time, was sent to fight the Philistines in Morocco, once they had been driven out of Canaan. The earliest real evidence of Jewish habitation, however, derives from tombstone inscriptions of the second century c.e. Later histories record that the early Jewish settlers in Morocco eagerly engaged in missionary activities and were successful in converting a number of local Berber tribes to Judaism. The Jewish population remained small, however, until the sixth century when it rapidly increased because of a large influx of Jews who fled the persecutions of the Visigoths in Spain. But it was not until after the Arab conquest of the seventh century that Morrocco began to flourish as a creative Jewish community. Between the eighth and 11th centuries, Morocco was a center of Jewish learning, with many scholars choosing Fez as their place of residence. During this period, other centers of Jewish settlement in North Africa also reached their creative heights; for fuller descriptions, see *Algeria, *Kairouan, *Tunisia.

Interior of a Jewish house in Fez, Morocco, typified by the high table, in contrast to the low tables in Arab homes.

The invasion, in the mid-1140s, of the Almohads, a fanatical Muslim tribe of central North Africa, put an end to this period of creativity; many Jews were forcibly converted to Islam and numerous communities were destroyed. The history of the Jews of Morocco thereafter is a history of relatively rapid rises and falls. In the 13th century the Jews were again allowed the freedom to prosper, and they soon gained complete control of the Sahara gold trade as well as the trade with the Christian countries of Northern Europe. But by the 15th century they were again in a steep decline, with this change of fortune marked most noticeably by the fact that the Jews of Fez were for the first time enclosed within a special quarter of the city, the *mellah* (similar to what came to be called the *ghetto in Europe).

During the last decades of the 15th century and throughout the 16th, Morocco, together with the other countries of Northern Africa, served as a haven for the tens of thousands of Spanish and Portuguese Jews who were forcibly expelled from their homelands. But Morocco was ill-prepared to receive so many immigrants, and many thousands died of disease and famine while camped in the fields surrounding the large coastal towns. Most of the exiles eventually made their way either to Turkey or to Italy, but substantial numbers did stay in Morocco although they were not well received by their coreligionists who feared them as economic rivals. The newcomers, who came to be collectively known as *megorashim* (literally: the expelled ones), jealously

preserved their own rituals and customs and set up their own communal institutions. (See *Tunisia for similar happenings elsewhere in North Africa.)

In the 17th and 18th centuries, most of Morocco's Jews were craftsmen, peddlers, or occasionally moneylenders. The majority lived in poverty and were beset by heavy taxes. Although their fortune might rise occasionally with a change in political leadership, Morocco's Jews continued to live a basically impoverished existence right into the 20th century, and in the 18th and 19th centuries, were even beset by a series of plagues and pogroms. When Morocco became a French protectorate in 1919, the lot of the Jews improved considerably, and in the decades prior to World War II, a Jewish middle class began to rise, with many Jews enjoying a higher education in Moroccan or French universities. Under Vichy French control during World War II, Morocco's Jews were spared destruction, but after the war and the declaration of Moroccan independence, there were violent anti-Jewish uprisings all over the country. Large-scale emigration to Israel began after 1960, and from a population of 160,000, only 22,000 remained by 1981.

Tangier, Casablanca and Agadir, the three main coastal towns of Morocco contained, until recent times, large settlements of Jews. All three acquired significant Jewish populations following the expulsions from Spain and Portugal in the last decade of the 15th century, but today all three contain only a handful of Jews, the majority having emigrated either to Israel or North America following World War II. Of the three, Casablanca boasted the largest and most developed Jewish community. At the beginning of the century, Casablanca had several synagogues, four *talmud torah* schools, four private schools and an *Alliance Israelite Universelle school.

1. Student in a Jewish school in Casablanca, Morocco.
2. Rabbi of the Ifrane congregation in Morocco standing outside his ancient synagogue.
3. Moroccan immigrants on a ship bound for Israel, 1950.

Many Casablanca Jews held high positions in commerce, industry and the liberal professions. The upper class of Casablanca's Jewish community founded numerous charitable organizations to care for the needs of the many poor Jews, but these have ceased functioning with the decline in the community.

MORTARA CASE concerned the kidnapping of a Jewish child by Catholics whose intent was the conversion of Jews. On the night of June 23-24, 1858, Edgardo Mortara, a six-year-old Jewish child from Bologna, Italy, was abducted by the Papal police and taken to the House of Catechumens in Rome, an institution for intended converts. The boy had been secretly baptized five years earlier by a Christian domestic servant who thought, she said later, that he was about to die. The parents tried in vain to get their child back. The case caused a universal outcry. Despite protests from such eminent persons as Napoleon III and Sir Moses Montefiore, Pope Pius IX rejected all petitions submitted to him. (It was partly in reaction to this case that the Alliance Israélite Universelle came into existence to "defend the civil and religious freedom of the Jews".) Only in 1870, when the secular power of the papacy ended, was Edgardo free to return to his family and religion. However, by this time he had taken the name Pius and was a novice in an Augustinian order, and refused to return. He preached eloquently in six languages and was so ardent a convert that he received the title of "apostolic missionary" from Pope Leo XIII. He became a church official in Rome and a professor of theology.

MOSCOW. Fortress for barbaric princes, spired city of czars, grim stronghold of Kremlin rulers, Moscow has been through time a window of the Soviet Union through which the history of Russian Jewry could be viewed.

Till the end of the 18th century, Jews were forbidden to reside in Moscow, though Polish and Lithuanian Jewish merchants did visit there. When Alexander II came to the throne (1855), Jewish merchants were permitted temporary residence and they played an important role in developing Russian trade. The number of Jews increased rapidly, and in 1865 Hayyim Berlin (see *Bar-Ilan, Meir) was appointed rabbi of the city.

Although throughout Russia anti-Jewish persecutions and decrees gained momentum in the 19th century, some liberality continued in Moscow. However, a new governor was appointed in 1891 whose aim was "to protect Moscow from Jewry." On March 28, 1891, the Jews of Moscow were expelled. Synagogues and prayer houses were closed.

After World War I, Jewish refugees again streamed into Moscow from German-occupied regions. Soon Moscow became a Jewish center where press, theater, publications and yeshivot flourished. In 1917 a conference for Hebrew education and culture was held in Moscow and the city became the center for organized Zionist activity.

Organized Jewish life was totally liquidated during the "black years" of Stalin's regime, but Jewish and pro-Israel sentiments were stimulated in 1948 by the establishment of the State of Israel and by Golda *Meir's arrival in the city as the ambassador of the

1. The kidnapping of Edgardo Mortara. Drawing by Moritz Oppenheim, 1858. 2. The Israel National Basketball team in Red Square, Moscow, 1953. To the left is Lenin's tomb and behind it the Kremlin.

1.   The Great Synagogue of Moscow.
2.   By misinterpreting a biblical passage, some Christians came to believe that Moses had horns. This sculpture by Michelangelo therefore shows Moses with horns protruding from his head.

1

new State. Later on, mass gatherings of young Jews, which took place on Jewish holidays (particularly Simḥat Torah), became a feature of Jewish life in Moscow. However, Soviet discriminatory practices against the Jews continued. Most synagogues were closed down and every year there were difficulties in obtaining *maẓẓot* for Passover. The Soviet secret police kept a close watch on the synagogue activities and often infiltrated the Jewish leadership with spies. A yeshivah exists in Moscow, but it is very closely supervised by the government and has very few students.

Until the rupture of diplomatic relations with Israel in 1967, contact was maintained through sport events, congresses and exhibitions. After the *Six-Day War in 1967, Moscow Jews began to demonstrate their pro-Israel feelings openly, which has resulted in the use of suppressive measures by the Communist regime.

MOSES. The greatest figure in Jewish history, Moses was a prophet and a political, religious and military leader who lived during the 13th century b.c.e. He led the Israelites out of slavery in Egypt, and received directly from God the Torah, Israel's Law of justice, holiness and lovingkindness. He translated the word of God into the realities of everyday life, and

transformed the Israelites from a horde of slaves into a civilized nation and potentially "a kingdom of priests" (Exodus 19:6).

The story of Moses is told in the Torah (which is also known as the Five Books of Moses), in Exodus, Leviticus, Numbers and Deteuronomy. He was born in Egypt to Jochebed and Amram of the tribe of Levi, at a time when the Israelites were suffering bitter persecution there. Pharaoh had enslaved them and commanded in addition that every newborn Hebrew boy be cast into the river Nile to die. Jochebed managed to hide her baby from the Egyptians for the first three months of his life. When she could no longer conceal him, she put him into a wicker basket made waterproof with pitch, and placed the basket among the reeds of the Nile where Pharaoh's daughter often came to bathe. Miriam, Jochebed's daughter, kept watch.

When Pharaoh's daughter came down to the river with her attendants she caught sight of the basket and had it brought to her. She opened it and saw the baby lying inside. Realizing that it must be an Israelite child, she decided to adopt it. A nurse was needed, and at this point Miriam emerged from her hiding-place and suggested her own mother.

Paradoxically therefore, Moses, the leader, prophet

2

Moses. Receiving the Tablets of the Law and passing them on to the Israelites. According to one rabbinic interpretation, God overturned Mt. Sinai and trapped the Israelites underneath until they agreed to accept the Law.

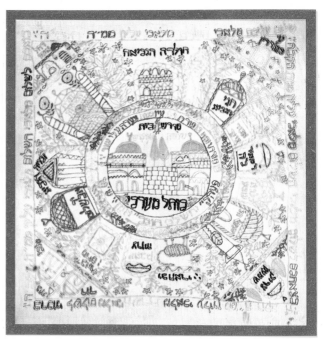

1. **Moses.** Page from the Sarajevo *Haggadah* showing the Israelite leader standing on top of the flaming Mt. Sinai, holding the Tablets of the Law. Spain, 14th century.
2. **Maps.** Map of Jerusalem embroidered in Persian style. 19th century.

1. Pharaoh's daughter finds the baby Moses among the reeds of the River Nile. Painting by Tintoretto, 16th century.

2. "Episodes in the Life of Moses." Right to left: Moses killing the Egyptian; meeting Zipporah at the well; kneeling before the burning bush; and leading the Israelites out of Egypt. Fresco by Botticelli in the Sistine Chapel in Rome.

and lawgiver of the Israelites, was brought up as a prince in Pharaoh's palace. Even his name contains an irony: Pharaoh's daughter called him *Moshe* (in English, Moses). In ancient Egyptian the name probably meant "son," but it is also connected with the Hebrew word-root which means "draws out" for the baby was drawn out of the river by the daughter of Pharaoh. Later on "draw out" was to be understood in another sense: Moses was to draw the Israelites out of Egypt.

Nursed by his mother through his early years, Moses learned from her a full consciousness of his Israelite identity. Although his upbringing and education were continued among the Egyptian royal family, he was revolted by the Egyptian way of life and longed for a nobler society. He also gained from his upbringing in Pharaoh's palace, however, for it gave him a freedom of outlook and action that the generations of enslaved Israelites did not and could not possess. He grew to be a man of high ideals and immense moral courage.

The conflict between his ideals and the values of the Egyptian slave-society of which he was part erupted suddenly in Moses' early manhood. He saw an Egyptian beating a Hebrew slave, and overcome by rage Moses slew the Egyptian and hid the body in the sand. A few days later he came across two Hebrews quarrelling. As he intervened to separate them, one cried, "Who made you chief and ruler over us? Do you mean to kill me as you killed the Egyptian?" Realizing that the murder was known, Moses fled from Pharoah's wrath to the nearby country of Midian. He was not yet ready to assume leadership of the Hebrews and they were not yet ready for their salvation. The small-minded, aggressive response of the Israelite to Moses' intervention showed him and his fellows to be slaves in spirit as well as in body, without even a true understanding of the horror of their bondage.

Wandering through Midian, Moses came to a well where the seven daughters of the priest, Reuel (also known as *Jethro), had come to water their father's flocks. They were involved in an argument over the use of the well with bullying local shepherds, and Moses, ever the champion of justice, took the part of Reuel's daughters. Following this incident he went to work for the priest as a shepherd and married one of his daughters, Zipporah. Thus Moses, like King David, a leader of the Israelites after him, spent his days tending flocks of sheep.

Time passed and he grew older, calmer and wise,

and it was here in the timeless desert that God spoke to him for the first time. Moses was in the wilderness near Horev with his flocks when he saw a bush that was on fire but did not burn. As he came towards the fire to investigate the marvel, the voice of God addressed him from the bush. God told Moses that he must return to Egypt, where a new pharaoh now reigned, and lead the Israelites out of their bondage. Moses protested that he was inadequate for the task of liberation leader, but God patiently answered all his objections and promised that He would help him. To convince the Israelites of his authority, God gave Moses three miraculous signs — but Moses was still reluctant. Finally God became angry. He conceded that Aaron, Moses' brother, should be spokesman and Moses at last accepted the commission.

Moses, now a freedom fighter, returned to Egypt with his wife and two sons and as God had instructed him, asked the new pharaoh to allow the Israelites to make a three-day journey into the wilderness to sacrifice to God. Pharaoh's reaction was not only to refuse, but to increase the hardship of his slaves by forcing them to make the bricks they used for building without straw. Both Moses and the Hebrews were discouraged; Pharaoh appeared immovable.

Moses breaking the Tablets of the Law in his anger at the sins of the Israelites.

Then God inflicted ten devastating plagues on Egypt (see also *Passover; *Plagues of Egypt). The last plague finally persuaded Pharaoh to surrender. Moses' rebellion had succeeded, and the Israelites prepared to leave the land of their bondage, hurried on their way by the now panic-stricken Egyptians.

Pharaoh quickly regretted freeing his Israelite slaves, and set off in pursuit of them. Moses had already led the people as far as the shores of the Red Sea guided by God's pillar of cloud and fire, when the thundering hooves of the pursuing Egyptians' horses were heard. The Hebrews in their fear, turned on Moses, blaming him for their plight — as they were to do again on many occasions during the 40 years ahead. Moses prayed to God. Then he lifted up his rod and the waters of the sea parted, and the Israelites crossed safely to the opposite shore. The Egyptians galloped after them, but the seas closed in on them and they perished beneath the waves. The song of praise which the Hebrews sang after this, their second deliverance from Egypt, praises only God. Moses would not allow himself to be considered a great man in his own right, nor anything other than God's servant.

Moses and the Israelites now headed into the wilderness towards the real purpose of their deliverance — the covenant with God. Freedom was not to be simply the end of slavery: it was to have a positive spiritual content, and to establish God as the One true God. In the third month of the Exodus they reached Mount Sinai. Moses ascended the mountain and remained there for forty days and nights, while he received God's Torah (see *Revelation). Whereas God reveals Himself to other prophets through dreams and visions, Moses came face to face with Him on the heights of the mountain.

Moses descended from his encounter with God holding the precious tablets of the Law to find the Israelites worshiping a golden calf. (See *Golden Calf.) The covenant with God was broken: the *Ten Commandments and the golden calf could not exist side by side, and Moses shattered the tablets of the law which God had given him. He ground the idol to dust, and with the help of the loyal tribe of Levi executed 3,000 of the idolators. He then begged God's forgiveness and climbed the mountain again to receive the tablets of the Law once more.

The forty years that followed marked a period of constant tension and crisis. Twelve spies were sent out to report on the land which God had promised the Israelites. Of the spies, ten brought back

Aaron (center) performs miracles before Pharaoh while Moses (right) turns the waters into blood in the first of the Ten Plagues. The *Cologne Bible,* 15th century.

discouraging reports saying that although the land was fertile the Israelites would be unable to conquer it. Only two of the spies, Joshua and Caleb, were optimistic, but they failed to convince the people. In consequence, the Israelites were condemned to wander in the desert for forty years till the generation which had come out of Egypt, which had worshiped the golden calf, and which had lacked confidence in God's promise, died there. Of that generation only Joshua and Caleb were to reach the Promised Land.

The years in the wilderness were hard ones. Not always content with *manna, the Hebrews often complained of hunger and thirst. On one occasion when God led Moses to a dry rock that could produce water, Moses, taunted by the jeers of the people, struck the rock instead of speaking to it as God commanded, and was himself condemned for lack of faith. Repeatedly the people murmured against him in discontent, and even threatened to appoint a new leader to take them back to Egypt. Moses' cousin *Korah, accused Moses and Aaron of self-aggrandizement and attempted a rebellion, but the rebels suffered a terrible punishment for the earth opened and swallowed them; thousands more of the rebels died from plague. Even Aaron and Miriam, the brother and sister of Moses, criticized him at one stage because of the woman he married — it is not clear in the Bible if this woman is Zipporah or someone else. As the forty years drew to a close and entry to the Promised Land was at last in sight, the Hebrews became engaged in desperate battles against the kings, Sihon and Og, on whose territories they encroached. Moses, the liberation leader in Egypt, the political leader of the forty years in the desert, training the people for democracy, now turned military leader and defeated the desert kings.

Moses, like the generation that he had led out of Egypt, was to be denied entry into the land. The commentator *Rashi explains that this was because Moses too showed lack of faith — he struck the rock instead of speaking to it. For whatever reason, God instead led Moses alone to the top of a mountain rising from the plains of Moab, and from here Moses looked towards the goal of his forty years of desert wanderings. Here on the mountain he died, and God Himself buried him — in a grave that was left unmarked, for Moses' burial place was not to become a shrine.

Through the forty difficult years of wandering, under Moses' leadership, Pharaoh's slaves threw off the mentality of their bondage. A new generation of men emerged from the desert, united by a new conception of God, a new faith, a new law of life and a new sense of common destiny. Moses, God's servant, had laid down the foundations for the entire future of the Jewish people, both spiritual and administrative.

As an aging leader, Moses gets his first and last glimpse of the Promised Land from the top of a desert mountain just before his death.

Because of the greatness of Moses as a man and because of his towering role in the history of the Jewish people, many stories and legends are told about him. Throughout the legends, however, although he is the most renowned of all Jewish teachers and the intermediary between God and man, there is no attempt to ascribe divine or even semi-divine attributes to him. In contrast to Christianity and Islam which center around a powerful, godlike personality, Moses is never made out to be more than a man — and it is emphasized that it is God and not Moses Who gave the Torah to Israel. Divine honors are denied Moses, but his human supremacy is consistently affirmed.

The rabbis say that God created him just a little lower than the angels, and that of the fifty levels of understanding that exist in the world, all but one were given to Moses. The *aggadah* relates that when he was born on the seventh day of *Adar, the whole house was filled with light, and that he was already circumcised at birth — that is, his covenant with God was already made. His beauty as a child was outstanding and even Pharaoh played with the baby, sometimes taking off his crown and placing it on Moses' head. God offered to make Moses the ancestor of a great nation, but Moses refused God's offer for fear that he would be accused of seeking only his own glory and not that of his people. He struck the rock because he was angered by the jeering impatience and disbelief of the Israelites, but he insisted that his sin be recorded in the Torah, so that future generations would not mistakenly ascribe other transgressions to him. He pleaded with God that he be allowed to enter the Promised Land with the Israelites, so that he might share their joy as he had shared their years of sorrow, but God refused him. Moses was the leader of the generation that came out of Egypt and that generation lay buried in the wilderness. As a leader he must remain with his followers. He died aged 120 on the seventh of Adar. God buried him in a grave which had been prepared for him since the eve of the Sabbath of the *Creation. In spite of the extravagant claims made for Moses in the *aggadah,* the rabbis and indeed Moses himself never pretend that he is more nor less than a man.

Christian tradition sees Moses as prefiguring Jesus. Although the Christians believe that Jesus surpasses Moses (being regarded as the son of God while Moses is but His servant), Christianity draws a parallel between them. Both have deep faith in God and both encounter continual incomprehension and hostility.

Moses is mentioned in the New Testament more than any other Old Testament figure. He occupies an important place in Islam too. His biography, with many variations on the biblical account, is told in full in the Koran and the Muslim religion believes that he prophesied the coming of Muhammad.

Moses has been popular with artists, writers and musicians through history, more so even than biblical figures such as David, Jacob, Joseph and Solomon. As early as the second century b.c.e. the Alexandrian writer, Ezekiel the Poet, wrote a drama about the Exodus from Egypt, *Exagoge.* A series of medieval plays center around Moses, and his popularity as a dramatic figure increased through the 18th, 19th and 20th centuries with both Jewish and non-Jewish writers, including the German Heinrich *Heine and the modern Israeli writer Ḥayyim Hazaz. Statues of Moses abounded in medieval churches, Michelangelo's horned sculpture in Rome being a famous example. Scenes from his life illuminated early manuscripts, including the seventh century Ashburnham Pentateuch and the 13th century St. Louis Psalter. Moses is pictured in the mosaics of St. Mark's Cathedral in Venice and in the frescoes of the Vatican's Sistine Chapel in Rome. Artists such as Botticelli, Poussin, Rubens, Rembrandt and Turner have portrayed him. He has inspired many musical compositions, from the time of the Renaissance onwards, by composers such as Monteverdi (1610), Vivaldi (1714), Handel (1739), Rossini (1818) and Schoenberg (1951). He figures too in American Negro spirituals — most notably the powerful *Go Down Moses* ("When Israel was in Egypt's land — Let My people go!") which has become an international favorite.

Many scholarly books of Bible criticism have been written on the subject of Moses. Some point out that his life contains many events common to the heroes of non-Jewish legends as well, and other critical scholars have raised doubts that Moses ever existed at all. Aside from the Torah itself, and the Book of Joshua, references to him in the Bible are surprisingly scant. In spite of these scholarly doubts however, there does seem to be every reason for accepting the story as it is told in the Bible as true, and acknowledging Moses as a historical figure.

MOSHAV. The moshav system of farming settlements, like the *kibbutz, was developed in Israel in response to local needs. The time and effort required to prepare land, neglected for centuries, to

A grape-growing *moshav*, Kefar Avigdor.

produce profitable crops once again, and also the unstable security situation, made it impossible for a farmer to hope to succeed on a private farm in Israel during the 1920s. At the same time, not everyone was willing to join a kibbutz in which there was no individual ownership of property. The solution lay in the moshav ovedim, the "workers settlement." The public buildings, barns, silos, etc., the heavy machinery and the land for cultivation was owned in common, and some property — the homes of the members, smaller fields which they could farm as they wished — was held privately. The moshav also served as a marketing outlet for the small farms and was able to use its larger combined output to obtain better prices for its produce. It performed as a sort of local government and provided community services such as schools, recreation and cultural facilities. The first moshav ovedim was Nahalal, founded in 1921, mostly by former members of kibbutzim. In 1980 there were 400 moshavim in Israel with a total population of 143,700.

Similar to the moshav ovedim is the moshav shittufi (collective moshav) which allows no private farming at all. Unlike a kibbutz, each family lives by itself and receives an income alloted by the moshav. Cooking, household matters and care of the children are private but the village provides community and medical services. The first moshav shittufi was founded in 1936. In 1980 there were 35 such moshavim with a total population of 8,100.

In recent years the moshav has been a model for

developing countries trying to solve agricultural problems. Many students and experts have come to moshavim in Israel to study their methods.

MOTION PICTURES. Since the early years of motion pictures, Jews have played a major role in the development of the industry and have been prominent in all its branches. This is true not only of Hollywood where the role played by Jews is generally known and acknowledged, but of the German film industry up to the Nazi era, Russian film production up to the time of the Stalinist purges of the 1930s, the British film industry up to the present, and contemporary "underground" motion pictures in the

United States. Several factors favored the early success of Jews in this area: the film business was new and had not developed a tradition of excluding Jews; participation in it required no intimate knowledge of the vernacular, since all early films were silent; and the motion picture was initially regarded with contempt as a low-grade form of entertainment suitable only for the uneducated. New immigrants therefore found it relatively easy to enter this field, and in the United States in particular, Jewish immigrants used the opportunity to transform the medium from a marginal branch of entertainment into a vast industry.

In the United States, many Jews moved into motion pictures from vaudeville, as actors, writers and agents, but most were concentrated in the production and distribution of films. Typically, they started out by owning a single theater, and then moved up to managing larger theater chains and the distribution and production companies that controlled the industry. Columbia, MGM, Paramount, 20th Century Fox, Universal, Warner Bros. were all founded by Jews. Only United Artists, a distribution company founded by actors who feared that the big producers might restrict their artistic freedom, was not. Among the most famous Jewish producers in the formative years of the industry were David Selznick *(Gone With the Wind),* Hal Roach (the Laurel and Hardy comedy series) and Sam Spiegel *(The African Queen).*

In Europe, Jews were prominent in the development of motion pictures, although their influence there was not as pervasive as in the U.S. German Jews, prior to the Nazi takeover, held a

1. Segullah, a *moshav ovedim* (workers' settlement) founded in 1953.
2. Scene from the movie "M" about a psychopathic child-killer, filmed in 1931. The girl in the photo is Hanna Meron, who is today a successful Israeli performer.
3. *Never on a Saturday,* Israeli film in which Robert Hirsch played 13 different roles, produced in 1964.

prestigious place in the film industry, in particular in the avant-garde, with creative directors such as Erich Pommer and Fritz Lang leading the way in undertaking daring artistic experiments and adopting techniques which later became standard. The greatest Russian film-maker Sergei Eisenstein (1898-1948) was Jewish as was Dziga Vertov (Denis Kaufman), the father of documentary film. There were even some Russian films in Yiddish until the Stalinist purges of the 1930s when Jews were excluded from all prominent positions. In Poland, beginnings were actually made towards the development of a distinctly Jewish film industry with the production of films in Yiddish and with Jewish themes, but World War II saw the destruction of Polish Jewry. The government of Israel, since the establishment of the State, has done much to encourage a local film industry, which has shown much promise in recent years. It also strongly encourages foreign companies from the United States and Europe to film on location in Israel.

Films on Jewish themes have been made since the very beginning of the industry. In 1902 a two-minute short *A Dance in Jerusalem,* was produced in Palestine, and in 1909, *The Yiddisher Cowboy*, a caricature of Jewish life on New York's Lower East Side appeared. In the 1920s, many films focused upon Jewish ethnic awareness and upon the conflicts between American Jews and the other immigrant minorities around them. After World War II, a considerable number of European films dealing with the *Holocaust were produced, but in America, only recently has the film industry begun to confront sensitively such themes as racism and anti-Semitism, and to portray Jewish characters as more than stereotypes.

Below is an alphabetical listing of some outstanding Jewish actors, producers and directors not already mentioned:

Arkin, Alan W. (1934-   ), U.S. actor. He first made his mark in Joseph Stein's *Enter Laughing* (1963), and later starred in *The Russians Are Coming* (1966), *The Heart is a Lonely Hunter,* and *Catch-22* (1970).

Buttons, Red (1919-), U.S. vaudeville and television comic. He is best known for his television series "The Red Buttons Show" which appeared between 1952-55. He won an Oscar for his starring role in the film *Sayonara* (1957), and he also appeared in *The Longest Day* (1961) and *They Shoot Horses, Don't They?* (1970).

Cantor, Eddie (1892-1964), U.S. stage and film

The Marx Brothers, among the most famous Jewish film personalities.

comedian. Cantor was born Isidor Iskowitch, on New York's Lower East Side, and at an early age began to play the vaudeville circuits. He toured the music halls of Europe and was given top billing in the Ziegfeld Follies. In the 1930s he appeared in several films, including *The Kid From Spain* and *Ali Baba Goes to Town* (1937). Songs which he sang became immediate big hits on the radio. He was active in Jewish and non-Jewish philanthropic organizations, and helped to raise large sums of money for Jewish refugees from Nazi Germany.

Cobb, Lee J. (1911-1976), U.S. actor, best known for his award-winning portrayal of Willy Loman in Arthur Miller's play *Death of a Salesman* (1949). He appeared in a large number of Broadway plays and films, including *On the Waterfront* (1954) and *Exodus* (1960).

Curtis, Tony (1925-   ), U.S. actor. He was born Bernard Schwartz in New York, and spent his early career performing in summer stock companies and off-Broadway shows. Following his first dramatic role in *Trapeze* (1956), he starred in many films, including *The Defiant Ones* (1957), *Some Like It Hot* (1959) and *Don't Make Waves* (1967).

Douglas, Kirk (1916-   ), U.S. stage and film actor. Born Issur Danilovich, in New York State, he first made his mark portraying a prizefighter in the 1949 film, *Champion.* He later appeared in *The Bad and* the *Beautiful* (1953), *Lust for Life* (1956), and *Lonely are the Brave* (1962). He then became a producer and formed his own company which made the anti-war film *Paths of Glory* (1957) and *Spartacus* (1960), in both of which he also starred. He identified himself with Israel causes in the U.S., and in 1966 played the lead in *Cast a Giant Shadow,* a film about Colonel David *Marcus.

Hoffmann, Dustin(1937-   ), U.S. actor. His starring role in *The Graduate* (1967) brought him instant fame. His subsequent films included *Midnight Cowboy* (1969), *Little Big Man* (1970), and *Papillon* (1973).

Holliday, Judy (1923-1965), U.S. actress. Born Judith Tuvim, in New York, she made her Broadway debut in *Kiss Them for Me* (1945) and later starred both in the Broadway play and film *Born Yesterday* for which she won an Academy Award in 1950. She appeared in numerous Broadway musicals, and in films including *The Solid Gold Cadillac* (1956).

***Jolson, Al** (1886-1950), U.S. stage, screen and radio star.

***Kaye, Danny**(1913-   ), U.S. actor and entertainer.

Levine, Joseph E. (1905-), U.S. motion picture producer. His best known films include *Jack the Ripper* (1959), *Boccacio '70, Divorce Italian Style,* and *The Carpetbaggers.*

Lewis, Jerry(1926-   ), U.S. comedian. He was born Joseph Levitch in Newark, New Jersey, and started his career at the age of 14 when he joined Dean Martin to form a successful comedy team. They made 16 films together and appeared extensively in nightclubs and on television. After 1956, Lewis parted from Martin and became a successful comedian on his own, directing and appearing in many films, including *Don't Give Up the Ship* (1959), *The Errand Boy* (1961) and *The Nutty Professor* (1963).

Loew, Marcus (1872-1927), U.S. motion picture executive. Loew began his career by showing films in rented halls. In 1919 he bought Metro Pictures Inc., and in 1924 he acquired Goldwyn Pictures. With the appointment of Louis B. Mayer as vice-president, M.G.M. was formed, with Loew as president. He built up the firm's studios in Hollywood into one of the largest in the world, and also developed Loew's Inc., one of the largest cinema chains in the United States.

Lorre, Peter (1904-1964), Hungarian-born film star. In his youth he appeared with German theatrical groups and worked for a time with the German dramatist, Bertold Brecht. He went on to London and appeared in several horror films directed by Alfred Hitchcock. He was a thickset man who could look both sinister and amiable, and after moving to Hollywood, appeared in many mystery and adventure films, the best-known of which were *The Maltese Falcon* (1941), *Casablanca* (1942), *Arsenic and Old Lace* (1944), and *20,000 Leagues Under the Sea* (1954).

***Marx Brothers**, U.S. theatrical comedy team.

Mostel, Zero (1915-1977), U.S. actor. Born Samuel Joel Mostel in Brooklyn, New York, he first acquired the name "Zero" because of his poor marks at school. Nevertheless, he finished college and began a career as a painting and drawing teacher. Only later did he begin to appear as an entertainer, but he soon established himself as a comedian and as a portrayer of corpulent villains in Broadway plays. In the 1950s he was blacklisted because of his leftist views and only after 1958 did his career actively resume, when he appeared as Leopold Bloom in an off-Broadway production of *Ulysses in Nighttown.* Stage and film successes followed with his appearances in *A Funny Thing Happened on the Way to the Forum* (1962) and *Fiddler on the Roof* (1964).

Scene from the Israeli film *Tevye and His Seven Daughters,* based on the story by Shalom Aleichem.

Muni, Paul (1895-1967), U.S. stage and film actor. Born Muni Weisenfreund, he began acting at the age of 12, and soon joined the new Yiddish-speaking Jewish Art Theater established by Maurice Schwartz in 1918. In 1926, he appeared in his first English role on Broadway and his success was immediate. He had a rich voice, good command of mime and facial expression and a capacity for varied characterization. In the late 1920s he appeared in a whole series of gangster films, but he resisted typecasting as a gangster and starred in *The Story of Louis Pasteur* (1934), for which he won an Academy Award. He later appeared in *The Good Earth* (1935), *The Life of Emile Zola* (1937) and *Juarez* (1939). These roles expressed his true stature as an interpreter of heroism in spirit rather than in violence. Among his last films were *Inherit the Wind* (1955) and *The Last Angry Man.*

Newman, Paul (1925-   ) U.S. actor. Among his notable films were *Cat on a Hot Tin Roof* (1958), *Exodus* (1960), *The Hustler* (1961), and *Butch Cassidy.*

Nichols, Mike (1931-   ), U.S. actor and director. Born Michael Igor Peschowsky, Nichols began his career as a cabaret performer and off-Broadway actor. In the 1960s he began to direct Broadway plays, many of which were popular successes, including *Barefoot in the the Park* (1963), *The Knack* (1964), *The Odd Couple* (1965), and *The Apple Tree* (1966). He then turned to movies and directed the film version of *Who's Afraid of Virginia Woolf?* (1966) and later, *The Graduate* and *Catch-22* (1970).

Preminger, Otto Ludwig (1906-   ), U.S. film and stage director and producer. Born in Vienna, Preminger went to the United States in 1935 and gained prominence in the theater with productions which included the anti-Nazi play *Margin for Error* (1943). He then took up film work and became one of the most important and controversial directors in Hollywood. His successes include *Laura* (1944), *The Moon is Blue* (1953), *Exodus* (1960), *Advise and Consent* (1962) and *The Cardinal* (1963).

Robinson, Edward G. (1893-1973), U.S. stage and film actor. Born in Hungary, Robinson came to prominence in the 1920s, when he appeared in *Peer Gynt* (1923), *The Adding Machine* (1923), and *Kibitzer.* In his first starring film role, he played a gangster in *The Racket* (1927), a portrayal that led to his being cast in the title role of *Little Caesar* (1931). His performance as a gang leader became a screen classic and he went on to play many such parts. He appeared in 150 films in the course of his career, including *All My Sons* (1948), *The Ten Commandments* (1956) and *The Prize* (1963).

Sellers, Peter (1925-1980), English actor and comedian. In the early 1950s, he appeared together with Spike Milligan and Harry Secombe in the radio comedy series *The Goon Show* which became a national favorite in Great Britain. He first won acclaim in the United States with *The Mouse that Roared* (1959), in which he played several roles. Most of his films since then have been comedies, including *Dr. Strangelove* (1963) and *What's New, Pussycat?* (1965).

*Streisand, Barbra (1942-   ), U.S. actress, singer and musical comedy star.

Todd, Mike (1909-1958), U.S. producer and impressario. The son of a Polish-born rabbi, Todd was born Avrom Hirsch Goldbogen in Minneapolis, Minnesota. He produced 21 Broadway shows (largely light musicals), and promoted two motion picture filming innovations, Cinerama and Todd-AO. In 1956, he made the $6.5 million film of Jules Verne's *Around the World in 80 Days* which grossed, by the time of his death in a plane crash, $33 million. His third marriage was to the film actress Elizabeth Taylor.

*Topol, Chaim (1935-   ), Israeli stage and film actor.

Winters, Shelley (1922-   ), U.S. actress. Born Shirley Schrift, in St. Louis, Missouri, she made her first successful film in 1942, *A Double Life.* In 1959 she won an Oscar for her role in *The Diary of Anne Frank,* and in 1965 she won another Academy Award for *A Patch of Blue.* Her other films include *Lolita* (1962) and *The Moving Target* (1965), and she appeared in the plays *Who's Afraid of Virginia Woolf?* and *The Night of the Iguana* (1962).

1. Kirk Douglas playing the role of Mickey Marcus in the movie *Cast a Giant Shadow.* It was filmed on location in the hills of Jerusalem in 1965.

2. Yiddish actor Jacob Mestel (1884-1958) in the film *Uncle Moses,* based on a story by Sholem Asch.

Wynn, Ed (1886-1966), U.S. comedian. Born Isaiah Edwin Leopold, he was known for 60 years as "The Perfect Fool." In the 1920s he staged the *Ed Wynn Carnival* and *The Grab Bag;* later he appeared in the films *Boys and Girls Together* (1940-41), *Marjorie Morning star* and *The Diary of Anne Frank* (1959).
Wynn, Keenan (1916-), U.S. actor. The son of Ed Wynn, Keenan toured in stock companies and appeared on the stage before making his screen debut in *See Here Private Hargrove* (1944). Subsequent films included *The Hucksters* (1947), *Kiss Me Kate* (1953), *The Americanization of Emily* (1964) and *MacKenna's Gold* (1969).

MOUNTAIN JEWS (Tats). Tucked away in the mountainous region of Dagestan and the surrounding areas of East Caucasus in the Soviet Union, there is a Jewish tribe which, due to its relative isolation from the rest of the world, has for centuries maintained its own unique Jewish lifestyle.

According to legend, these Mountain Jews and their neighbors, the Jews of Georgia, originated from the *Ten Lost Tribes. And, in fact, the Talmud mentions a Jewish community in the region as early as the third century c.e.

Apparently the community flourished during the Middle Ages. Travelers spoke of the dense Jewish population in the Derbent region and the area became known as *Zhidy* ("Land of the Jews"), or *Chufut-Dag* ("Mountain of the Jews").

Until the annexation of Dagestan by Russia at the beginning of the 19th century, the Mountain Jews were completely cut off from the rest of the world, and changes in their way of life came slowly. A 19th-century historian records that the Mountain Jews were then mostly illiterate farmers and hunters who lived in mud huts and carried daggers or similar weapons. They were prepared to defend their families and their honor by the sword and until recently practiced the custom of vendetta. But at the same time they carefully preserved their Jewish traditions. The synagogue, its exterior resembling a mosque, served as a *heder* for the children. They observed most Jewish festivals, circumcised all males, and held religious wedding ceremonies.

In 1917 the Mountain Jews fought alongside the Red Army against the anti-Semitic Czarist regime. But their situation was not much better under the Communists. As in the rest of the Soviet Union, the Mountain Jews had to contend with attempts at forced assimilation. They were ordered to change the alphabet of their Judeo-Tat dialect (which is similar to Iranian in origin) from Hebrew to Latin and then to Russian Cyrillic letters.

Communist propaganda against the Mountain Jews continues and in 1970 only four of their synagogues remained intact. But they have persisted in maintaining their Judaism and there are no reported instances of assimilation.

The Mountain Jews are also very enthusiastic Zionists despite official anti-Israel propaganda.

MUHAMMAD (c. 571-632). The founder and prophet of the Islamic faith, Muhammad was born into the Arabian tribe of Quraysh at Mecca and in his youth traveled with trading caravans to Syria, as steward to the rich widow, Khadīja. She was perhaps 40 and he 25 when she proposed marriage and he accepted. While she lived, Muhammad took no other wife; she bore him six children, including Fatima, the only one to give him a lasting line of descendants. Nothing more is known of Muhammad's life for 15 years thereafter.

From about 610 c.e. Muhammad claimed to have visions and to have been commanded, as messenger of God (Allah),to recite certain verses which came to his mind. In order to win over the Arabs to his new religion Muhammad realized that his appeal would have to be national and not aligned to either the Christianity of Byzantium or the Judaism of Babylonia. The holy book of Islam, the Koran, soon attracted a small community of devotees, and its message at this time concentrated on God's goodness and power, the return to God and final judgment, the necessity for man to be humble and grateful to God and to worship Him, and the obligation of generosity and respect for the rights of the poor and defenseless.

The ruling clique in Mecca began to fear that it might be overthrown. When Muhammad began to attack the traditional worship of many gods

Some Muslim sects believe that Muhammad really did appoint a successor, named Ali, before his death. That appointment is here depicted by a 16th-century artist.

(polytheism), opposition to him grew. His insistence that only the annual pilgrimage shrine, the Ka'ba in Mecca, be considered the shrine to the one God, became a point of contention and he was forced to leave Mecca for a while. The climax of his career came in 620. A delegation from Medina sought his arbitration in a conflict there and in return promised to accept him as prophet. He sent an agent to Medina to instruct the people in Islam. Two years later almost all the Arab clans of Medina pledged themselves to fight on the prophet's behalf. Medina, at this time, an oasis about 250 miles north of Mecca, contained some 20 Jewish tribes which were culturally hardly distinguishable from their Arab neighbors. The Jews were included in the federation of the eight major Medinian Arab clans with Muhammad's followers who emigrated from Mecca in 622; from this date is measured the Islamic era. Muhammad was anxious that the Jews acknowledge him as a prophet. He stressed the continuity of his message with that of earlier prophets and adopted Jerusalem as the direction to be faced in prayer. Friday afternoon became the time of weekly communal worship. But the Jews, especially the three major clans, were unimpressed. From the start they found fault with Muhammad's assertions.

Muhammad soon abandoned the attempt to win over the Jews and henceforth changed the direction of prayer toward Mecca. He claimed that Islam had been the true religion of *Abraham, who was not a Jew, and that any differences between himself and Jews and Christians stemmed from their corruptions of the truth or downright lies. From 624, relations between the Jewish tribes and the followers of Muhammad deteriorated, certainly to a large extent because of his personal hostility. The 600 men of the Jewish Qurayza tribe were put to death and their women and children sold into slavery. Other minor Jewish tribes, which maintained neutrality, were allowed to remain in Medina unmolested. Thus Muhammad attacked not the Jews as such, but those who undermined by criticism the ideology of Islam or who gave support to his opponents. In January 630 Muhammad set out for Mecca with 10,000 men; the city surrendered to him without resistance. He gave a general amnesty and forbade pillage. A few anti-Muslim propagandists were executed and the Ka'ba cleansed of idols. In the same month Muhammad defeated 20,000 Bedouin in the battle of Hunayn, near Mecca. He was now the most powerful leader in Arabia. Tribes all over the Arab world allied with him and became Muslims. Forbidden to fight against each other, they turned their military might northward. Returning to Medina after leading the greater pilgrimage, the *hajj,* in March 632, Muhammad died on June 8, making no provision for a successor. See also *Arabs, *Islam.

MUNICH, capital of Bavaria in southwest Germany, appears to have had a sizeable Jewish community by the 13th century. The Jews lived in their own quarter, had a synagogue and a *mikveh* (ritual bath) and a hospital but until modern times their history was one of recurring expulsions. In 1285, 180 Jews were burned to death in the synagogue following a *blood libel. In 1287 permission was granted for the rebuilding of the synagogue, but the community remained small and suffered various restrictions for several centuries thereafter. During the *Black Death (1348-49) the whole community was annihilated. By 1369 there were Jews in the city once more and in 1375 Duke Frederick of Bavaria granted them the privilege of paying the same rate of customs duties as non-Jews. Munich Jews lost all their assets when Emperor Wenceslaus (1378-1400) canceled all debts owed to them. In 1413 they were accused of

The remains of a synagogue in Munich after the destructive rampages of *Kristallnacht,* 1938.

1. Title-page of *Sefer Even Israel* by Israel Lipkin, founder and spiritual leader of the Musar Movement. The book consists of a collection of his discourses assembled by his pupils.

2. Over 80,000 people gather for the memorial ceremony in the Munich stadium in honor of the 13 Israeli sportsmen killed by Palestinian terrorists during the 1972 Olympics.

*desecration of the Host and again suffered persecution. In 1442 the clergy had the Jews of Upper Bavaria expelled. Eight years later they were also driven out of Lower Bavaria. The synagogue in Munich was converted into a church. For three centuries Jews were excluded from the city and from the Bavarian state.

During the Austrian occupation Jews were readmitted to Bavaria but in 1715 they were again expelled. A few settled again in Munich by the late 1720s. *Court Jews were exempted from the general ban on Jewish entry into the city in 1750. Apart from these the only Jews allowed to remain were those who had been commissioned as purveyors or had made loans to the state. A body tax was levied on the others, who were again expelled. In 1794 there were 153 Jews in Munich, earning their livings as contractors for the army and royal mint, as merchants, moneylenders, and peddlers. They had no legal rights. In 1805 they were granted the right of inherited domicile, and allowed to conduct religious services, and to reside in all parts of the city.

Following the Napoleonic Wars there were 451

Jews in Munich by 1814. A synagogue was dedicated in 1827. By 1900 there were 8,739 Jews, and by 1910 20% of Bavarian Jews lived in the capital (11,000). There was also a steady immigration from Eastern Europe. After World War I, a revolutionary government was formed on the Soviet model, and a number of Jews were prominent members. It was routed by right wing forces who instigated a reign of terror against communists, socialists, and Jews. During the political and economic upheavals of the 1920s and 1930s, Munich became a center of anti-Semitism, and the cradle of the Nazi Party (see *Nazism). When *Hitler took power in 1933, the Munich police came under the control of Reinhold Heydrich and Heinrich Himmler. The first *concentration camp, Dachau, was erected near Munich. A Jewish cultural and religious revival was sparked off by the increasing hostility of the Nazis to the 10,000 Jewish inhabitants. On July 8, 1938, Hitler ordered the destruction of the main synagogue. During the war 4,500 Jews were deported from Munich (most of the others having left earlier); 160 managed to survive the war in the city. After the war a new Jewish community was formed by camp inmates, refugees and displaced persons. In the following years about 120,000 Jews passed through Munich on their way to Israel. In March 1970 the Jewish home for the aged was burned down, seven people dying in the flames. As if to brand the city's vicious treatment of its Jews on the conscience of the world, a massacre of 11 unarmed Israeli sportsmen was perpetrated by Palestinian terrorists during the 1972 *Olympic Games in Munich.

In 1980 there were 3,920 Jews living in Munich but they were repeatedly troubled by acts of desecration and vandalism.

MUSAR MOVEMENT. The Hebrew word *musar* in the Bible means chastisement, but in later times it came to mean ethical and moral behavior which is the meaning in modern Hebrew. The Musar Movement which developed in the mid-19th century in Lithuania and Russia in Orthodox Jewish circles had as its aim the strengthening of the ethical and moral dimensions of Judaism and Jewish life. The idea was started by one of the outstanding rabbinical authorities of his day, Israel *Lipkin, who was better-known by the name Salanter, after his birthplace. He felt that the Jews were seeing Judaism as a ritualistic religion and were observing the *mitzvot* in a mechanical manner and ignoring the fact that

Judaism requires of man to be as good and ethical as he can possibly be. He believed that this could be corrected only by intensive study of texts which discuss the proper behavior required and the way to achieve it; and he inaugurated a movement to make such study an integral part of the curriculum of the yeshivot and to establish a small "*musar* room" in every neighborhood where people would go for a short period every day to "check up on their spiritual wellbeing."

Salanter's plans at first met with opposition from many rabbis, yeshivah heads and communal leaders who felt that the observance of the *mitzvot* and the study of Torah were sufficient to ensure that a person has a good character; but little by little the *musar* idea caught on and ultimately pervaded most — if not all — of the great Lithuanian yeshivot which appointed a special faculty member (known as the *mashgiah*) to supervise this aspect of the curriculum.

Israel Salanter had several outstanding disciples and over the years different methods and techniques developed to achieve the aim of the movement. Some yeshivot adopted extreme ways to inculcate in their

students the conviction that what other people think about a person is immaterial as long as that person does what is right. For this purpose students were given practical exercises to deliberately make themselves ridiculous in order to immunize them against taking other people's opinions seriously. Other yeshivot were less extreme. Common to all the schools, however, was the insistence on regular study of *musar* texts and constant self-examination particularly with regard to one's motivations and ethical life. Very many present-day yeshivot still operate according to the principles of the Musar Movement.

MUSEUMS. The establishment of museums to preserve Jewish material culture is a relatively recent innovation. Before the 19th century, the nearest thing to a Jewish museum was a collection of ritual objects bequeathed to a synagogue in Brunswick, Germany, in the 1700s. Later, a number of secular museums opened Jewish sections, devoted mainly to biblical and Palestinian antiquities. And in 1878 the first exhibition of Jewish ritual art was held at the Universal Exhibition in Paris. But the first actual Jewish museum — the Juedische Museum in Vienna — opened only in 1897.

1. Lecture at the Hebron yeshivah which follows the Musar trend being delivered by the late Rabbi Ezekiel Sarna.
2. Courtyard of the Rockefeller Museum of Antiquities in East Jerusalem.

1.   Interior of the Shrine of
the Book containing the
Dead Sea Scrolls, at the
Israel Museum, Jerusalem.
2.   The former Wolf
Museum in the Eisenstadt
ghetto, Austria, where
Jewish ritual objects were
displayed.
3.   The Billy Rose Sculpture
Garden at the Israel
Museum, Jerusalem.

Once the precedent was established however, Jewish museums were developed all over Europe. Famous collections were found in Munich, Budapest, Prague, Warsaw, Vilna and many other cities.

Most of the European museums were destroyed when the Nazis gained control. Fortunately a considerable amount of material was saved and transferred to other collections.

A strange fate befell the Jewish Museum of Prague when the Nazis decided to establish a "Museum of the Extinct People," intending to justify the destruction of the Jews. Ritual objects were collected throughout Eastern Europe and placed in the Klaus synagogue in Prague. At the end of the war its collection totalled more than 200,000 art objects, and forms the basis for today's Prague Jewish Museum.

At present there are hundreds of Jewish museums all over the world. The Jewish Museum in London, largest of the numerous Jewish collections in the city, was established in 1932 and has a superb collection. The Musée d'Art Juif in Paris, the Jewish Museum in Copenhagen, the Judisches Museum des Schweiz in Basle, and the Jewish Historical Museum in Amsterdam also have impressive displays. In Spain, the 14th century synagogue of Toledo, built by Samuel *Abulafia, has been designated an official museum illustrating the history of Sephardi Jews. New York City houses several Judaica collections, the largest of which is the Jewish Museum of New York. There are also many other Jewish museums throughout the United States.

The State of Israel is a land of museums. The largest is the Israel Museum in Jerusalem incorporating the Bezalel National Art Museum, the Shrine of the Book with the Dead Sea Scrolls, and the Rockefeller Museum which possesses a very large archaeological collection. Several museums are dedicated to the Holocaust and the Jewish resistance movements, e.g., *Yad Vashem in Jerusalem, *Yad Mordechai in the kibbutz of that name, and the Ghetto Fighters Museum located at Kibbutz Loḥamei ha-Getta'ot. Bet Hatefutsoth — The Naḥum Goldmann Museum of the Jewish Diaspora is in Tel Aviv.

MUSIC. Whether there is such a thing as "Jewish music" is a very difficult question to answer. This is mainly because the Jews have been scattered throughout the countries of the world for nearly 2,000 years and have adopted the musical traditions of their host nations and adapted them to their own needs. One great Jewish musicologist, Curt Sachs, defined Jewish music as "that music which is made by Jews, for Jews, as Jews." This, however, is a very wide definition and a complicated one because it is not clear what is meant by "as Jews." Be that as it may, music in all its aspects has been and is important for Jews. Music is used extensively in the synagogue rituals as well as in the home; Jewish themes have inspired great music, and there have been a great number of outstanding composers and performers who were Jews. In this article we will try to give you an overall picture of the subject to help you in your thinking.

In the Bible. According to the biblical tradition (Genesis 4:21), Jubal was "the ancestor of all who play the lyre and the pipe." Jubal was the sixth generation after Cain, the son of Adam; so we see that music started very early.

When King David brought the Ark of the Covenant to Jerusalem the procession was accompanied by the playing of lyres, drums, rattles and cymbals, and later on in the Temple, both instrumental and vocal music played a part in the service. It is clear from biblical sources that there were families of Temple singers, presumably Levites. Many of the Psalms are also headed by musical superscriptions which indicate that their recitation was accompanied by instrumental music.

In the Temple — and earlier in the wanderings in the desert after the Exodus from Egypt — the *shofar* and the trumpets played an important role. Sounding the *shofar* is still the main ritual of *Rosh Ha-Shanah today. In addition to the Temple, music was evident in many other activities. The rejoicing at military victories involved singing, dancing and drumming and the Bible describes music at popular feasts and at the meals of the aristocracy and the royal court. We are also told that the prophet Elisha needed to hear music to bring him to the state in which he could prophesy, and David used to sing and play for King Saul in order to soothe his troubled spirit.

In the Bible about 19 different musical instruments are mentioned; these include wind, percussion, and stringed instruments.

In the Second Temple there was an orchestra which accompanied the sacrifical services and the singing reached a high level. Some scholars are of the opinion that there was an instrument that resembled an organ — but this is very doubtful. Some passages in the Mishnah give a detailed description of the musical activities in the Second Temple, presumably from eye-witness accounts.

The Attitude of the Rabbis. In the Talmud and midrashic literature, music is highly thought of. There are many legends about King David's lyre (a type of harp) which was played by the midnight wind, and they also pictured even plants singing praises to God. It was the rabbis who first created the idea of the celestial music of the angels which became a universal source of artistic inspiration. Although the rabbis disapproved of the sound of a woman singing, feeling that it might excite a man's baser feelings, they really viewed music and song as an act of worship. One of the greatest rabbis of the modern period, the *Gaon

1. Title page of the Song of Songs, a biblical book from which many song lyrics have been adapted. The illustration shows a musician playing a lute before King Solomon who is believed to be the author of the book. From a 15th-century Florentine prayerbook.
2. A Persian youth serenading his bride. Late 18th-century painting.

1. Orchestra of a Jewish boarding school in Poland, 1894.

2. American violinist Isaac Stern (left) playing with two Supreme Court Justices, Moshe Landau (Israel) at the piano and Abe Fortas (U.S.) on the second violin. This unique event took place at the America-Israel Culture House in New York.

of Vilna, is reputed to have said that after the study of Torah, music is the most important of the arts. *Ḥasidism laid great stress on music as a means of serving God and in recent years a sort of "pop-ḥasidic" music has developed.

Cantillation. An important aspect of Jewish music is the way in which the Torah and the other sections of the Bible are read in public. These are chanted according to very ancient traditions which are indicated in the text by cantillation signs above and below the words. The signs, which were written down by the masoretes (for more on this see *Masorah) indicate how the verse is to be broken up and to what tune the words are to be chanted. The exact rendering of the music varies from community to community — the way the Yemenite Jews chant the

text is quite different from the way European Jews do — but these cantillation signs are in fact musical notations.

In addition to the traditional cantillation, many Jewish communities, particularly Oriental ones, have developed distinctive musical styles for the reading of Psalms and even Mishnah.

The first known musical notations on a Jewish text were made by Obadiah, the Norman proselyte (11th/12th centuries), a Catholic priest who converted to Judaism and annotated *piyyutim* (liturgical poems) with musical notations indicating the chant.

In the Synagogue. As even an occasional visitor to the synagogue can immediately see, Jewish prayer is musical. Entire sections are sung by the congregations and the services are led by a cantor or *ḥazzan* who starts and finishes every passage with a musical rendition. Each festival has its distinctive melodies in keeping with the mood of the occasion. Very often synagogues have choirs to accompany the *ḥazzan* and together they execute very complicated and sophisticated pieces of singing. When the *Reform movement started, it introduced the organ into the synagogue as a means of making the services more attractive. This move met with the firm opposition of the Orthodox rabbis, but it is still a feature of Reform synagogues throughout the world.

Not all synagogue music is the same. The Jewish community has always been influenced in its musical taste by the non-Jewish surroundings. This results in the fact that the music in an Oriental synagogue sounds like what Europeans think is Arabic music whereas to an Oriental Jew, Ashkenazi synagogue music sounds like European music.

In Israel. Just as there is a question as to whether Jewish music exists, so too with regard to Israel music. Because Israel is populated by immigrants from all parts of the world, Israeli composers try to combine and amalgamate all the different musical traditions. But it is hard to say definitely that there is Israeli music. Pop music in Israel sounds much the same as pop music throughout the world except that the text is in Hebrew — often biblical verses. However, each composer — whether of classical music or pop — writes the music he feels and in this he is undoubtedly influenced by what happens around him.

NABATEANS were a Semitic people, considered to have been Arabs, who established a kingdom in the ancient territory of *Edom, east of the Jordan River. The Nabateans have left no written records and knowledge of their history is obtained chiefly from Greek and Latin sources, mostly from the fourth century b.c.e. to the second century c.e.

The first recorded contact between the Jews and the Nabateans was in 169 b.c.e. With the rise of the *Hasmonean dynasty, the two nations were apparently drawn together because of their common Syrian enemy. Soon afterward, however, conflict arose between Judea and the Nabatean kingdom as both sought to annex territories. The Nabatean ruler in this period may have been Aretas, referred to in the sources as "king of the Arabs." When Aretas I died in 96 b.c.e., Avadat, king of Nabato, took the throne and became involved in open warfare with the Hasmonean leader Alexander *Yannai.

A succession of Nabatean rulers then fought a series of battles against the Syrians, the Greeks and the Romans, culminating with their first century c.e. struggle against *Herod, the Roman-appointed ruler of Judea.

The Romans deprived the Nabateans of their political independence early in the second century c.e., but they nevertheless maintained their religion and culture, which received its final blow when the Byzantines converted the inhabitants of their area to Christianity. The Nabateans passed out of history with the advent of Islam in the seventh century, but the ruins of some of their cities, such as Shivta, Kurnub, and Avedat in the Negev, and the magnificent Petra built into the red cliffs of Jordan, still remain.

NAGID. Toward the end of the eighth century, the *Abbasid caliphate was divided into independent kingdoms, in most of which there were Christian and Jewish minorities. The ruler of each kingdom appointed leaders for these non-Muslim groups, and the Jewish leader was called *nagid.* Most large Jewish communities were headed by a *nagid* who was probably chosen from among the Jews of high rank at the court of the sultan or caliph. The duty of the *nagid* was to serve as officer of the Muslim state and to see to it that Jews fulfilled the covenant of *Omar. He also looked after the interests of the Jews in internal community matters as well as protecting them from oppression. The position differed somewhat from that of the*exilarch under the earlier Abbasid rule: the *nagid* did not claim descent from the house of David, and the post was not a hereditary one. The *nagid* was usually appointed with the consent of the community on the strength of his own achievements. Ḥisdai ibn Shaprut and *Samuel ha-Nagid were influential *negidim* in 10th and 11th century Spain. They were able to accomplish a great deal for Jews in Spain and for Jewish communities and yeshivot in other parts of the world. In Egypt, Abraham, the son of Maimonides was an influential *nagid.* From the 16th to the 19th century in North Africa, the *nagid* served only his own local community, rather than an entire province. In 19th century Egypt, the *nagid* was replaced by the *hakham,* or chief rabbi.

NAHALAL, the first *moshav ovedim (workers' settlement) in Erez Israel. It was founded in 1921 in the western Jezreel Valley by veteran pioneers of the Second Aliyah, some of whom had been members of the first kibbutz, *Deganyah. The 80 settling families each received 25 acres (100 dunams) of land, and then proceeded to drain the malaria-infested swamps, which had prevented two previous attempts at settlement.

The village layout in Nahalal, devised by architect Richard Kauffmann, became the pattern for many of the moshavim established before 1948; it is based on concentric circles, with the public buildings (school, administrative and cultural offices, cooperative shops and warehouses) in the center, the homesteads in the innermost circle, the farm buildings in the next, and beyond those, ever-widening circles of gardens and fields.

In 1929 a Girls' Agricultural Training Farm was established at Nahalal by WIZO (Women's

Aerial photo of a reconstructed Nabatean farm at Avedat in the Negev, Israel. Notice the terraced field and the pipes along the hillside for conveying water to the crops.

1. Aerial view of Nahalal, designed by the architect R. Kaufmann.
2. The Ramban synagogue in the Old City of Jerusalem, believed to be the one originally built by Nahmanides in 1267. The synagogue has been restored several times over the centuries.

International Zionist Organization), and in the 1940s it became a coeducational farming school of the *Youth Aliyah movement.

Nahalal is now one of the principal centers of the moshav movement, with a population of about 1,100. In biblical times, Nahalal was a town in the territory of the tribe of Zebulun, the exact site of which is still in dispute.

NAHMANIDES

NAHMANIDES (1194-1270), Spanish rabbi, *halakhic* scholar, Bible commentator, kabbalist and community leader, known in rabbinic literature as RaMBaN, the acronym of Rabbi Moses ben Nahman.

Nahmanides spent all but the last four of his 76 years in Gerona, a little town in north-central Spain, but the fame he achieved in his lifetime was world-wide, and the writings he left have continued to challenge students and scholars alike to this very day. In his youth he was a student of some of the greatest *halakhic* scholars of northern and southern France. As a young adult, he set up his own yeshivah in Gerona and proceeded to rear a generation of disciples who later followed him as the acknowledged leaders of Spanish Jewry. He held no official communal position, but his stature as a scholar and teacher was so great that during his lifetime it was customary throughout Spain to refer to him simply as "the teacher," while later generations of Spanish rabbis would refer to him in their writings as "the trustworthy teacher" *(harav ha-ne'eman).* In 1232, at the height of the bitter controversy that erupted over the writings of *Maimonides, Nahmanides boldly stepped forward to attempt to bring together the

warring factions. (For a full description see *Maimonides.) His compromise proposal, however, was rejected by extremists in both camps, and the controversy continued to smolder for about 70 years, until the wisdom of his position was recognized and accepted by all. In 1263, he was called upon to undertake the awesome task of defending Judaism and all the Jews of Spain in a public *disputation with a Jewish apostate. The disputation was held in the presence of the King of Spain and all the leaders of the Spanish Church, and forced Nahmanides to draw upon all his scholarly and rhetorical talents in order to counter the carefully prepared arguments of his opponent. The Hebrew record of the debate which Nahmanides himself prepared, reveals that Nahmanides emerged victorious. However, as a consequence, he was forced to flee Spain in fear for his life, and at the age of 72, he reached Erez Israel and settled in Jerusalem. He quickly set out to reorganize the remnants of the Jewish community he found there, and then he moved on to Acre where he assumed the position of community leader. He died there in 1270, but his place of burial is unknown.

More than 50 works written by Nahmanides have been preserved, and all of them bear the stamp of his extraordinary mind — lucid thinking, rigidly logical order, intellectual boldness and profundity. In the realm of *halakhah,* he produced a series of lengthy works covering the major portions of talmudic literature. A large proportion of these consist of critical annotations to the main *halakhic* writings produced in the preceding generation. Nahmanides' goal in formulating these comments was to vindicate

the interpretations offered by earlier scholars in face of the critical attack of the later scholars. Included in this class of writings is Nahmanides' critique of Maimonides' novel classification and arrangement of the commandments found in his *Sefer Ha-Mitzvot*. To this very day, Nahmanides' annotations are studied, both by students in yeshivot and by advanced scholars, because of their penetrating insights into the problems of talmudic argumentation.

It is, however, as a Bible commentator that Nahmanides made his greatest mark. He wrote an extensive commentary on the whole Pentateuch and on the Book of Job which pioneered a new style and method in biblical interpretation. It combined a basic concern with understanding individual words and phrases together with a broad search for reaching a philosophical and mystical appreciation of the text as a whole. It was the first Bible commentary ever to be written which openly included kabbalistic allusions, and because of its wide popularity played a major role in spreading knowledge of the *Kabbalah to a wide audience. It became a classic almost immediately upon its appearance, and has continued to be used until today, together with the commentaries of *Rashi and Abraham *Ibn Ezra, as an indispensable aid in understanding the Bible.

NAHMAN OF BRATSLAV (1772-1811), hasidic *zaddik in the Ukraine, originator of a radical theology which made him a center of controversy all his life and founder of a sect of *Hasidism which is still in existence today.

1. The chair of Nahman of Bratslav, now used by his followers as a Chair of Elijah during circumcision ceremonies.
2. Interior of the synagogue of the Bratslaver Hasidim in the Me'ah She'arim quarter of Jerusalem.

Nahman was the great-grandson of the *Ba'al Shem Tov, the founder of Hasidism, and his mother was said to "possess the holy spirit." He was thus brought up in a thoroughly hasidic and mystical atmosphere. While he was only in his teens, he began to attract disciples who became his Hasidim, and he assumed the role of a *zaddik*. The doctrines he preached, however, were considered to be heretical by many of his contemporaries, and he was not able to stay in any one place for any length of time because of the controversies which he aroused. He made an extensive visit to Erez Israel, and then wandered around the Ukraine, settling finally in Bratslav, where he remained until shortly before his death. He died at the age of 39, after suffering for many years from tuberculosis.

After Nahman's death, no one succeeded him as *rebbe*. The members of his sect continued to venerate only him, and preserved with utmost reverence the chair upon which he used to sit. Used only on the occasion of circumcisions, the chair was carefully dismantled and each piece smuggled into Erez Israel when the Bratslaver Hasidim fled Europe prior to the outbreak of World War II. In Jerusalem, the Bratslaver Hasidim reassembled the chair, and it now stands in the Bratslaver synagogue in the Mea Shearim quarter of Jerusalem.

In contrast to all other hasidic sects, the Bratslaver Hasidim have no living *rebbe,* and thus they are sometimes referred to as the *Toite* (dead) Hasidim. The reason for this lies in Nahman's controversial theory of the *zaddik*. He claimed that there was only one true *zaddik* — himself — and that he was destined to reappear as the Messiah. The *ẓaddik* was to be venerated almost as a godlike figure, for the *ẓaddik* "simulates the Creator." He was the channel through which the community's prayers were directed to God and as a result all were obligated to confess before him so that he could bring about their spiritual elevation and redeem the world.

Naḥman did not record his theology in any systematic fashion. His disciples copied down a large number of allegorical stories and fables which he used to relate, and these have been carefully preserved. They are still studied with great care by the Bratslaver Hasidim to this day.

NAHUM OF GIMZO, an influential sage of the Mishnah who lived at the end of the first century and the beginning of the second century c.e. Only meager information has been preserved of his teaching and his life, but it is known that Rabbi *Akiva was a pupil of his and that he occupied himself mainly with *aggadah*. He is best known for his radically optimistic philosophy articulated in an epigram which also served as a pun on his name – *Gam Zo leTovah* – "This too is for the good" he was wont to say even in face of misfortune and catastrophe. Many stories are told about him in the Talmud, including one about the time he was carrying a casket full of jewels as a gift to the Roman emperor which were stolen from him at an inn and replaced with earth. "This too is for the good," he declared, and presented the earth to the emperor. The emperor threatened to put him to death for mocking him, but he was vindicated for his optimism when the prophet Elijah appeared in the guise of a senator and suggested that this was the legendary earth which turned into deadly arrows when thrown at the enemy in battle. And on being put to the test, it did indeed prove to be that earth.

NAMES are more than just arbitrary labels for people. Each Jewish name tells a story of its own and very often reflects the nature of the time, place and atmosphere in which it was chosen.

The most important source for Hebrew proper names is the Bible, and biblical names were usually descriptive and meaningful, often incorporating the name of God in praise or gratitude; thus, Nethanel (God has given), Eleazar (God has helped), Joshua (God the Savior). Other biblical names describe the circumstances surrounding the birth. Thus Abraham called his son Yizḥak [Isaac] from the Hebrew word for laughter, because Sarah had laughed at the idea of

1. Imperial decree by Napoleon, issued at Bayonne, France, on July 20, 1808, ordering all Jews to adopt surnames.
2. Page from a book in which name-changes were registered, Mainz, 1808.

bearing a child in her old age. And Yizḥak named one of his sons Ya'akov [Jacob], a play on the Hebrew word *akev* ("heel"), because he was born grasping the heel of his twin brother Esau.

The Talmud attaches great importance to the preservation of Hebrew names, viewing foreign names as a sign of assimilation. According to the Talmud, one reason for the deliverance of the Children of Israel from Egyptian bondage was the fact that they did not change their names. Yet, despite this subtle warning, Jews have tended to adapt their Hebrew names to the language of their neighbors or to take on purely non-Jewish names. This tendency, first noticeable during the Middle Ages, accelerated during the late 18th and 19th centuries. Some governments encouraged the process by passing laws which forced Jews to adopt European names. Napoleon issued such a decree, hoping to assimilate the Jews.

It was during the Middle Ages that Jews began taking on surnames to add to their Jewish forenames. These second names, which have since evolved into family names, were at first used as descriptions to identify the individual. The most traditional method was to add the name of the father to the forename, e.g. Ibn Ezra (son of Ezra), or Jacobson (son of Jacob). The surnames Cohen and Levy were usually used to show direct descent from the *priests and Levites who served in the Temple. Other sources of surnames were the occupation (Miller, Goldsmith), birthplace (Berliner, Moscowitz), or physical characteristics (Alt= old, Klein= small, Schwartz= swarthy) of the individual. Some well-known surnames are really *abbreviations whose original meanings reflect the history of the family. For instance, Katz is short for *Kohen Zedek* (Righteous priest), and Zachs is an abbreviation of *Zer'a Kedoshei Speyer* (descendants of the martyrs of Speyer — a city in Germany whose Jewish population was almost wiped out during the Crusades).

Like most peoples of the world, the Jews have evolved certain traditions regarding the use of names. For example, Ashkenazi Jews consider it wrong to name a child after a living father or grandfather, whereas Sephardim consider it an honor to do so for a grandparent. According to the *Hasidei Ashkenaz, it is wrong to marry a woman with the same name as the husband's mother. The reason for this seems to be because of respect; the man might tell his wife to do something and the mother might think he meant her.

Jewish boys are officially named at the *circumcision ceremony eight days after birth, and a girl's Jewish name is publicly announced when the father is first called to the Torah after her birth. Converts are also given new names — usually ben Abraham or bat Abraham (son or daughter of Abraham) because conversion is equated with rebirth.

In modern times, names have changed to suit the location and environment of the bearer. In the United States Jews have adopted shortened, Anglicized versions of their names and in Israel, with the revival of Zionism and the Hebrew language, many have adopted modern Hebraized names. (Golda *Meir was once Golda Myerson, *Ben-Gurion was Gruen, and *Ben-Zvi was Shimshelevitz.) The result of this environmental influence is that very often cousins and even brothers have different family names.

NAMIER (Bernstein-Namierowski), **SIR LEWIS** (1888-1960), English historian and Zionist, was born of well-to-do landowning parents in eastern Galicia, where anti-Semitism early turned him into a dedicated Zionist. He was 20 when he reached England, an eccentric and self-centered young man who alienated many of his contemporaries with his forcefully expressed opinions. He studied at Balliol College, Oxford, with men such as T.E. Lawrence and Arnold J. Toynbee. During World War I he served in the British army and acted as an adviser on eastern Europe at the Versailles Peace Conference in 1918.

In 1931 he was appointed professor of modern history at the University of Manchester. His work centered on the theme of cohesion versus disintegration, and he pioneered a new theme of historical scholarship.

He devoted himself to the Zionist cause: from 1927 to 1931 he was political secretary to the Zionist executive and one of the founders of the *Jewish Agency. He served as deputy to Chaim *Weizmann on the Anglo-Jewish committee for refugees from Germany, and during World War II he worked full-time for the Jewish Agency. His Zionism was a romantic nationalism — a vision of a historic breakthrough in messianic terms.

NAPLES. The first Jewish settlement in this city which was also the former kingdom of southern Italy probably dates back to the first century c.e. By the fourth century the community had achieved considerable size and economic importance, and by the 12th century *Benjamin of Tudela, who visited there, reported 500 Jews living in Naples, with their own synagogue and school, enjoying the right to own real estate and dispose of it as they wished (a right rarely granted Jews in those days).

But their good fortune was reversed when, in the 13th century, Dominican preachers incited anti-Jewish riots which reached their peak in 1290.

In 1330, Robert of Anjou invited Jews from the Balearic Islands to settle in Naples and the rest of his kingdom, promising them protection against attack and the same taxation rights as those enjoyed by Christians. This was the beginning of a more tolerant era for the Jews of Naples, and the favorable conditions there attracted Jews from various parts of Europe, among them Don Isaac *Abrabanel, who became fiscal adviser to King Ferdinand I and King Alfonso II.

In the 15th century a Hebrew press was established in the city and Naples became the center for book printing and the book trade. The first Jewish printer there was the German Joseph ben Jacob Gunzenhausen, who was followed in 1490 by Joshua Solomon *Soncino.

Hard times returned for the Jews of Naples when

in 1495 the kingdom was conquered by Spain and in 1496 a decree for the expulsion of the Jews was issued. Though not implemented immediately, the decree was finally carried out in 1510 and only 200 wealthy families were allowed to remain, on condition that they pay an exhorbitant tax. In 1541 even these remaining Jews were expelled by Emperor Charles V.

It was not until 1735, when the kingdom passed to the house of Bourbons, that Jews were readmitted to Naples. Even then, however, the reprieve was short-lived as pressure from the Church caused the Jews to be expelled once more in 1746.

At the beginning of the 19th century several Jewish families again settled in Naples, and by 1931 there were 998 Jews there. After World War II only 534 remained and there are still about that number in the city.

1. Title page of the volume containing the decisions of the French Sanhedrin set up by Napoleon in 1807 to deal with Jewish legal matters.
2. Medal issued in honor of Napoleon's decree emancipating the Jews of Westphalia in 1808. The decree was later revoked by the Germans after the fall of Napoleon, and the Jews reverted to their subservient status.

DÉCISIONS DOCTRINALES
DU
GRAND SANHÉDRIN
QUI S'EST TENU A PARIS AU MOIS D'ADAR PREMIER,
L'AN DE LA CRÉATION 5567 (*Février 1807*),

SOUS LES AUSPICES
DE
NAPOLÉON - LE - GRAND,
Avec la traduction littérale du texte Français en Hébreu.

PARIS,
IMPRIMERIE HÉBRAÏQUE , FRANCAISE ET DE LANGUES ORIENTALES
DE L.-P. SÉTIER FILS,
IMPRIMEUR DU CONSISTOIRE CENTRAL DES ISRAÉLITES.

1812.

NAPOLEON BONAPARTE (1769-1821), French emperor who left a mixed legacy of both generosity and intolerance towards the Jews. Adhering to the French revolutionary code of liberty and equality, Napoleon emancipated European Jews from their ghetto existence and then reportedly issued a manifesto in Palestine (never to be fulfilled) promising Jews their return to the Holy Land. But his greed for personal power led him to deny the Jews certain freedoms and he attempted to destroy their independent, nationalistic spirit.

His greatest contribution to Jewish history took place during the years 1806-1808 when he set up a variety of Jewish political, religious and social organizations in France. He gathered rabbis and Jewish communal leaders from all parts of the French empire to convene an Assembly of Jewish Notables whose job it was to clarify relations between the Napoleonic state and the Jews. He also established the French Sanhedrin to deal with Jewish legal matters, and the Consistory — the official organ of the French Jewish community. Napoleon's purpose in establishing these Jewish institutions was to separate the political from the religious elements in Judaism, and thereby gain greater control over the former. But the long-range effect was to help the Jews organize their own independent functioning community.(For details of this organization, see *Consistory.)

The euphoric mood created among Jews by these reforms was shattered, however, when on March 17, 1808, Napoleon issued an order restricting the economic activity and the freedom of movement of

the Jews in the eastern part of the empire for a period of ten years. This order became known among Jews as the "Infamous Decree."

Napoleon's influence was not limited to Europe. In February 1799, his conquering armies moved into Palestine, capturing the coastal towns of El Arish, Ramleh, Jaffa and Haifa. They met heavy resistance at Acre, however, and by June, 1799, his decimated army retreated to Egypt.

With the fall of the Napoleonic empire, the status of the Jews deteriorated. The Congress of Vienna, convened after his defeat, refused to ratify the rights of the Jews acquired under the Napoleonic conquest and numerous anti-Semitic riots ensued.

NASI, prince or leader. In biblical use, *nasi* refers to a person of importance, a leader, a tribal ruler or a king. Under the Roman occupation of Erez Israel toward the end of the period of the second Temple, when there was no independent Jewish leadership, the term *nasi* was used by Jewish rulers to show their authority while not claiming kingship. Ancient coins of Simeon *Bar Kokhba, on display now in the Israel Museum, bear the inscription *Shimon nesi Yisrael,* Simeon, prince of Israel.

The title is best known for its reference to the presiding judge of the *Sanhedrin (high court) although some sources claim the term was first applied to *Judah ha-Nasi who was head of the Sanhedrin toward the end of the second century. The *nasi* presided over court sessions; proclaimed the new *moon and fixed the *calendar and festivals;

legislated halakhic rulings and kept in touch with Jewish communities in the Diaspora. After the destruction of the Temple in 70 c.e. the Roman governors probably utilized the authority of the *nasi* in their control of the subjugated Jews. The title *nasi* persisted for many centuries and in many lands throughout later history, sometimes as the head of a Jewish community or institution, sometimes as a title of honor for members of illustrious families. The fabulous family of Portuguese Marranos took the name Nasi (see *Nasi, Gracia) and were indeed leaders of the oppressed Jews. In recent modern times *nasi* is the Hebrew word used for the title "president" and is used to designate the president of the State of Israel (see also *Nagid).

NASI, GRACIA (c. 1510-1569), wealthy Portuguese stateswoman who used her power and influence to help her fellow-Jews escape persecution.

Gracia Nasi was a member of the first generation of Portuguese *Marranos (Jews who were forced to convert to Christianity) and her original name as a

Christian was Beatrice de Luna. In 1528 she married Francisco Mendes, also a Marrano and member of an important banking family. When Francisco died in 1537, his widow — heiress to a large share of the family wealth — left Lisbon with her only child, Reyna, and her nephew Joao Micas, and went to join her brother-in-law Diogo Mendes in Antwerp. There she became active in aristocratic society and assisted in efforts to aid Marranos escape the *Inquisition. With the help of her nephew Joao, who acted as her business manager, she is said to have established personal ties with many of the world's rulers, including the Emperor Charles V, the Queen Regent of the Netherlands, and the sultan of Turkey.

But even her great wealth and important position could not protect her from the wave of anti-Semitism spreading through Europe, and when Diogo died she was forced to flee to Venice, leaving much of her property behind. In Venice she was betrayed to the Inquisition by her own sister for secretly practicing Judaism and escaped punishment only because the Turkish authorities intervened in her behalf. Such diplomatic maneuvering, rare on any occasion and almost unheard of in cases concerning Jews, was proof of the great power and influence she had acquired.

From Venice she moved to Spain and in 1553 settled in Constantinople. It was during this period that she totally abandoned Christianity and openly embraced Judaism. She took on the Jewish name of Gracia Nasi and her nephew became known as Joseph

1. The Sanhedrin (high court) of the Jews, as it may have looked almost 2,000 years ago, with the *Nasi* seated in the center.
2. Gracia Nasi honored in a 16th-century medal.

Nasi. A short while later Joseph married his cousin Reyna.

In Constantinople Gracia continued her remarkable work on behalf of Marranos, while Joseph continued the family's financial expansion. They controlled the major part of the spice trade in northern Europe, the largest market at that time, and conducted commercial activities with various European countries. When Pope Paul IV burned 26 Marranos in 1556 as renegades from the Christian faith, Gracia Nasi retaliated by organizing a boycott of the Ancona port, single-handedly forcing the Turks to intervene and save some of the accused. This boycott represented the first attempt by Jews to use economic power as a weapon in international affairs.

Gracia and Joseph contributed large sums to Jewish causes, establishing yeshivot, supporting Jewish scholars, and helping start a Hebrew press in Constantinople. Through its extensive influence, the Nasi family obtained permission from the Turkish sultan to rebuild the ruined Palestinian city of *Tiberias. Gracia settled there, opened a yeshivah, and encouraged Jewish immigration. It is believed that she died in Erez Israel in 1569.

NASSER, GAMAL ABDUL (1918-1970), president of the United Arab Republic (Egypt), whose extremely belligerent attitude toward Israel aggravated the already tense Middle East situation.

Nasser participated as an officer in Egypt's invasion of Israel in 1948. Shortly afterward, as a founder of the revolutionary "free officers" group, he led the 1952 military coup in Egypt, forcing King Farouk to abdicate and making General Mohammed Naguib head of the new republic. In 1954, Nasser became premier and ousted Naguib, and in 1956, as the only candidate on the ballot, he was elected Egypt's first president.

As one of the most powerful Arab leaders, Nasser encouraged other Middle Eastern countries to join in his anti-Israel policy. He intensified the economic *boycott of Israel, supported armed infiltration, and insisted that Arabs refuse to recognize Israel or negotiate with her. By barring Israel shipping from the Suez Canal and, in 1956, nationalizing the Suez Canal Company, he helped precipitate the *Suez Campaign.

Nasser initiated economic and social reforms in his country, but he also nationalized the press and silenced his critics. He made Egypt militarily and economically dependant on the USSR, and initiated the arms race between Israel and her Arab neighbors.

On June 9, 1967, after Egypt's defeat in the *Six-Day War, Nasser resigned for a few hours, but reassumed power in response to mass demonstrations by his supporters. He then tried to place the blame for defeat on others, and had several military leaders convicted in show trials.

Gamal Abdul Nasser died suddenly in September 1970, and was replaced by President Anwar Sadat.

NATIONAL JEWISH WELFARE BOARD (JWB). Organized in 1917, the JWB was originally meant to serve the religious needs of Jewish soldiers and sailors in the United States armed forces during World War I. It has since served hundreds of thousands of young men in the course of several wars, and has also assumed various community functions.

The JWB is made up of representatives from the YMHAs, synagogues, and community organizations. In its military capacity it is responsible for organizing religious services and holiday programs in military

1. Cartoon which appeared in the Egyptian paper, *Al-Jarida*, on May 25, 1967, shortly after President Nasser blockaded the Gulf of Akaba to Israel shipping and a week before the outbreak of the Six-Day War. It shows Nasser, with the armies of Iraq, Lebanon, and Syria behind him, kicking Israel, represented by a stereotyped caricature of the Jew, over the edge of a cliff.
2. A Hanukkah service organized by the National Jewish Welfare Board for American Jewish sailors.

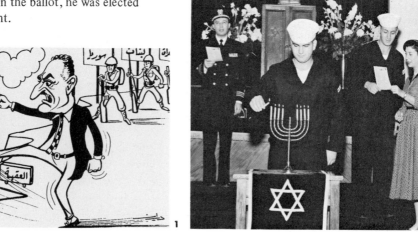

bases, obtaining furloughs for Jewish soldiers on religious holidays, preparing an abridged prayer book, and recruiting Jewish military chaplans – the first 26 of whom served in World War I.

During World War II, the JWB established a close relationship with the United Service Organizations for National Defense (USO) and greatly expanded its war work, recruiting 311 rabbis to serve as chaplains.

The organization did not cease to function during peace time and, in fact, turned much of its effort to the civilian population – specifically to the establishment of Jewish community centers across the country. In 1921, the JWB merged with the Council of Young Men's Hebrew and Kindred Associations (YHMA and KA), acting as sponsor and organizer of these cultural-recreational bodies. In 1922, a JWB Lecture Bureau was formed which encourages lectures, forums, and classes in the community centers. A World Federation of YMHAs and Jewish Community Centers was organized in 1946 which provides teenage activities, camping facilities, old-age functions and family programing in various communities throughout the world. The Jewish Book Council and the Jewish Music Council, both sponsored by JWB since 1944, also provide Jewish cultural activities.

A rift developed within the ranks of the JWB however, with regard to the Jewish character of the community centers. Those who favored non-sectarianism felt that any emphasis on Jewish religion and culture would be discriminatory and segregationist. Others felt that the whole point of the YMHA system was to have a distinctively Jewish chain of community centers. This ambivalence is reflected even in today's centers, many of which accept non-Jewish members and sanction non-Jewish programing.

NATIONAL PARKS OF ISRAEL. An excursion to any one of Israel's national parks can be an unforgettable recreational and educational experience. One can board a cable car to the top of *Masada's famed archaeological excavation and watch the sun rise over the Dead Sea, or enjoy the lush foliage and natural pools at the desert oasis of *En Gedi. Tourists and local residents alike can picnic in the landscaped seashore gardens of *Ashkelon, listen to concerts in the Roman amphitheater at *Caesarea, or just wander leisurely through the parkland areas of the Carmel forests.

The National Parks Authority of Israel is

responsible for maintaining over 34 sites throughout the country, designated as national parks. Most of these parks have been linked with historical sites, where the remains of ancient settlements are often augmented by picturesque gardens and tourist facilities. Such historical sites included Mt. Zion in Jerusalem, the Jerusalem national park circling the Old City walls, the Crusader ruins at Aqua Bella (Ein Hemed) and the ancient synagogues at *Bet Alfa, Baram and Hammath.

Aerial view of the natural spring and bathing pools of Ma'yan Ḥarod, one of Israel's many national parks.

1. The gnarled trunk of an aged tree, preserved in Ḥurshat Tal, a national park in the Upper Galille.
2. Itzhak Navon, fifth President of the State of Israel.

Occasionally, purely archaeological sites are taken over from the Department of Antiquities by the National Parks Authority. This is usually the case when the excavations have been particularly impressive and attract a large number of visitors, such as those at Masada, Ḥazor, *Acre, and Caesarea.

There are also numerous parks chosen not for their historical significance but for their natural beauty and scenic locations. For example, Ḥurshat Tal in the Upper Galilee with its streams, pond, lawns, and woods makes a lovely picnic, hiking and camping area. Similarly, the natural spring in Mayan Ḥarod in the Valley of Jezreel, and the three natural pools of Gan ha-Sheloshah also in Jezreel are ideal vacation spots, enchancing the beauty and preserving the natural wonders of Israel. (See also *Archaeology, *Capernaum, *Holy Places in Israel, *Megiddo, and *Yad Mordekhai.)

NATURE. All natural phenomena are represented in the Bible as the creative handiwork of God. This perspective is explicitly and dramatically formulated in the story of *Creation, but it is the common assumption underlying all the biblical writings. In the words of the Psalmist, "The heavens declare the glory of God" — they reveal in their grandeur and awesomeness the majesty of God who created them.

Having been created by God, the universe is also totally subject to His control. As a result, God can impose His will upon the workings of the natural world as He pleases (the miracles of the Bible) but He can also transfer some of His controling power to others. This God did when He created and blessed man. Although part of the natural world, man was given dominion over it, and told that the natural world was to serve his greater interests.

For the ancient Greek philosophers, nature and the physical universe constituted a central focus of philosophic investigation, but the rabbis of the Mishnah and Talmud did not share this speculative interest. For them, as for the biblical authors, the contemplation of nature served primarily to reveal the wonderful ways of the Creator and to point the way for man in his search for understanding God. (For the rabbis' understanding of miracles, see *Miracles.)

For *Philo and the medieval Jewish philosophers, however, nature was an important subject of philosophic study. In general they adopted without modification the accepted physical theories of their day which claimed, among others, that the natural order operated in accordance with immutable laws of physics and that all substances were composed of four basic elements. These assumptions forced them to undertake novel explanations of many parts of the Bible, notably the *Creation story and the miracles. However, a central feature of the philosophy of most of them was the emphasis upon the fact that the study of nature was a necessary prerequisite for attaining a true understanding of God, since God's essential nature could not itself be known, but could be approached through understanding His creation.

In the writings of many of the medieval kabbalists, a strong tendency towards a pantheistic appreciation of nature can often be found. A central feature of later kabbalistic thinking is the notion that in the initial process of Creation, sparks of the divine were scattered throughout the Universe, and are contained within all matter. This notion was developed in the 20th century by Rabbi Abraham Isaac *Kook, who explained the evolution of the natural world as a purposeful drive of all Creation striving for reunification with God.

NAVON, ITZHAK (1921-   ), fifth president of the State of Israel. Navon was born in Jerusalem to an old Sephardi family which settled in Erez Israel in the 17th century. After graduating from the Hebrew University he became a teacher. From 1946 to 1949 he was active in the Arabic Department of the Haganah. After serving in the Israel Embassy in Argentina and Uruguay (1949-50), he was appointed political secretary to the foreign minister, Moshe Sharett. He was political secretary to David Ben Gurion and head of the prime minister's office (1952-63) and director of the cultural division of the Ministry of Education and Culture (1963-65). Navon later joined the Rafi party and was elected to the Knesset in 1965 where he became one of the deputy speakers and served as chairman of the Committee on Foreign Affairs and Defense. At the 28th Zionist Congress (1972) he was elected chairman of the General Zionist Council.

Navon wrote the text for two musical plays based on Sephardi folklore, *Sephardic Romancero* (1968) and *Bustan Sephardi* ("Spanish Garden," 1970).

In 1978 he was elected president of the State of Israel in succession to Prof. Ephraim Katzir, thus becoming the first native-born president of the modern Jewish state. In October 1980 he paid an official visit to Egypt, the first by a president of Israel to an Arab state. **2**

NAZARETH, a city in Galilee, sacred to Christians as the home of *Jesus, Mary and Joseph. According to the new Testament, Jesus' birth was announced to Mary in Nazareth. Jesus was brought up in the town, and although he did almost all his preaching outside of Nazareth, he was known in his lifetime as "Jesus of Nazareth." Early Christians were contemptuously called "Nazarenes" by their enemies, and the Hebrew and Arabic terms for Christian are derived from the town's name.

During the first centuries of Christianity, Nazareth does not seem to have had a Christian community, but by the sixth century a church had been established in a converted synagogue. During the Crusades the town was repeatedly fought over by the Crusader and Muslim armies, changing hands several times. In 1263 it was totally destroyed and remained in ruins for 400 years. Only towards the middle of the 18th century was the city rebuilt. By the early decades of the 20th century the population numbered some 8,000, both Muslim and Christian, and served as a market center for the surrounding Jezreel Valley as well as a pilgrimage and tourist center. In July 1948 the city was captured by the Israel army and remained in Israeli hands after the armistice was signed. Its population was rapidly augmented by Arabs who had left other locations, to the extent that it became, prior to the *Six-Day War of 1967, the largest Arab center in the State of Israel. By 1969 it had a population of 33,000 with a slight majority of Muslims over Christians.

The city of Nazareth.

In 1957 Naẓerat Illit, a Jewish development town was built in the heights overlooking the city. It developed rapidly, becoming a center for large industrial enterprises (such as car manufacturing) and in recent years has served as one of the main absorption centers of new immigrants, particularly from the Soviet Union.

NAZIRITE was a person who vowed for a specific period to abstain from grapes or grape-products, from cutting his hair, and from touching a corpse. Through this abstinence, he attained a certain symbolic sanctity.

A person could choose to dedicate himself for a few weeks or a few years. When the period of the vow was not specified, it was understood to be 30 days. The most famous Nazirites in Jewish history — *Samson and *Samuel — were consecrated as such by their parents from the moment of their conception, with the intention that they remain Nazirites all their lives. Samson's Nazirite period was, of course, ended prematurely when his hair was cut by his enemies.

The uncut hair of the Nazirite was his distinguishing feature. Since hair continues to grow throughout life, it was considered by the ancients to

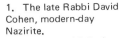

1. The late Rabbi David Cohen, modern-day Nazirite.
2. Samson, a biblical Nazirite, who derived extraordinary strength from his uncut hair.
3. Nazis humiliating a Polish Jew by publicly and brutally cutting off his beard.

be the source of man's vitality and life-force. Thus, the symbolic connection between Samson's superhuman strength and his unshorn locks.

If the Nazirite wanted to end his period of sanctity before the sworn date, he had to make a reparation offering at the Temple and undergo a ritual involving the sprinkling with purifying waters and the shaving of his head. If he completed the vow period, he was allowed to bring a thanksgiving offering, including some of his freshly cut hair.

It was considered a great honor to be able to bring such a thanksgiving offering, and some pious people took the Nazirite vow just so that they would have this opportunity. Others became Nazirites for the fulfillment of a wish, such as the birth of a child.

The Nazirite vow was severely discouraged by the rabbis, since *asceticism was considered to be against the spirit of Judaism. However, the observance of the Nazirite vow seems to have persisted for centuries until its virtual disappearance in the Middle Ages. In modern times, Nazirite practices were observed in Jerusalem by Rabbi David Cohen, a disciple of Chief Rabbi A.I. *Kook.

NAZISM, the political movement and ideological system which, under the leadership of Adolf *Hilter, dominated Germany between 1933 and the end of World War II in 1945. Based upon a mixture of extreme racialist and nationalist ideas, of which unrestrained anti-Semitism formed the main element, Nazism succeeded in implementing a Europe-wide program of exterminating Jews which resulted in what is known today as the *Holocaust of European Jewry.

The term "Nazi" originates from the German pronunciation of the first two syllables of

Nationalsozialistische Deutsche Arbeiterpartei
("National Socialist German Workers' Party), the name
of Hitler's political party. Founded immediately after
World War I, the party quickly won over a large
segment of the German population by employing
propaganda which took advantage of the unbearable
economic situation of the German people that
followed their massive defeat in the war. Under the
sign of the swastika, Nazism projected an emotional
appeal that almost had the character of a new religion.
The ideology of the party, clearly spelled out in Hitler's
own book, *Mein Kampf* ("My Struggle"), asserted that
the German people constituted an elite Aryan race
whose purity was being threatened by the "pollution"
of Jewish blood. The Jews, he declared, were calculating
and unpatriotic, and were blamed for Germany's
defeat in World War I. They were profiteers,
materialists, base in character, supporters of both
capitalism and communism, and parasites of the
nation.

Using slogans such as "When Jewish blood spurts
from the knife, things will go well," and "Germany,
Awake ! Judah, drop dead ! " as well as classic
anti-Semitic propaganda literature, such as the
*Protocols of the Learned Elders of Zion, the Nazi
party whipped up strong anti-Jewish feelings across
Germany. In 1933, when Hitler became chancellor and
assumed virtual dictatorial powers, he began to
implement a program that aimed at making Germany
"Judenrein" (free of Jews). Laws promulgated at
*Nuremberg eliminated Jews from citizenship, public
office and the professions, prohibited Jewish children
from attending public schools, severely restricted
Jewish businesses, and established the requirement of
special identity cards for Jews. With the start of

World War II, even more diabolic plans were put into
effect to deal with the Jews of the European
countries overrun by the German armies. In the east,
mass executions of Jews took place, while in central
Europe concentration camps were set up and the
systematic murder of millions of Jews carried out. In
the end, as a result of Nazism, six million Jews
perished, and the Jewish communities of central and
eastern Europe were almost completely destroyed.
(For further details see *Germany, *Hitler, and
*Holocaust.)

Nazism was officially abolished in Germany with
the death of Hitler and the capitulation of the
German armies, but it had received massive support
both inside and outside Germany, and supporters of
the Nazi ideology are still found today in many parts
of the world.

NEBUCHADNEZZAR was the king of Babylon who,
in 586 b.c.e., destroyed the first Temple in Jerusalem
and exiled the majority of the Jewish population of
Judea. He reigned from 605 to 562 b.c.e., a period in
which Babylon and Egypt were the two great powers
of the civilized world, and during most of that time
he was engaged in almost continuous battle with
Egypt over the territories of Syria, Palestine and the
surrounding region. In 597 he captured Jerusalem for
the first time, deposed the Judean king, *Jehoiachin,
and appointed in his place a king of his own choice,
Zedekiah. Several years later, while he was engaged in
battle in the far east, Zedekiah together with the king

1. Jews lined up against a
wall after arrest by Nazis.
2. At the height of their
power, thousands of Nazis
gather for their annual party
rally in Nuremberg.

1. Nebuchadnezzar, depicted in his madness as half-animal, half-man, a fate which the prophet Daniel predicted would befall this Babylonian king. Watercolor by 18th-century British artist, William Blake.
2. Negro and Jewish leaders of America marching side by side in their struggle for equal rights. Left to right: Martin Luther King Jr., Ralph Bunche, and Rabbi Abraham Heschel at a civil rights demonstration in Alabama, 1962.

of Syria revolted against his rule, but he returned in 588 and laid seige to Jerusalem. In 586, he captured the city, and on *Tish'ah be-Av he had the Temple destroyed, carried off a large part of the population into captivity and put Zedekiah and other Judean notables to death. *Daniel and the prophets *Jeremiah and *Ezekiel were eyewitnesses to all these events and the biblical books bearing their names testify to the political and spiritual crises which confronted Judea during this period. According to the Book of Daniel, Nebuchadnezzar suffered greatly for destroying the Temple. He was beset by dreams which he could not understand. One of them, a vision of a magnificent tree cut down in its prime was interpreted by Daniel for the king as a personal warning of many years of madness that were about to come upon him, during which time he would eat grass and live like an animal.

NEGRO-JEWISH RELATIONS in the United States. In the early days of America, Jews had little contact with Blacks or with the whole Negro slavery issue. Some Jewish merchants were slave traders and southern Jews, conforming to the lifestyle of their neighbors, owned slaves. But only a few Jews became actively involved in the debate. Rabbi David *Einhorn emerged as a leading rabbinical abolitionist and, on the other side, Rabbi Issac Mayer *Wise condemned radical abolitionists as "warmongers."

It was not until the 20th century that Jews became active in the Negro struggle. Jews helped found the National Association for the Advancement of Colored People (NAACP) and two of these Jewish founders — Joel Spingarn and his brother Arthur — served as chairmen while Louis Marshall and Rabbi Stephen S. Wise were also prominent in this originally radical Black organization. Julius Rosenwald, another American Jew, gave millions of dollars for recreational and educational institutions and model housing for Blacks.

After the 1954 Supreme Court decisions on school desegregation, the civil rights movement accelerated, especially among young people. Many Jewish college students joined Blacks in marches, sit-ins, and demonstrations both in the Southern towns and Northern ghettos. Prominent members of the Jewish community such as Rabbi Abraham Joshua *Heschel also joined in the cause. In 1965, three young Jewish civil rights workers were killed in the South by racists and became, to some extent, symbolic of the Jewish dedication and sacrifice in the struggle for equality.

But by the late 1960s a distinct change had taken place in the relationship between Blacks and Jews. Young people became disenchanted with the movement and many — including Jews — dropped out. Blacks became alienated from the White society which they blamed for their disappointments. Jewish support began to be looked upon as outside intervention in a personal cause and Jews became increasingly unwelcome in Black civil rights organizations.

The situation in urban centers was especially explosive, where Jewish shopkeepers, landlords, social

workers, and teachers were often the only Whites in all-Black neighborhoods. The Black demand for immediate integration on all levels caused serious crises in the major cities. Blacks felt, for example, that schools with an overwhelming majority of Black students should also have a majority of Black teachers who could better cope with the student body. This change-over was resisted by the White Jewish teachers who feared for their jobs, and led to the racially tense 1968-69 New York City teachers' strike. Similarly, Black integration of previously all-White (and usually Jewish) neighborhoods aroused latent fears and led to the establishment of the Jewish Defense League (see article on *Self-defense). In addition, many Black leaders adopted an anti-Israel position with regard to the Middle-East. This was particularly so among the Black Muslims. Nevertheless, Black moderate leaders have rejected the militant anti-Semitic stand of their radical fellows and many Jews, especially lawyers and political leaders, continue to participate in the civil rights movement.

NEHEMIAH (c. 400 b.c.e.), cupbearer (a very important office) at the Persian court of Artaxerxes I and later governor of Judea. When Cyrus, king of Persia, had conquered Babylon, he permitted the exiled Jews to return to Judea to rebuild their Temple and to reestablish their homeland. But the Judeans were beset with many problems. The neighboring Samaritans were constantly attacking and the Jews themselves were demoralized. Many of them had intermarried; they were careless of the Sabbath and of other *mitzvot*. The rich oppressed the poor, and Jerusalem was a neglected ruin. Nehemiah requested permission to try to restore order and was appointed governor of Judea. He organized a labor force to rebuild the walls of Jerusalem for protection, and then to build houses inside for people to live in to restore the city. With *Ezra the Scribe, he urged his people to rededicate themselves to the study of Torah and to the faithful observance of *mitzvot*. Through the wise and devoted use of his authority he was able to accomplish a new and just social order. His own deep religious feeling inspired others to follow his example. Many mixed marriages were dissolved, the sanctity of the Sabbath, of the Temple and of the sabbatical year were restored. The Book of Nehemiah appears in the Bible at the end of the Book of Ezra.

NETUREI KARTA, a group of ultrareligious extremists, mainly in Jerusalem, who regard the establishment of a secular Jewish state in Erez Israel as a sin and a denial of God, and therefore do not recognize the State of Israel. Their name, which is Aramaic for "guardians of the City," comes from a passage in the Jerusalem Talmud which states that

1

2

1. Nehemiah the prophet, portrayed wearing Renaissance clothes and a Persian turban.
2. Members of the Neturei Karta sect object to having their pictures taken. This youngster is therefore trying to hide his face from the photographer.

Wearing sackcloth as a sign of mourning, members of Neturei Karta observe Israel Independence Day as a sorrowful occasion.

religious scholars are the guardians and defenders of the city. Most of them come from the old *yishuv*, the settlement which existed in Palestine before the 20th century, but they have been joined by some immigrants from Hungary, disciples of Rabbi Joel Teitelbaum of Satmar.

Neturei Karta broke away from Agudat Israel in 1935 and first adopted the name *Ḥevrat ha-Ḥayyim,* after Rabbi Joseph Ḥayyim Sonnenfeld. It aimed at creating "a circle free from the influence of the contemporary spirit and its fallacious opinions." A condition of membership was "the education of sons and daughters in the traditional Jewish manner," which means, the language of instruction may not be Hebrew, only Yiddish. The name Neturei Karta was first used in 1938. During the War of Independence, Neturei Karta opposed the creation of a Jewish state and Israel's control of Jerusalem, and tried to bring about the internationalization of the city.

The most consistent members refuse to accept Israeli identity cards, to recognize the Israeli courts, and to vote in municipal or general elections. They consist of only a few dozen families concentrated in the Me'ah She'arim quarter of Jerusalem and in Bene Berak. Occasionally they gain some support in wider Orthodox circles by creating religious controversies, such as their demonstrations against Sabbath violation and mixed bathing. In 1966 Neturei Karta split, following the marriage of their leader Rabbi Amram Blau (1894-1974) to a convert, Ruth Ben-David. Members of Neturei Karta derive their livelihood mostly from small trade and contributions from abroad, notably from disciples of the Satmar *rebbe* in the United States.

Congregation Shaare Shamayim - G.N.J.C.
Verree Road above Welsh Road
Philadelphia, Penna.   19115